Mind Gym

Chelsea,

achieve more
by thinking
differently

*Great to meet a
kindred spirit,*

mindgym

Sebastian Bailey, Ph.D., & Octavius Black

[signature]

HarperOne
An Imprint of HarperCollinsPublishers

HarperCollins books may be purchased for educational, business, or sales promotional use. For information please e-mail the Special Markets Department at SPsales@harpercollins.com.

HarperCollins website: http://www.harpercollins.com

FIRST HARPERCOLLINS PAPERBACK EDITION PUBLISHED IN 2016

Designed by Terry McGrath

ISBN 978–0–06–233145–8

Library of Congress Cataloging-in-Publication Data
Bailey, Sebastian.
Mind gym : achieve more by thinking differently / Sebastian Bailey and Octavius Black. — First edition.
    pages cm
Includes index.
ISBN 978–0–06–233144–1 (hardcover)
1. Thought and thinking. 2. Creative thinking. 3. Behavior modification. 4. Success. I. Black, Octavius. II. Title.
BF441.B263 2014
153.4'2—dc23
                        2014012011

16 17 18 19 20   RRD(H)   10 9 8 7 6 5 4 3 2

Contents

A Fitness Program for Your Mind

Do you feel overwhelmed? Overworked? Overloaded? Do you feel that despite your best efforts, you are not performing at your best? You are not alone. More than ever we are under constant pressure to succeed. We are asked to do more at work in less time and with fewer resources; and we are stretched thin at home as we balance professional responsibilities, take care of our homes, pay bills, look after our children, care for our aging parents, and nurture our most intimate relationships—all while posting Facebook updates that make our friends jealous. Keeping up with our daily lives is challenging enough. Taking the time and creating the space to consider more fundamental questions—*Am I building a meaningful life? What choices should I make to maximize my chances of happiness?*—seems like a luxury few of us can afford.

To thrive in this breakneck environment, our best bet is to leverage our most powerful assets: our internal resources. We need to think smarter, make better decisions, relate more strongly to others, work brilliantly, and manage our stress. The good news is that there is a wealth of scientific information on *how* to leverage these resources to excel personally and professionally.

The bad news? The majority of that enlightening science is buried in complex academic papers and books. Some has made its way to the popular media—for better or worse. There seems to be an endless supply of "pop psychology" theories that promise a more fulfilling life, success at work, a better understanding of yourself, stronger relationships with others, and the secret to everything else. Not all these shiny theories are bad. But it is often impossible to tell the snake oil from the fairy dust, or the gimmicks from the truth.

Not anymore.

We wrote this book with two goals in mind: to make the best, most rigorous research findings on the science of success and fulfillment accessible to everyone and to help you apply these insights so you can effect radical change in your life as quickly as possible. *Mind Gym* will explain why you get trapped in negative thought patterns, why your relationships fail or succeed, why your conversations don't turn out the way you expected them to, why you get stressed, and why you can't get your creative juices flowing. But more important, *Mind Gym* will provide tools and exercises to help you change what you think and how you approach these challenges, so you can optimize your most powerful ally: your mind. When your mind is fit, you get more out of life, more out of work, more out of your relationships, more out of everything.

A Gym for the Mind

The original idea for Mind Gym was born in 1999, during a casual conversation over dinner when the topic turned to cultural trends in society. We discussed the 1980s obsession with physical improvement (the birth of jogging and Jane Fonda's workouts) and the 1990s focus on the soul (yoga, alternative medicine, and meditation). We asked ourselves, *What will the new millennium be about?* The mind. We all agreed that as the pace of technology and life increased, a sharp mind would be essential to our success and fulfillment.

What we needed, we agreed that night, were personal trainers for our minds. Just as a physical trainer identifies the best equipment and exercises that will help us achieve our fitness goals, we all need an expert to help us navigate the complexity of our minds and help us get them into the best possible shape. A year later, we launched a series of "workouts" for the mind to do just that. These short, sharp workshops were grounded in robust science and packed with practical tools that could be applied immediately and exercises that were fun to do.

Since our company, Mind Gym, launched in 2000, more than one million people in thirty countries have participated in our trademark ninety-minute workouts. Some of the world's most progressive corporations—including Google, Tory Burch, PepsiCo, and Unilever—have brought these workouts to their organizations to help train their people to achieve more by thinking differently. And the vast majority of participants love them. An incredible 95 percent of participants have said they would apply what they'd learned to their lives, and 93 percent would recommend the experience to others.

To develop these workouts, we explored a century of psychological research to identify the best and most helpful insights on how to optimize our minds and behaviors. When necessary, we adapted and combined different theories from the psychological sciences to make them more relevant to the needs of people today. Over the years, we've had a chance to test and refine the hundreds of techniques and exercises, first on the Mind Gym team and then, when they were found to be effective, on hundreds of thousands of participants in our workouts. The result is a wealth of practical and road-tested advice on how to think and communicate more effectively.

Because not everyone can attend our workouts, we wrote this book so you can experience Mind Gym workouts and exercise your mind wherever you are—at home, in your office, on a plane, or anywhere you can sneak away to read and try out these techniques for a few minutes.

The Mind Gym Philosophy

The science-backed techniques and exercises we offer in this book are informed by a set of assumptions that lie behind everything Mind Gym does:

- *We can choose how we think.* We are not preprogrammed to perceive and interpret the world in a certain way, but we are largely free to decide *how* we think and how we communicate.

- *We can choose to improve.* Just like exercising at the local gym helps us become more physically fit, we can all improve our mental performance by choosing to exercise our minds. No, we can't turn ourselves into brilliant thinkers like Albert Einstein or Leonardo da Vinci, any more than multiple trips to the gym will turn us into Dwayne "The Rock" Johnson. But we *can* become the best version of ourselves.

- *We can choose to be smarter.* Intelligence, in its broadest sense, involves much more than abstract problem solving or IQ. In addition to systematic thinking, intelligence includes physical and social skills, as well as perception, imagination, emotional self-regulation, and many aspects of personality. All of these can be enhanced.

- *We can choose our habits.* Most of us tend to underestimate the extent to which we behave on autopilot, reflecting mental "default settings" that we have forgotten we can reset. By uncovering more of the options that are available, we'll find it easier to escape our current habits or "settings."

At Mind Gym, we believe everyone can change radically—if they make a conscious decision to do so. If you are ready to change, ready to get your mind into the best shape it's ever been, start your exercise program now.

How to Use this Book

Mind Gym is designed to meet your specific needs. We've divided the book into seven parts, each tackling some of the most common challenges people face:

- How to adopt a positive mind-set

- How to increase productivity

- How to repair broken relationships

- How to influence others

- How to resolve conflict successfully

- How to be more creative

- How to minimize stress and maximize bliss

Each part starts with a brief summary of the content covered in its chapters. If your priority is to manage stress or be more creative, then go straight to the relevant section. Having trouble deciding whether or not to stick with a relationship? There's a section on that too. Each chapter within the section offers specific tools that you can use immediately, and they are crafted to help you achieve results right away. At the end of each chapter we've put together some exercises for you, called "Give Your Mind a Workout." The beginner exercises are to get you started and the advanced exercises are there once you're ready for something more challenging.

Of course, you can read this book cover to cover if you prefer. Or you may choose to follow one of our pre-designed programs. Just like a physical fitness regime can be designed for strength or stamina, each of our programs has been developed to help address common desires.

There are four basic programs to help you get what you need from *Mind Gym* as quickly and efficiently as possible:

Get What You Want

This program is especially helpful if you know what you want—both professionally and in your relationships—but don't know how to get it, particularly when obstacles keep getting in the way. (Read chapters 1, 2, 3, 5, 9, 11, and 15.)

Be Liked

This is a program for those of you who struggle in social situations, have difficulty maintaining relationships, or simply would like to deepen your connection to colleagues and friends. Do you want to be more charismatic? Do you want that special person to look your way? This program is for you. (Read chapters 1, 6, 7, 8, 12, and 14.)

Be Respected

This is a big one. It's a program for those of you who want to be admired or at least treated as an equal by others. Do you often feel like you're getting the short end of the stick? Follow this program. (Read chapters 3, 9, 10, 11, 13, and 16.)

Overcome Adversity

If you are facing a difficult time in your life or want to be ready to deal with unexpected challenges, you'll love this program. It helps you realize how and why you internalize chaos, and how others might be adding to your challenges. And it helps you understand the ruts that you need to get out of. (Read chapters 1, 2, 3, 12, 13, 14, 18, 19, and 20.)

Whether you choose to follow one of these programs or read individual chapters that fit your needs, we hope the book will lead you to new paths and reveal aspects of yourself you didn't quite know were there. By getting your mind in top shape, your life will change: You'll work smarter. You'll have stronger and richer relationships. You'll be more fulfilled. You'll thrive.

Have a fantastic workout!

PART ONE

Reset Your Mind

THE COMPUTER CRASHES before you could save that all-important document. You forget to buy the vital ingredient in the meal you're cooking for your hot date. The bad weather is going to make you miss your flight connection. All of these circumstances could make you believe that you're unlucky or that the world is somehow conspiring to get you. But is it? Or are these just random circumstances you have no control over? Maybe the real question you should be asking yourself is this: *Is my mind conspiring against me—creating negative thoughts around innocuous situations or unrealistically positive thoughts around truly negative situations?*

It may surprise you to know that one of the most significant discoveries in contemporary psychology is that we all choose how we think, react, and respond to situations. Sounds obvious, right? Well, it's not. For years experts thought we were preprogrammed in our early, formative years, that our minds were hardwired like a computer. The theory was that when a person encountered a specific stimulus, only a specific reaction would occur. Of course, there were other experts back then who challenged this theory. But at the time, these experts theorized that our thinking, reactions, and responses to stimuli could only be changed as a result of our being rewarded or punished. Basically, we weren't given credit for a powerful ability: choice.

The truth is, you have control of your thoughts, reactions, and responses. And once you understand how powerful that choice can be, you'll be able to change more aspects of your life than you can imagine.

In this first part of the book, you'll learn how often you operate on autopilot—a state of "going through the motions" of your life without really paying attention to choice. Being stuck in autopilot can not only lead you down the wrong paths in life and at work, because you're not paying attention to possible pitfalls, but it can also result in fantastic opportunities passing you by—a new relationship, a career opportunity, or an experience of a lifetime.

You'll also learn how and when to flip the switch on habits, keeping the good habits and eliminating the bad. If you're unaware of your habits, you'll soon become aware—and be able to swap bad habits for positive lifestyle choices that can get you where you want to be in a heartbeat. Maybe you want a job promotion. What bad habits are holding you back? Do you want more money? What good habits should you focus on more?

Finally, we'll show you how your perception of the world impacts your behavior. You'll learn how to adopt a positive mind-set and how to turn good thinking into good activity, which, in turn, creates phenomenal results. In fact, as many Mind Gym users report, this simple switch in thinking is the single biggest catapult that can change everything.

Most important, the first two chapters that follow are going to prepare your mind for the rest of the book, where we'll dive into specific areas of your life.

Get ready to get set—your new mind-set.

CHAPTER 1

Flip the Switch
on Automatic Thinking

This is your life. You have goals you want to achieve, dreams you want to pursue, milestones you want to reach. To get there, you need to think deliberately and make the right choices day in and day out in order to reach your highest potential. Unfortunately, your hectic life often leads you to simply go through the motions, doing the same things over and over, following familiar habits of behavior and thinking. In short, you get stuck in autopilot.

Sometimes these habits are tremendously helpful—thank goodness you don't need to figure out how to use your toothbrush every time you use it. But there are times when your mental habits—or thinking shortcuts—need revisiting. Like with many other habits (such as using a toothbrush), you may not even realize that you've created a mental habit. This chapter explores how to spot your mental shortcuts, how to switch to more helpful thinking modes, and how to break bad mental habits.

Attention! Attention!

Imagine for a second that you could tune in and listen to other people's thoughts. What would you hear? If you listen in to our friend Janelle's inner monologue, you would hear the equivalent of a talk radio program—a nonstop conversation about everything and anything: *What if interest rates go up? Where would that leave me? Perhaps I should pay off my loans. Then again, it would be great to go hiking in the Himalayas.*

Without pausing, Janelle moves abruptly in her mind from subject to subject. *Oh look, broccoli is on sale. I wonder if something is wrong with it. Is it old? Is it covered in pesticides? Maybe I should just buy a frozen dinner instead. There is a low-fat version I could buy. I better not. It might be disgusting. But I should stick with my healthy diet. Then again, Kate has put on weight recently. She'll probably get offended if she sees me only buying healthy food. I wonder when is the best time to go hiking in the Himalayas.*

To put it mildly, there's a lot of chatter happening in Janelle's head. However, if you asked her what she was thinking about at any specific moment, she would be able to confidently share her thoughts, in detail and at length. But not everyone's like Janelle.

Our friend Catherine's internal dialogue is extremely different. Her mind sounds more like static noise—a consistent buzz without much focus. If you asked her what she was thinking at any given second, she might actually be startled by your question and reply, "Um, I was just zoning out." Or she might say, "I can't get this song out of my head." Or, "I wasn't really thinking about anything specific."

Catherine's static noise plays in her head while she fumbles through the motions of familiar routines, like grocery shopping, cleaning, or commuting to and from work. How many of us have driven past our destination because we were zoning out? How many of us have arrived at our destination and "snapped out of a trance" with only a vague recollection of how we arrived there?

The difference between Janelle and Catherine is their focus. Janelle is an example of someone with an exclusively internal focus: she is always aware of what she is doing and what she is thinking, almost like an observer of her own mind. Catherine, by contrast, has an entirely external focus: she is oblivious to how she is thinking and what she is doing—she is just doing it.

Internal Focus

When your focus is internal, it's much like you're having a conversation with yourself. Consider the voice you hear in your head as you read this book. Even while you're reading our words, another dialogue might be asking if it's worth continuing to read this chapter or if now is the time to have a cup of coffee. You might also be thinking about whether you left the oven on, where to go on vacation next, or how to deal with a cranky coworker.

When your focus is internal, you are conscious of the fact that you are thinking; you can hear and pay attention to the running commentary in your head.

External Focus

Assess where you are at the moment. What is happening around you? What noises do you hear? Who is nearby? What colors do you see? What do you notice that is new or different?

External focus is an awareness of the things outside your own head. And when you focus in this way, you aren't aware of what you're thinking. Your attention is on what is going on, not on what you think about it, how to interpret it, or whether it could have an impact on your future.

When you are really caught up in something, whether it's the thrill of a football game or the latest twist in your favorite reality show, you are externally focused. And when you find yourself thinking, *Why am I wasting time watching this ridiculous reality show?* you have returned to an internal focus.

Of course, as soon as you ask yourself where your focus is, your focus automatically becomes internal, which is one of the reasons why it is easier to move to an internal focus than to an external one.

Where Should Your Focus Be?

Your mind is always occupied in one of two places: what is going on inside your head or what is going on outside your head. It is impossible to focus at the same time on both what's internal and what's external, just as it is to focus on neither. What is possible, though, is to switch between them, which, with a little mental discipline, you can do pretty much whenever you want.

Try it for yourself: Grab a blank sheet of paper and a pen, and draw a picture of a house in the countryside on a sunny day. While you are drawing, there will be times when you think to yourself, *Am I doing this right?* or *I really can't draw very well.* At other instances, you will be so absorbed in, for example, making the smoke coming out of the chimney look realistic that you won't be aware of what you are doing. You will find it impossible to be aware of the conversation in your head and be absorbed in your artwork at the same time. But you can quickly move between the two, going internal by asking yourself a question, like *How well am I doing this task?* and going external by focusing on the picture or some element of it, like *The smoke is heavy and thick.*

So, which is best? Do you want to be more like Janelle—internally focused—or more like Catherine—externally focused?

The answer is neither, or both. Different personality types tend to spend more of their time in one world than the other, but all of us spend time in both, and we need to. It is both natural and sensible to switch between an internal focus and an external focus. Both have a helpful side and a harmful side.

Either focus, internal or external, is helpful when it increases your likelihood of success, effectiveness, efficiency, or elegance. And it is harmful when it keeps you from achieving your goals or performing at your best, whether you are trying to relax, give a presentation, or argue with your partner.

The Four States of Mind

Combining the different *types* of focus (internal and external) with the different *ways* of focusing (helpful and harmful) generates four distinct states of mind: autopilot, critical, thinking, and engaged.

Your challenge is to spend as much time as possible in the helpful states and learn to swap neatly between *thinking* and *engaged* to

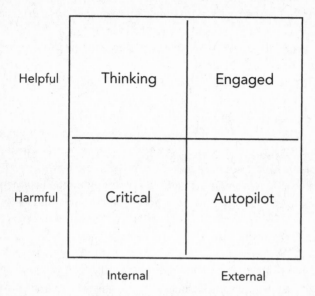

support your desires. To accomplish this you need, first, to be good at spotting which state of mind you are in.

Autopilot: Recognizing Habits of the Mind

Imagine waking up tomorrow morning and hearing this: "Good morning. My name is Mark and I will be your autopilot for the day. We will be setting off for work this morning five minutes late, as usual, and then traveling along the same route we have taken every day for the past three years. Later, someone will ask how we are, and we will reply 'Fine, thank you' without a moment's thought. There is a possibility of turbulence at the one P.M. meeting, when someone makes a statement we disagree with. But don't worry: we have a stock response of tired and familiar arguments we can shoot back at them."

Silly as this scenario may seem, everyone has an autopilot inside that is taking mental shortcuts every day. Without these mental shortcuts, you would get very little done. However, because you take these shortcuts, you tend to miss out on opportunities and fail to perform at your best. In effect, the lights are on but no one is home.

Autopilot kicks in when you allow what was once exciting and challenging to become boring or mundane. You stop thinking about the situation and, instead, respond in preprogrammed ways. There are several factors that can turn on the autopilot (and turn off your thinking mind):

The Familiarity Trap

We label things and experiences to help us understand how they fit with the world around us. For example, you see someone crying and automatically think, *Crying equals sad;* therefore, that person must be upset. Your automatic response prevents you from considering alternative explanations. The person crying could be acting, chopping onions, or laughing so hard that tears are streaming down his or her face. But when you are caught in the familiarity trap, you are unlikely to consider these alternatives. The familiarity trap explains, say, why security officials at the airport rotate roles. If a person looks at an X-ray screen for long enough, a nuclear bomb might go through without that person noticing. Some pianists learn their pieces away from a keyboard so they won't become too familiar with it and fall into autopilot when they perform.

The Single View

Of course, we all see the world through our own eyes. My eyes are different from your eyes. But when we try to consider an issue or solve a problem, we tend to assume that the way we see the world is the *right* way to see it. Why wouldn't we? And yet our view isn't always the right one. Thinking creatively demands that you look at a familiar problem with fresh eyes—using a perspective different from your own. To actually achieve this, you need to recognize that your mind is functioning on autopilot, temporarily fixed by your worldview and your life experiences.

Pressure

To demonstrate that pressure often leads us to behave in autopilot mode, psychologists John Darley and Daniel Batson asked a group of seminary students to prepare a talk on the Good Samaritan parable.[1] With the parable at the forefront of their minds, the seminarians were then asked to walk to the location where they were expected to deliver their talk. So far, the task seems pretty straightforward. However, this is where the cunning psychologists made life difficult. They had arranged for the seminarians to come across someone lying in the road, coughing, spluttering, and calling for help. To make matters more difficult, the psychologists had told half the seminarians that they were late for their talk and the other half that they had plenty of time. How many would stop to help the injured person? And which ones? Of those who were told they had plenty of time to reach their destination, 61 percent stopped to help, but of those who were told they were late, only 10 percent stopped. According to the observations of the psychologists, some seminarians literally stepped over the actor pretending to be injured. The slight change of situation moved the rushed seminarians into autopilot, making them forget what had been on their minds just moments before.

There is nothing wrong with letting your autopilot direct mundane activities you have to do and have no desire to change, like mowing the lawn or folding laundry. But as the study just described shows, there are times when you must take control of your thinking or risk missing key opportunities (in the case of the seminarians, the opportunity to put into action the very message they were about to deliver at a lecture). Being in autopilot is unhelpful when

- you want to achieve something you haven't done before,

- you have to perform a task in circumstances different from the circumstances in which you have performed that task in the past,

- you want to do something better than you have done it in the past, or

- you want to explore better ways to do something that you're used to doing in one particular way every time.

Critical: Monitoring Self-Commentary

Sports commentators are not always complimentary about the sports stars they report on: "Oh, that was a cheap shot on the field!" or "He's playing like a rookie." Similarly, when you are in a critical state of mind, you hear an inner voice giving a running commentary on what you are doing and what you should be doing differently: *I'm making a fool of myself onstage* or *I'm paralyzed—I can't decide what I need to do next* or *I think she would like me if I said something witty and charming, but I can't think of anything, so she's probably going to hate me.*

This state of mind is accurately described by the expression "You are your own worst enemy." In sports terms, it is the equivalent of that old commentary cliché: "They're playing against two teams tonight: the opponents and themselves." Critical noise or chatter often peaks when you are doing something that matters to you: playing tennis, making a point in an important meeting, negotiating with the plumber, or sharing a passionate embrace. A voice pops up and starts talking to you about what you are doing, how you are doing it, and whether you are doing it right.

You may be fooled into thinking that this voice is helpful, but in fact it is a distraction. It's a bit like when you try to get to sleep but can't. The more you tell yourself, *I must get to sleep, I must get to sleep,* the more anxious you are about falling sleep, and thus, you actually become more awake. When you interact with people, your critical mind can be particularly distracting. It might instruct you with what to say to sound smart or it might observe, *I'm being boring* or *Come on, I should have shared better ideas with this person by now.* These instructions distract you, knock your confidence, and get in the way of what you are truly trying to accomplish.

When you are in a critical state of mind, you also suffer from what is called the "impostor syndrome."[2] If you have ever thought, *I'm not able to do this; it's only a question of time before they find out I'm faking,* then you have suffered from impostor syndrome.[3] And it's okay to admit that you've had these thoughts. It's more common than you might assume. In fact, almost all white-collar workers suffer from impostor syndrome at some stage in their careers, and some of the more successful people experience it throughout their working lives.[4] This means that all those people you are worried might expose you as an impostor are probably busy worrying that you are about to show them up. What a relief!

Thinking: Actively Analyzing Your Thoughts

You are in a thinking state of mind when you are assessing options, deciding on a course of action, working through a problem, estimating the likely consequences or chain of events, or simply organizing your thoughts to make more sense of them. When you're at your best in this state, your thoughts feel clear, precise, and positive. This state of mind is particularly useful when:

Solving Problems and Making Decisions

In this state you "think through a problem" and then decide what you ought to do and how you ought to do it. For example, you weigh the pros and cons of taking a new job; you decide whether you prefer grapefruit or orange juice for breakfast; you consider where to go on vacation or how to spend your weekend; or you plan how to have a difficult conversation with your boss.

Correcting Mistakes

When things don't seem to be going the way you want them to, you need to rethink your course of action or plan and react accordingly. Moving into a thinking state of mind allows you to consider what is happening and the options available to you (as opposed to being in the critical state of mind, in which you punish yourself for being in a bad situation in the first place).

Reflecting on the Past

One of the most effective ways of improving yourself is to learn from your past experiences, consider what you did well, and decide what you could do better in the future if you were in a similar situation. This kind of reflection, best accomplished when in the thinking state of mind, helps you become more self-aware, more knowledgeable, and, in due course, more capable.

Making Sense of a Situation

You want to be in a thinking state when asking yourself questions to make sense of your current life situation. *Why do my personal relationships start so passionately and end so abruptly? Why do I want to change jobs? Am I redecorating my home to increase its value or to make it a nicer place for me to live?* Asking, and trying to answer, some of the "big" questions can be a very helpful mental tool, so long as you ask the right questions and do something with your answers (otherwise it can turn into self-indulgent navel-gazing).

Most of the suggestions in this book are designed to trigger your thinking state of mind by suggesting approaches and techniques to help you think differently. But when it comes to putting these techniques into practice—as opposed to deciding which techniques to use—being in an engaged state of mind is key.

Engaged: Getting "into the Zone"

There are many phrases used to describe the engaged state of mind: "captivated," "absorbed," "in the sweet spot." An engaged state of mind exists when your focus is external, on something in your immediate environment, and when you're performing at your best. If you can drive, you might recall the moment when you first drove somewhere on your own without thinking, *Check mirror, change gear, right blinker,* but instead your attention was completely on the road ahead and the other motorists while you sang along to the radio. Or you might recall the first time you skied to the bottom of a slope and you were not quite sure how you got there, but it felt great. Equally, it could be writing an email, contributing in a meeting, talking with people at a party, or reading a book. The key is that while you were performing a task, you didn't have any distractions, either internal ones (voices telling you what you should or shouldn't be doing) or external ones (checking a clock or looking around for other people to talk with).

When you are absorbed by what you are doing, you are engaged and totally present. By not judging yourself, you interfere less with the task at hand and allow your potential to take over. Mihaly Csikszentmihalyi (pronounced *chick-sent-me-high*) describes this state as finding "flow."[5] It is where you are likely to feel peak performance and immersion in what you do.

Move from Harmful to Helpful States of Mind

Leading in the 1950 Monaco Grand Prix, Juan Manuel Fangio approached a blind corner, and instead of continuing at his typical 100 miles per hour, for some reason he braked hard and took the bend at a crawl. As he rounded the turn, he saw a nine-car pileup. If he had been traveling at his usual speed he would almost certainly have been caught in the crash and might well have died. Instead, he drove safely past.

So, what was it that caused Fangio to brake suddenly and for no obvious reason? It wasn't until some time later that even Fangio could explain why he slowed down. Without being aware of it at the time, a part of his mind had noticed that the faces of the spectators in the stand ahead, which would usually be fixed on him as the race leader, were turned away toward the crash.

If he had been in a thinking state of mind, it would have taken too long to process this piece of information to react in time, and if he had been in autopilot, he wouldn't have spotted that anything was different. But Fangio was completely engaged, as any Grand Prix champion would be, so he picked up on this unusual detail, realized that it could mean danger, and took an intuitive, split-second decision that saved his life and won him the race.

Learning to move away from harmful states of mind and into helpful states is critical—keeping yourself mentally on your toes to live the life you truly want to live.

Switch Back to Manual

Need to turn the autopilot off? Here are the best ways to switch back to manual:

- *Look for something new.* Practice scanning your environment, consciously looking for what is new, different, and unusual. Ask yourself questions, like *How has this street changed since the last time I walked down it? What are the differences between the people on the train? What do I notice today about my colleagues?* These questions might seem silly, but they force you to live in, think about, and focus on the present—to become aware of your surroundings and not slip back into autopilot.

- *Learn that "always" isn't absolute.* One of the reasons why all of us can get caught in autopilot is that we tend to see the world as a set of absolutes. You are apt to believe that such and such will always happen, because so far it always has. This is a mental shortcut, which saves you from having to think about it again. As a result, your thinking falls into patterns of your own making and you are, in effect, switching on the autopilot.

- *Accept other people's perspectives.* Have you ever had a boss or colleague you thought was overbearing, dogmatic, aggressive, or rude? Do you think they saw themselves in that way? Surprisingly enough, they might not. If they were asked to describe themselves, they might say they were assertive, direct, honest, and candid. One of the reasons why conflicts can get so ugly is that it's easy to fall into a state of autopilot and respond to others without thinking or without considering others' perspectives. By staying alert to other people's perspectives, you can move out of autopilot and into a more constructive state of awareness.

Remove the Critical Noise

Right now you might be hearing critical noise in your head. You might be asking yourself, *Can I do this? Will this work? Can I really become engaged?* The answer is yes. But you need to start with getting rid of the critical noise.

When you want to move from the critical state of mind to the thinking state, do the following:

- Bring objectivity and analysis into your thinking. Ask yourself, *What are the facts of the situation at hand and what are simply my assumptions?*

- Think like an attentive optimist (chapter 2).

Build Reflection Time into Your Routine

How do you move to a reflective state of mind? After completing any task, think back on what you have achieved, what you did well, and what you would like to have done differently. Golfers can practice reflection between shots but not while taking them. Parents can practice reflection after disciplining a child. Salespeople can reflect back after pitches and presentations. All of us would benefit from practicing reflection at the end of each day.

When you want to move to a more reflective state of mind, do the following:

- Schedule quiet moments in your day. Don't eat lunch at your desk while answering emails, but find a place where you have the space to think.

- Take advantage of "dead time"—standing in line, commuting, waiting for other people. Use that time to reflect on what you are trying to achieve, what you've learned, and what you can do better.

- Relax. See chapter 20 to find ways to calm your mind into a state where you're reflections will be at their most astute.

Get Engaged

When you want to engage in a task but you hear the critical noise make its entrance (*You don't want to do* that) or you find yourself busy thinking rather than being absorbed in the moment, there are several things you can do:

Recognize the Vital Components of a Situation

Vital components are part of what you are doing, and may indeed be essential, but they aren't tied directly to the outcome of a situation. For example, if you are talking with a person on the telephone, a vital component is the other person's tone of voice. If you are playing tennis, a vital component is the speed of the ball. If you are being interviewed, a vital component is the posture of the interviewer. The trick with these vital components is to not allow critical noise to start: *He's folded his arms; I'm clearly boring him.* Instead, you need to observe or report on what is happening without commenting on it, and trust yourself to do what is right as a result. Focusing on vital components makes you more present and aware of your surroundings. Most important, it moves you toward an external focus, which helps silence the critical noise.

Focus on Process, Not Outcome

When you focus on an eventual outcome, it is all too easy for the critical state of mind to take center stage. Your critical voice starts spewing negative thoughts: *I'm never going to make it to the top of the mountain. The sales targets are impossible. It'll be years before we finish redecorating the house.* To quiet this voice and get engaged, focus on the steps you are taking to get the task accomplished. A mountain climber will focus on getting to the next ridge or, when really exhausted, on simply taking the next step, one at a time. A salesperson will concentrate on the call to a specific potential client, rather than on reaching his or her quarterly sales number. A DIY hobbyist will devote him- or herself to each stroke of the brush. By focusing on the steps you need to take to get where you want to go, rather than on the eventual outcome, your mind switches from critical noise to being engaged.

Balance Challenge and Skill

The balance between challenge and skill is a sensitive one. If a task is too challenging (e.g., preparing a meal for twenty-five guests) for your level of skill (e.g., you can't even boil an egg), you might feel anxious about completing the task. If you have more talent or skills (e.g., you are a celebrity chef) than is required to complete a task (e.g., toasting bread), you can feel apathetic toward it. If neither skill nor challenge is needed, you are bored. However, if you are skilled in something and there is a challenge to meet, you can become immersed and enjoy what you are doing. You are also more likely to achieve your potential by managing this balance between skill and challenge.

Try to make even the most mundane tasks more challenging: when mowing the lawn, for example, focus on how well you mow, try mowing in strips as if it were a football field, or challenge yourself to mow in the quickest time but still have the neatest lines.

The Ideal State of Mind

An ideal state of mind fluctuates between thinking and engaged— whatever a current situation demands of you. There isn't a formula that dictates when you should be in one state and when you should be in the other, but much like dancing, you need to find a rhythm and delicately move as the situation (or music) requires.

Claire thinks, *What should I wear? I have the big marketing meeting today, so I'd better look sophisticated.* She chooses her favorite suit and then thinks no more about it as she returns to her automatic routine for getting ready for work. During her drive to work, however, she is fully engaged in her environment, noticing that road construction is planned for next month. *I'll need to find another route,* she thinks.

On the way up to her office, Claire bumps into Peter, her old boss, who was recently made a director. "Congratulations," she says enthusiastically, totally engaged in the conversation. It is only when Peter starts explaining his new role that she thinks, *He could be a useful sponsor for my project. I wonder how I can persuade him.* Claire quickly develops an influencing strategy (see chapter 9), and when there is a suitable moment in the conversation, she broaches the subject: "Peter, when you say . . ."

What seems to Claire like only seconds later, though it has been several minutes, Peter suggests a meeting with his whole management team. As Claire gets herself coffee, she reflects on what she did well that helped gain Peter's support and whether she can apply any of these lessons when it comes to the marketing meeting.

Claire glides between the different modes as the situation requires. Most of the time she is in either an engaged or a thinking state, moving to an internal focus (thinking) when she needs to assess a situation or decide what to do and then to an external focus (engaged) when she executes her decisions and plans, getting completely involved in what she is doing.

With the help of this book, you'll learn to do much the same.

The End of the Beginning

Autopilot should now be turned off. And that's a good thing, because if you really want this book to work for you—to positively impact the way you live, work, and build relationships with people—you need to be thinking and engaged. In this chapter, you've learned about how to change your mind. The next challenge is much harder: putting the theory included in the pages that follow into practice.

It's time to get busy.

GIVE YOUR MIND A WORKOUT

Beginner: Become Aware

We are all guilty of negative, critical self-talk from time to time, but some of us have a continuous stream of critical noise within our minds. Before you can change your inner voice, you need to become intimately acquainted with it.

1. Listen to your thoughts. The first step in changing your inner critic into your inner fan is changing your awareness. Think of yourself objectively, as if you were a third party, and listen to the thoughts that regularly go through your mind.

2. Don't critique yourself. While you listen and catalog your thoughts, don't pass any judgment on them or on yourself. If you hear your inner critic say nasty things, don't critique your inner critic and set yourself off on a never-ending spiral of criticism.

3. Stay neutral. Reflect neutrally on what you hear inside your head so you become more aware of the ways in which you are critical of yourself. Once you fully understand the ways in which you sabotage yourself, you'll more easily change your state of mind.

Advanced: Become Engaged

One of the things you can do to move closer to an engaged state of mind is focus on the vital components (described earlier in this chapter) of the situations and places you find yourself in.

1. Notice more. Go to a coffee shop or somewhere busy in public. Make a list of ten things you notice, and then list ten more, then ten more. Don't just describe your surroundings; expand your focus to people, interactions, tones of voice, and nonverbal signals. Use all your senses.

2. Practice with people. Repeat what you did in the previous step (but without writing anything down) in an interaction with a group of friends or at a work meeting. Don't allow any critical noise to come

in; just practice nonjudgmental awareness of your surroundings and the people within it.

3. Be present. See what you can learn by just externally focused, non-judgmental observation, and notice while you're observing how present you feel in your surroundings—no longer lost somewhere in your mind but very much present in the room.

CHAPTER 2

Think like an Attentive Optimist

Some people have all the luck. Or at least that is how it seems.

Luck is a bit like magic: You think it is incredible until you realize it's just an illusion—a trick on the mind. Once the mystery is gone, the secret is obvious. This is great news. If you can understand what makes some people apparently luckier than others, you can also start to adopt some of their habits and become lucky yourself.[1] A lucky you won't happen instantly. Just like with magic tricks, it takes determination and practice to master new habits and make them appear effortless. As you become more accomplished, things will increasingly work out as you'd like—the world will seemingly turn in your favor. To everyone else, this will appear as if you are either extremely lucky or extremely talented, or maybe both.

The techniques in this book are designed to help you achieve what you want and so, in some way, to help you appear luckier. This chapter, in particular, will show you that the ways in which you perceive and interpret the world around you have an enormous effect on how fortunate or unfortunate you are. Adopting the way of thinking outlined in the pages that follow will mean that, along with numerous other benefits, you

- achieve more,

- live longer,

- are better liked, and

- have better relationships.

This way of thinking is called "attentive optimism."

The Difference Between Optimists and Pessimists

Believe it or not, the way we think and perceive the world around us greatly affects the way things work out for us. Optimists and pessimists perceive the world in very different ways. Even when they experience a similar event, they draw much different conclusions and describe the event in very different terms.

Consider this story. One night Mike and Ashley host a highly successful barbecue for a group of friends and neighbors. The following morning, Mike wakes up with a slight hangover and remembers the night before. He smiles and thinks, *We always throw such great parties.* On the other side of the bed, Ashley rouses from her slumber and slowly recalls the same event. *We were lucky,* she thinks. *Last night there was just the right group of people for a get-together.*

Mike's analysis of events shows all the characteristics of an optimist. He applies the success of the barbecue to a wide range of other parties (he thinks, *We throw great parties* as opposed to *We throw really nice casual barbecues for six people*) spanning a long period of time (*We always host great parties,* not *Yesterday we hosted a good barbecue*).

Ashley's reaction, by contrast, shows the traits of a pessimist. She associates her success with a very specific type of event (an intimate get-together) and associates it with one moment in time (last night only). She believes she got lucky.

Like Mike and Ashley, we all have an explanatory style—that is, a pattern of communication that reveals whether we perceive a particular event as either positive or negative. There are two dimensions that help illustrate the differences between how an optimist and a pessimist explain events: scope and time span.

Scope

This is how a person explains the depth or scope of a situation. It ranges from a highly specific, particular case (barbecues for six people) to a universal, generalized category (being good at entertaining guests). The phrase "making a mountain out of a molehill" was invented for people who expand the scope of a situation.

Time Span

This is the way in which a person uses time or consistency to explain events. Descriptions range from one-off or temporary (last night) to typical (usual) and all the way to permanent (always).

When considering positive past events, an optimist explains them as universal and permanent, as Mike did. Pessimists, like Ashley, see them as specific and temporary. By contrast, when it comes to analyzing negative past events, the opposite occurs: the optimist sees them as temporary and specific; the pessimist sees them as universal and permanent. Here's an example: After a busy summer full of barbecues and picnics, Mike and Ashley have gained a little extra weight. Mike looks at his bulging stomach and thinks, *All these summer parties haven't been good for my stomach.* Ashley, on the other hand, avoids looking in the mirror as she passes by and tells herself, *I'm destined to be overweight.* Mike, the optimist, explains the situation by making it temporary (this summer) and specific (these parties).[2] Ashley, the pessimist, does the opposite, making it permanent and applying it to the rest of her life.

In short, an optimist explains negative events as caused by environment (external) and as transient and temporary—the negativity only corresponds to a specific instance. A pessimist explains negative events as caused by his or her own actions (internal) and as recurring or permanent. In this way, negative events are deemed likely to happen again and are seen as part of his or her whole life, not attached to one specific instance alone.

The Benefits of Optimism

According to hundreds of well-controlled studies, optimists tend to be better off than pessimists. Time and again research has shown that optimists live longer, are healthier, achieve more, and have better, stronger relationships.[3] They are, however, more often wrong than their pessimist counterparts. But does it really matter? Let's look at what the experts say about a few of those points.

Optimists Live Longer

There aren't many concrete things you can do to greatly increase your chances of living longer. Sure, regular exercise and consuming five servings of fruits or vegetables a day (assuming you know what size a serving is) will help. Other statistics point to healthy relationships, certain financial markers, and other standards of well-being greatly impacting your longevity. However, one thing that has been scientifically shown to increase life expectancy is thinking optimistically.

Mayo Clinic researchers tested the theory for themselves.[4] They selected almost nine hundred people who had sought medical care. When these people were originally admitted to the clinic, they took a series of examinations and, as part of the series, were tested for their level of optimism. Thirty years later, two hundred of the original nine hundred had died, with the optimists living 19 percent longer than the pessimists. Those are impressive numbers.

For all the skeptics reading this book, you might be thinking that there could have been a lot of other variables in play—and the researchers can't possibly know that optimism is the big divider. Diet, work pressure, sexually transmitted diseases, and lifestyle habits could play a major role. So, how can anyone claim that optimism makes a true difference? A study in which all the different variables were excluded would be impossible, wouldn't it? It would. Unless you conducted your study in a convent.

A group of psychologists analyzed the autobiographical essays nuns had written just before completing their final vows and entering a convent in the 1930s and 1940s. The scientists discovered that 90 percent of the nuns they considered the most optimistic in their essays were still alive at age eighty-four. In contrast, only 34 percent of the least optimistic were still alive.[5] Same lifestyle. Same diet. Different outlook. Furthermore, 54 percent of the most positive were still alive at age ninety-four. And after the researchers studied many other factors, the nuns' level of optimism was the only one that had a significant correlation with life span.

But it's not just one study that proves the advantages of optimism for our health. A 2012 study with heart transplant patients showed that optimistic patients had a higher quality of life after transplantation and for an additional five years. Pessimistic patients, on the other hand, reported greater depression immediately after and for five years post-transplant, even if they showed no signs of depression beforehand.[6]

Optimists Achieve More

Yes, it's true: optimists get more things done. And it's not just because they live longer. They tend to be more persistent and resilient and so tend to achieve results—in almost any endeavor. In a large-scale experiment conducted by the pioneering psychologist Martin Seligman, a group of optimists and pessimists were recruited to become insurance sales agents. The intention of the study was to compare the sales agents' performance. By the second year of the experiment, the optimists were outselling the pessimists by 57 percent.[7] Hey, optimism is great for business.

Optimism also boosts achievements in athletics. Research has shown that runners who explain events optimistically perform better after receiving feedback that their time trial was somewhat slower than expected, whereas pessimists did even worse after this feedback.[8]

Pessimists Are More Likely to Be Right

Not everything in life goes an optimist's way. Actually, far from it. For all their good fortune, you might be surprised how often optimists tend to get things wrong.[9]

In Seligman's study, comparing insurance sales agents' performance, the pessimists were far more accurate about predicting the conversion rates of sales calls—that is, the number of calls that resulted in an actual sale. The optimists generally got the conversion rate wrong, typically thinking it was less difficult to convert a lead into revenue. In fact, the optimists were way off in their assumptions. But did it matter? The pessimists gave up making calls earlier than the optimists, who persevered and got the extra sales. But the pessimists were right.

Some pessimists prefer to label themselves "realists." And that is a fair assessment: they are more realistic than optimists in their analysis of a situation—in fact, they are typically right about their assessments. The realist school justifies their mode of thinking by arguing that by being realistic about the world, they will never be disappointed or let down by events. That sounds rational. But does it work?

The irony is that even with this play-it-safe behavior, realists are still more likely to be disappointed than optimists. This is because when something apparently bad does happen, an optimist tends to focus on the upside, while a realist focuses on the downside. Say, for example, both an optimist and a realist are turned down for a bank loan. The realist thinks, *I suspected as much,* and congratulates him- or herself on not having built up false hopes. The optimist, however, thinks, *I now know what I need to do to increase my chances of being approved next time,* and goes back for a second attempt. Guess who actually has better odds at eventually getting the loan. Yep, the optimist.

The Best Kind of Optimism

In the early academic thinking on optimism, it was believed that optimists took responsibility for positive events and put the responsibility for negative events on external factors. (Pessimists, of course, were believed to do the opposite.) In the previous example of Mike and Ashley, Mike takes credit for the barbecue and blames the summer parties for his tummy. A danger does exist that if someone gets carried away with their optimism, they might end up ducking responsibility: they might ignore a problem until it grows out of proportion or they rely too much on wishful thinking as a route to achieve their aims.

An attentive optimist is the kind of person who treads a careful path between taking too much responsibility and taking far too little. After an event that results in a positive outcome, an attentive optimist will take some credit but only what that person feels is his or her due. Consider a professional athlete who scores the winning points of a game and gives credit to his teammates during a postgame interview for making the play possible—it's a humble and gracious public act. But rest assured, in private the attentive optimist athlete is still extremely proud of his accomplishments.

By contrast, an undiluted optimist is inclined to see this one example as definitive proof of his athletic superiority and never-ending good fortune. *That's just how great I really am,* he might tell himself. And a pessimist, as suggested previously, will give the credit to external factors (perhaps other people) and so reap very little or no satisfaction from his own contribution. He might think, *My winning point doesn't really count because my team is so good* or *The opposition is so bad that a monkey could have made the play.*

An attentive optimist will accept appropriate responsibility when a task, event, or situation goes wrong, and then explore what can be learned from the experience. This is likely to include lessons for the future, which is in sharp contrast to the undiluted optimists, who tend to place the responsibility elsewhere.

An attentive optimist, then, is the kind of person we should all strive to be. But how much of one are you?

Are You an Attentive Optimist?

The following diagnostic is designed to help you determine how much of an optimist you already are and which ways you can adapt yourself to become an attentive optimist, if you want to.

For each of the following statements, imagine the described situation and allocate a total of 10 points between the four options (*a, b, c,* and *d*). This could be a combination of 3, 3, 4, 0 or 10, 0, 0, 0 or 7, 0, 2, 1—whatever you think best represents your inclination in each situation. The only rule is that the total points for each statement equal 10.

Example:

0. My favorite color is blue.

   a. Only on weekends _2_

   b. Unless it's paired with orange _4_

   c. Because it feels cool _0_

   d. Because it brings out my eyes _4_   (Total points: 10)

Your Optimism/Pessimism Diagnostic

1. Someone is rude to me for no obvious reason.

    a. She is having a bad day. ____

    b. She is a rude person. ____

    c. I barely noticed. ____

    d. I must have done something wrong. ____

2. My proposal for a new project at work is rejected.

    a. I can learn from this for next time. ____

    b. I messed up. ____

    c. They wouldn't know a great idea if it was in front of their noses. ____

    d. That destroys my chances of promotion. ____

3. I phone my favorite local restaurant to reserve a table, but it is already fully booked.

    a. I may as well find somewhere better. ____

    b. It's my own fault for not calling earlier to make a reservation. ____

    c. Why is it always me who has to book the restaurant anyway? ____

    d. I've ruined the whole evening. ____

4. I cook dinner for friends, and although they say it is delicious, most of them barely touch the food on their plates.

    a. In the future, I'll practice a new dish before trying it on guests. ____

    b. I'm embarrassed. I am a terrible host. ____

    c. My friends said it was delicious and I've no reason to doubt they were telling the truth. ____

    d. My friends will never want to visit me again. ____

5. I get lost on my way to visit a friend.

    a. I can see where I went wrong; it'll be easier next time. ____

    b. I am a lousy navigator. ____

    c. My friend's directions are useless. ____

    d. My friend will be very upset that I'm late. ____

6. I read an article in the newspaper that gives me the information
   I need to impress a client.

   a. It's a good thing I keep up to date with current affairs. ____

   b. What a fluke. ____

   c. Good things happen to me. ____

   d. I suspect my client knows the information already. ____

7. My team wins a game in a two-on-two basketball tournament.

   a. We're a great team. ____

   b. The opposition must not be very good. ____

   c. I am a fantastic basketball player. ____

   d. It was all thanks to my partner. ____

8. My partner / close friend really likes the birthday present
   I bought her.

   a. I am good at buying presents. ____

   b. Thank goodness she gave me a hint. ____

   c. I bet there aren't many partners/friends who would have chosen
      so well. ____

   d. I'll never be able to get her something as good for Christmas. ____

9. I cook dinner for friends and they praise my food.

   a. I'm a good cook. ____

   b. My friends are easily pleased. ____

   c. When I really try at something, I can make a success of it. ____

   d. There wasn't anything special about it. They must have low
      expectations about my abilities. ____

10. Someone compliments me on my clothes.

    a. I do look good in this outfit. ____

    b. He clearly doesn't have much of an idea about style himself. ____

    c. He must really like me. ____

    d. What a nice thing to say. ____

Your Results

Total your points for each option (*a, b, c, d*) in the diagnostic and enter the numbers here:

a: _____   b: _____   c: _____   d: _____

To see how much of an optimist or pessimist you tend to be, use this formula to calculate your points:

$$(a + c) - (b + d) = \text{_____}$$

If your total is a positive number, then you tend to think optimistically; if it is negative, then you tend to look at things pessimistically. The higher the number, the more you tend to think in this way (the maximum is 100 on either side, positive or negative).

What Kind of Optimist Are You?

The *a* responses represent an attentive optimist's typical viewpoint and *c* are the responses of an undiluted optimist. If your total *c* points are higher than your total *a* points, then your optimism probably needs reining in or it will be counterproductive. You are likely missing out on the "attentive" part of attentive optimism.

If you gave 2 or more points to a *c* response for any statement, it suggests certain types of unrealistic optimism:

Statements	Unrealistic Optimism Types
1, 2, 4	*You ignore problems.* This suggests a tendency to dismiss problems that may need to be addressed. The danger is that the problem grows, though you could have taken action earlier to keep it in proportion.
3, 5	*You duck responsibility.* This suggests that you may not accept your share of the blame when things go wrong. This not only annoys others but also means that you will be less likely to make important changes to yourself, and so the same problem may recur.
6, 7, 9	*You tend toward wishful thinking.* This implies that you are looking through rose-colored glasses and extrapolating more than appears reasonable about your abilities or prospects. The danger here is that you assume things will just happen, and so you may not make enough effort to ensure they actually do.

Statements	Unrealistic Optimism Types
8, 10	*You overinterpret.* This is similar to wishful thinking. It happens when you decide you know what other people are thinking, or are capable of doing, without much evidence to support your assumptions. You may well misinterpret their motives or underestimate their capabilities as a result.

What Kind of Pessimist Are You?

The two pessimistic responses—*b* and *d*—have different meanings too. A *b* response is straightforward pessimism based on the explanatory style described earlier. A *d* response represents more accentuated pessimism.

If your pessimism is mainly of the *b* type, then the best way to go about becoming more of an optimist is to explain situations differently to yourself after you've experienced them. When something goes wrong, try describing the situation as specific and temporary (e.g., *The shower curtain didn't stay up* this time), and when things go well, describe them in a universal, permanent, and personal way (e.g., *I'm great at all home repair projects*).

If you gave 2 or more points to a *d* response for any statement, it suggests certain things other than your explanatory style are worth looking at if you want to benefit from attentive optimism. Review your *d* responses to any of the statements outlined in the following list, because this will give you further insight into your type of pessimism.

Statements	Unrealistic Pessimism Types
1, 3	*You overidentify.* This indicates that you may be in danger of taking more responsibility for a negative outcome than is reasonable.
2, 6, 8, 9	*You maximize/minimize problems.* You run the risk of exaggerating a negative impact or dismissing a positive aspect.
4, 5	*You overinterpret.* Much like undiluted optimists, you assume what other people are thinking or are capable of doing without much or any evidence.

Statements	Unrealistic Pessimism Types
7, 10	*You misallocate responsibility.* You are generous in your praise, but you may not value your own contribution enough. This modesty could be attractive to others, but it may also leave you with less appreciation of your strengths.

When Pessimism Pays

So far, we have suggested that optimism is preferable to pessimism, and broadly speaking this is true. However, there are a handful of circumstances in which it is better to switch to a more pessimistic outlook. One of the tricks to being an attentive optimist lies in knowing when to be optimistic and when to be pessimistic. In summary, there are three situations when it is best to adopt a pessimistic outlook:

When You're Making Major Decisions

The optimism that helped you succeed in your day job could be a disadvantage when you are considering big decisions, such as changing your lifestyle completely. Too much optimism in this situation can result in wishful thinking.

When the Implications of Being Wrong Would Be Extremely Serious

How comfortable would you be if you knew that the pilot of your plane was being optimistic about having enough fuel to get to your destination? Yeah. Serious.

When You Are Trying to Comfort Someone Who Is Very Unhappy

Try telling someone whose mother has just died that they are really lucky because they will inherit a lot of money and will no longer have to spend Christmas being reminded of all their faults. Try it. We can pretty much guarantee that this conversation ends very badly.

In almost all other situations, you are better off being broadly optimistic.

Optimism, Meet Pessimism:
Why Arguing with Yourself Is Good

Kevin likes playing chess. The person Kevin most often plays chess with is himself. When his friend Alan saw him playing white and then swapping seats and playing black, Alan was confused. "Don't you always lose?" he asked. "No," replied Kevin, "I always win."

This story not only highlights the difference between an optimistic thinker, Kevin, and a pessimistic one, Alan, but also poses an interesting question: How can you develop your own strategy when you know how you'll play against yourself and, therefore, will be more than capable of defeating yourself? Kevin contends that he deliberately blocks his previous thoughts and, by physically moving to the other side of the board, looks at the problem with a fresh perspective. He admits that it isn't quite the same as playing against another person, but he is confident that it has helped him improve his game.

When it comes to the idea of arguing with yourself, your reaction is likely to be more similar to Alan's than to Kevin's—most of us find arguing with ourselves a struggle because we assume that we are right in the first place, so how can we possibly argue against ourselves? After all, if we didn't think we were right, we would have changed our view already. Right? Or wrong?

The weak point of this argument (yet here we are, arguing with a previous paragraph we wrote) is the *assumption* of being right. We all assume we're right. And once we make that assumption, we don't seriously consider the possibility we could be wrong. Through a combination of mental idleness (autopilot) and a desire to reinforce our self-perception, we rarely open our assumptions up to scrutiny.

Actually, the strongest reason for arguing with yourself is that your beliefs may be limiting you from achieving everything you are capable of. If you believe you're not good at learning new languages, then you don't try to improve your Spanish. If you believe your significant other will never come around to seeing your point of view, you're unlikely to continue trying to persuade them to. Instead, you'll simply say, "You're wrong."

Still, there is great value in allowing your optimist voice to argue with your pessimist voice, and vice versa. It's like the cartoons where the devil is sitting on one shoulder and an angel is sitting on the other, tugging at your decision-making process. It's your job to let them argue. And it's your job to play the role of judge and choose sides in the end. The only question is, How do you get good at arguing with yourself?

The Six Steps of Arguing with Yourself

Sean was a participant at a Mind Gym workout. During the course of the workout, the following discussion happened between Sean and a Mind Gym coach, though it could quite as easily have happened inside Sean's head. The important point is the thought process that unfolded—a six-step process of self-analysis we can all learn from and apply to our own internal arguments.

Step One: Your Belief

Sean believed he was bad at giving presentations. As a result, he tried to avoid taking any role that required standing up and talking to groups of people (even though he had to make a presentation roughly every eight weeks in his current job). This limited Sean's exposure in his company and in his industry, which meant that he had not been promoted into the position someone with his track record would expect.

"Whenever I make a presentation," Sean explained, "there is always someone who disagrees with me. They ask me questions that I can't answer on the spot, and it looks like everything I am saying is just a bunch of hot air. Plus, my boss always interrupts when he is there, making points that I hadn't considered; everyone looks at me with totally blank faces; I always have to use notes; and throughout my entire career, not one single person has ever said they thought I made a good presentation. I'm not making it up. I really am a bad presenter."

At first glance, Sean's argument that he is a bad presenter seems strong. But there is always a danger with a pessimistic opinion that it is a self-fulfilling prophecy: we are so determined to maintain our self-belief that we will go out of our way to prove it is correct, even if we suffer as a result. Is this what Sean was subconsciously up to?

Step Two: Your Evidence

After the Mind Gym coach asked Sean a few questions, a different picture started to emerge. Sean admitted that people didn't *always* stare with blank faces. Sometimes they actually nodded and took notes, even though he gave out copies of the slides he used. This actually could be a sign that they were interested in remembering what he had said rather than, as Sean saw it, proof that his visual materials weren't any good.

Sean also agreed that, over the years, some people had made comments like "That was interesting" or "I wish I had heard that presentation before my last project." So, while Sean's audiences didn't directly compliment his presentation style, they clearly valued the content of his presentations. Sean also accepted that in his company culture, compliments were rare, and when you did something well, most people assumed that you were just doing your job. The culture, however, also favored quickly pointing out when things went wrong. Had anyone ever told Sean he was a bad presenter? The answer was no, even though Sean had done eighteen different presentations.

It turned out that the difficult questions Sean was so afraid of getting asked at these presentations came from representatives of the same department during every presentation. In fact, the reason Sean couldn't answer the questions was because they weren't relevant and they weren't geared toward his area of responsibility. But because Sean believed that, as the presenter, he should be able to answer whatever question came his way (another false belief), he floundered and apologized, which made him appear less convincing.

When scrutinized, Sean's evidence that he was a poor presenter didn't look quite so strong. Yet even though his arguments were dismissed due to largely false evidence, Sean maintained a pessimistic outlook on his situation and insisted that he was a horrible presenter. And it's his perception that matters, not anyone else's.

Step Three: Your Alternative Explanations

If the evidence itself is not enough to disprove an argument, then the next step is to look for alternative explanations.

Sean's presentations were often about quite technical and complex subjects and were delivered to people from other parts of the organization, not to his immediate colleagues, who would have been more familiar with the content being discussed. As a result, the blank faces Sean saw were likely signs of deep concentration rather than disbelief or boredom.

As for Sean's boss interrupting him, maybe he wasn't doing so because Sean was a poor presenter but because he wanted to take some of the credit for the content of the presentation for himself. When this was suggested to Sean, he immediately thought of other times when his boss had taken some of the glory for his work. And as far as Sean's belief that he wasn't a good presenter because he relied on his notes, many good presenters use them, especially when they are talking about complex subjects.

The general assumptions behind Sean's arguments needed to be considered. Quite often, when people see themselves as "failing" it's due to a misguided definition of success. In this instance, the question was, What does a good presentation consist of? Some people (Sean included) think that it is about making people laugh, speaking fluently, and not using notes. Certainly, if you are a stand-up comedian this is true, but not necessarily if you are a presenter in business.

Step Four: Your Consequences

By this stage, Sean was beginning to see that there might be another side to his argument. But what if he hadn't considered changing his view? When both the evidence and the alternatives aren't very convincing, the next question to ask is, *What might be the consequences of my perceptions?*

In Sean's case, what would be the consequences if his initial assumption—that he is not a good presenter—was true? Sean's perception of his presentation skills was clear. As a "bad presenter," he damaged his reputation each time he stood up to speak. As a result, he typically tried to stay out of the spotlight because he thought he was failing and wasn't being considered for new roles or promotions. Also, senior roles in his company tended to require more presentations, so he steered clear of discussing those roles, because he assumed no one would even consider him. At just thirty-two years old, Sean had presumed he had hit a ceiling in his career.

When pressed further about the consequences of being a bad presenter, Sean, it seemed, had exaggerated the effect. He agreed that there were people more senior than him who weren't great presenters either. They'd succeeded either by joining up with someone who was a more proficient communicator or by writing papers that were widely shared and published. The consequences of being a poor presenter were actually less serious than Sean had initially assumed.

Step Five: Your Wasted Thoughts

When all the arguments presented in steps one through four have been tried and found wanting, the last resort is to ask yourself, *Is there any use in holding on to my perception?* For Sean, the value in seeing himself as a bad presenter was, well, zero. For that reason, it would be well worth his effort to change his view. The only way his self-belief about being a bad presenter could be helpful is if he uses it as a prompt to take action and therefore become a better presenter.

Step Six: Your Call to Action

Challenging the way you look at a situation is probably the single most powerful thing you can do when it comes to altering your beliefs and trying to change from a pessimistic to an optimistic viewpoint. It is certainly possible that Sean, by simply thinking differently about his capabilities, could become a more confident and effective presenter. Perhaps if he grew less bothered by his lack of polish, he could gain authority in his subjects. But thinking differently is not the only thing Sean could do. He could tackle his perceived weaknesses head-on. He could be coached to answer difficult questions more effectively; he could spend more time anticipating the questions that might be asked and so prepare some answers; and he could develop some standard techniques for questions he doesn't know the answers to. No doubt, there is plenty more that Sean could do to become a better presenter.

When you change your perspective of a situation by arguing with yourself, you will then be ready to quash pessimistic habits (*I am not good enough and there's nothing I can do about it*) and, instead, do something positive (*I am capable. Now let me get on with it and do something to make me even better*). Next, you need to decide what sort of change to make and when to make it.

The Six Steps: Your Summary of the Disputation Process

In the previous six steps, we charted the "argument" Sean had during a Mind Gym workout. As a result, he

• considered himself a perfectly adequate presenter,

- appreciated that the level of his presenting skills wasn't as critical to his future success as he had previously thought, and

- knew what he could do to become a better presenter.

This argument happened between two people—Sean and the Mind Gym coach—but it could just as easily have happened in Sean's head. It is a process any of us can use when we have a pessimistic or negative assumption we want to challenge or change.

Win Yourself Over

The tone of the "inner voice" you have an argument with is up to you, though the tougher and firmer that voice, the more likely it is to win any argument. Imagine, for example, that your inner voice takes the persona of a courtroom attorney or a character from one of your favorite crime shows—a cop or judge who wouldn't let you get away with any shenanigans. Always be sharp but fair and don't let yourself dodge questions or responsibility. If you're going to have the hardest argument you'll ever have, you might as well do it properly. You can handle the truth.

ARGUING WITH YOURSELF: A SUMMARY OF THE SIX STEPS	
1. What is your belief?	This will be a pessimistic view. If you are already thinking optimistically about a situation, then you don't need to argue with yourself about it.
2. What evidence is there to challenge this view (i.e., the case for the prosecution)?	Work hard to unearth all the evidence against this view. Imagine you are Columbo and Sherlock Holmes rolled into one.
3. If the evidence isn't enough, what alternative explanations are there to explain the situation?	There are almost certainly other reasons. Come up with as many alternative explanations as you can before picking out the ones that are most likely to be valid.

4. If the alternative explanations and the evidence aren't enough, what are the real consequences if your belief is correct? (i.e., so what?)	You might well have built this belief up into an enormous thing in your mind. A reality check will help put it back into perspective. Indeed, so much so that the belief may become largely irrelevant.
5. If you are still holding on to your original belief, how useful is it to have this view?	Even when all other arguments haven't worked, holding on to this negative belief is unlikely to help. Better to see it differently, say, as a good base from which to build.
6. Given this argument with yourself, what will you do to improve the situation?	There are usually lots of things you can do to improve the situation. Write them all down before deciding what to do (otherwise, you will face roughly the same situation the next time, and since your previous approach to the situation didn't work, it probably won't work next time either). Then, of all the possible actions you've listed, decide which you will actually do and when.

Avoid Optimistic or Pessimistic Ruts

Most of us have decided how we look at life, and we tend to use the same approach for most everything. Quite simply, this is your mind-set. If you've found that a sense of realism is helpful in one part of your life—say, buying a house or submitting weekly reports at work—then you are likely to use the same sense of realism in every other part of your life, even if it is having the opposite effect from the one that you want. Your upbringing also has a strong influence on how you approach your life.

Once you are aware of how you tend to look at things and of your explanatory style, you can decide whether to change. This chapter and the diagnostic hopefully helped you realize how you can change the way you look at things, how you can be more attentively optimistic—and, for that matter, pessimistic when it will work to your advantage.

Of course, knowing is one thing, doing is quite another. This is an exercise book. You won't get the true benefits until you work out.

GIVE YOUR MIND A WORKOUT

Beginner: Look for the Upside

Learn to Spot Optimism

Before you know what to look for in yourself, learn to spot optimism and pessimism in others.

1. Scan for pessimists. Watch and listen to find friends, colleagues, and celebrities being interviewed on the radio or TV—anyone who is entirely pessimistic in the way they present their situation. Listen intently as they describe negative events as universal and permanent, and positive events as mere circumstances.

2. Scan for optimists. Watch and listen for people being entirely optimistic in the way they present their situation. Listen intently as they describe positive events as universal and permanent, and negative events as mere circumstances.

Find the Positive

Psychologist Martin Seligman came up with the following "Three Good Things" exercise and tested its validity in increasing optimistic feelings.[10] His research demonstrates that this exercise provides lasting happiness and fewer depressive feelings, which continues months after completing the exercise. So why not give it a try?

1. Every night for a month, write down three good things that happened that day and what caused them.

2. After each good thing, write what it means to you. Keep this in a journal or notebook so you can return to it and review what you wrote. They say it's the little things that count, and after this month, you'll likely agree.

Advanced: Argue with Yourself

Think of this exercise not as a lesson in understanding but as an activity that results in a winning argument.

1. Choose a perception you have about yourself that you would like to change—for example, a negative perception of what you are capable of.

2. Don't become too entrenched in your position to start with. If you do, be willing to agree in principle that you will compromise or change your view if the arguments are compelling.

3. Imagine you are a prosecutor in a courtroom challenging your original hypothesis; give it everything you can. As the prosecutor, you don't need to be fair; you need to make the best case possible. Don't put up a defense as you go along but assemble all the arguments against your original view first.

4. Is there a case for the prosecution? If so, accept this without necessarily launching a counterattack.

5. Search for alternative explanations. There is almost always more than one reason. We tend to overemphasize the examples that support our beliefs and underplay any counterexamples that suggest alternative causes.

6. Try to find the right path between firm and supportive: too lenient and your views won't change; too aggressive and you won't want to change.

7. Challenge your assumptions about the importance of your view. So what if you can't play a musical instrument or master all the functions on your mobile phone?

8. The ultimate fallback is to decide whether your view is helping or hindering. Even if, in your opinion, your view is true, that isn't enough of a reason to hold on to it. If the belief is getting in the way, then it's best to put it to one side.

9. The hardest part of arguing with yourself is being willing to be swayed. Ask yourself if you are being obstinate.

PART TWO

Take Control

HOW MUCH CONTROL do you have over your life? It's a question that has puzzled philosophers, great academics, and people stuck at airport gates waiting for delayed flights.

The truth is that you have much more control over your life than first meets the eye. Rather than being a pawn, pushed around in some great game of existential chess, you have the ability to choose what you do, how you do it, and when you do it.

As wonderful as this choice is, it also has disadvantages. Are you procrastinating about a big project? Are you timid about asking that special person out on a date because you assume they'll reject you? Are you frustrated by a situation at work that could actually open a door to a new opportunity? Why?

The chapters in this part of the book are filled with techniques to help you think differently, react differently, and regain control of your life.

This section starts with a chapter titled "Take Charge." In it, you'll learn ways to approach everyday challenges, such as being more proactive so things get done rather than hang over you like a cartoon rain cloud. You'll learn how to take charge of your thinking when circumstances seem like they're out of your control. And you'll discover tools that not only allow you to choose how you think, feel, and react to situations but also give you control of those situations.

Next, in "Start a New Chapter" you'll explore bigger issues, like *Where's my life going?* The tools in this chapter will help you answer the big burning questions: *Am I doing the right things to get what I want in life? Am I at least headed in the right direction?* You'll quickly learn how to clear your most common hurdles. You'll better understand many of the things that may have held you back in the past. What's more, you'll almost immediately discover how to re-chart your future course.

Finally, the last chapter in this section, "End Procrastination Now," will help those who want to change but don't know where, how, or when to begin the process. In this chapter, you'll examine why you procrastinate. Are you trying to avoid uncomfortable situations? Are you complacent? Are you an "action illusionist"? You'll find out. And you'll gain all the tools you need to stop procrastinating and start living, working, and building stronger relationships today.

No, you can't control every situation in your life. But you can choose to take control of your thoughts, your actions, and your reactions. Dive into this next part. Wrap these chapters around certain areas of your life. You will be surprised by how much you can improve aspects of your life that you didn't even know needed improvement.

CHAPTER 3

Take Charge

The thoughts and preaching of Reinhold Niebuhr, a theologian born in the nineteenth century, may not be the most obvious place to start when considering how you can take control of a challenging situation, but a truism he described in a prayer still has much resonance today: "God, grant me the serenity to accept the things I cannot change, the courage to change the things I can, and the wisdom to know the difference."

Over a century later, absolute wisdom may still be beyond the reach of humankind, but the ability to differentiate between what is in our control and what is not is very firmly within our grasp. Sometimes the difference is not obvious. For example, if you wanted a friend to read this book, you could recommend it. You could offer them a reward to read it, you could tell them why you think it is worth their while, you could even buy them a copy—all these things are in your control. But whether that person reads it or not, and likes it or not, is out of your control. This ability to distinguish and act on what is in or out of your control makes the difference between those who can banish the worry monsters and those who can't.

Reactive Versus Proactive Mind-Set

Danny is concerned about selling his house. The market is soft. The real estate agent doesn't seem very efficient. The last people who made an offer pulled out, and Danny won't be able to afford the mortgage when it increases next month. He is losing sleep and it is affecting his work. *Please will someone fall in love with my house and make an offer today?* he says to himself.

The chances are no one will. Danny is focusing on what is out of his control: the market, the agent's efficiency, the reaction of the last people who made an offer, the end of the discount on his mortgage. As a result, he is likely to feel powerless and use lots of mental energy without achieving very much. Danny is in "victim" mode—at best reacting to events and at worst waiting passively for them to show him his destiny, which is unlikely to be a particularly rosy one. This is not a good place to be. Danny would be better off summoning the courage, as Reinhold Niebuhr put it, to focus on changing the things he can.

Let's take a look at Danny's worries and the possible actions he could take to overcome them:

Danny's Worries	What He Can Do
The soft market	• Find out if similar properties are being sold for less and what they're selling for. • Reduce the asking price of his house.
The real estate agent's efficiency	• Give the agent a time limit to sell the house. • Talk with the agent about why he is finding it difficult to sell the house and what can make a sale easier.
The cancellation of the last offer	• Ask the agent why the last people decided not to buy the house. • Make some cosmetic improvements, such as repainting.
The mortgage increase	• Talk to the bank and explain his situation. The bank may offer a refinance option that allows him to keep the house. • See if another bank will take on the loan at the same terms (and if there is a penalty clause for leaving his existing bank).

A skeptic might argue that there is no guarantee these proposed actions, or any others, will solve Danny's problems. That skeptic would be absolutely right. There is no guarantee. What is 100 percent certain is that Danny can choose to focus on the left column of the list—his worries—or the right column of the list—what he can do about them.

People like Danny, who focus on their worries, have a "reactive" mind-set; they worry about all the things that might go wrong and feel they can't do anything to change them. People with reactive mind-sets are likely to

- respond to what happens, often feeling like a victim;

- spend a lot of time worrying in ways that drain their energy but won't improve the situation;

- blame and accuse other people for the problems and challenges in their lives;

- put off doing things for as long as possible and, in the end, work harder to achieve the same or a poorer result; and

- fail to take action that would likely improve their circumstances.

People who focus on what they can do to make a situation better have a "proactive" mind-set. These people create a plan of action to tackle their problems and turn their attention to all the things they can do to positively influence the situation. People with a proactive mind-set are more likely to

- take action proactively, doing things that will help;

- feel in control of the situation and their lives;

- have more free time to do what they want; and

- be viewed as leaders or as strong.

If Danny focuses his attention on what he can do, two things will start to happen. First, he will feel better about his real estate problem, because rather than feeling impotent about the situation he will feel he can make a difference. Second, he will deploy his energy toward thinking about and doing things that could help.

A proactive mind-set is likely to also lead to a third benefit: As Danny starts to take action, new opportunities will emerge that he hadn't even considered. Perhaps when he talks with the real estate agent, he discovers that he could help with Internet marketing, inexpensively improve the landscaping of the house, or clear out the spare room so that it appears larger and more desirable.

Proactive thinkers always focus on what they can do to improve a situation. As a direct result, they achieve more and feel more in control. They are in charge.

The Science Behind Being in Charge

The idea of having a "locus" of control was put forward by Julian Rotter in 1954.[1] He suggested that individuals with an external locus of control—people with a reactive mind-set—typically believe that rewards in life are determined by forces such as fate, luck, or other people. Individuals with an internal locus of control—people with a proactive mind-set—tend to believe events are triggered by their own behavior or capability. Further research has suggested there are numerous benefits to having an internal locus of control, or a proactive mind-set, including

- greater job performance and job satisfaction,[2]
- decreased likelihood of depression or anxiety,[3]
- healthier relationships,
- higher academic achievements,
- longer life expectancy,[4]
- less stress, and
- less illness.[5]

Social scientists generally believe that people with parents who were controlling or authoritarian are more likely to develop an externalized locus of control or reactive mind-set. Similarly, individuals who have experienced stressful life events, like the death of a parent or sibling, particularly when they were young, also tend to develop a reactive mind-set.

By contrast, those whose parents encouraged them to do things that produced direct and measurable results from their efforts, like learning to play a musical instrument, are more likely to have an internalized locus or proactive mind-set. Kindness also makes a difference: Children with an internal locus also seem to have parents who showed affection and love.

How to Spot a Proactive or Reactive Mind-Set

One way to spot how proactive or reactive you are is to notice the way you think about a situation. Imagine that you are frustrated because your boss keeps changing her mind and makes unreasonable demands of you. Here are some different ways to think about this problem, split between a focus on being out of control and a focus on being in control.

Out of Control (Reactive)	In Control (Proactive)
She's an unreasonable person who doesn't appreciate the pressure I'm under.	I need to set up some early morning meetings so we can agree on the priorities of the day.
She has problems in her personal life and is taking them out on me.	I'll take her out for coffee and see if there is anything I can do to help—maybe alleviate some of her stress at work so she can deal with her personal stuff.
Her own boss is being unreasonable (too).	I'll talk to my coworkers to see what they do to get the best from her.
	I'll choose areas where I must stand my ground to set a precedent.

Of course, it's easier to find oneself in the "Out of Control" column. In the short term, it may even be necessary—for example, when someone grieves the death of a friend or relative. However, if you stay in that column, the situation is probably going to get worse. Choose the "In Control" column and you are much more likely to improve the situation.

Going for a run three times a week may be hard work to start with, but it will make you fitter than slouching in front of the TV. In the same way, focusing your energy on what is in your control will make you more proactive, less stressed, and far more likely to achieve your goals.

There's Always Something You Can Do

Are there times when nothing can be done? Not many. Sometimes, it's true, there is very little that you can do. Yet even when a problem seems too big to tackle, or so big that your efforts might not make a difference, there are still things you can do.

For example, imagine that you're extremely concerned about the damage being done to the environment. While it is true that no single action you take will resolve the environmental problems in our world, a few actions on your part can make a big difference. You could

- vote for the political candidate or party that supports your cause,
- buy products that are environmentally friendly,
- recycle,
- write to newspapers, bloggers, and companies that share your concerns,
- invest exclusively in environmentally friendly funds, or
- take part in peaceful protests.

These actions aren't going to lead to an immediate or enormous difference in the hole in the ozone layer or instantly replant the Amazonian rain forests, but they are more likely to help than your doing nothing at all.

There's always something you can do to impact or positively change a problem. But the hardest step is often just understanding that your mind-set is limiting your action.

GIVE YOUR MIND A WORKOUT

Beginner: Understand Locus of Control

1. Next time you sit down for a chat with a friend, listen carefully to what he or she says and try to determine where their locus of control tends to be: external (reactive) or internal (proactive). You will hear people using a reactive mind-set when

   • they describe their worries as being outside their control,

   • they blame others for the situation they find themselves in, or

   • they avoid taking action.

   If someone is doing two or all three of these, they probably have an external locus of control.

2. As you start to talk about what is going on in your life, see if you can spot where your locus of control is. Listen to yourself talk to a friend about what is going on in your life and reflect on what you say and how you say it.

3. Take the time to reflect on how you view your life. Do you see a lot of challenges that you cannot solve, or do you see opportunities for creative solutions? Do you feel out of control, or do you feel ready to tackle the challenges? Are you someone who procrastinates because doing anything feels futile? The answers to these questions will clue you in as to where your locus of control lies. If you have an external locus of control—you feel reactive and out of control—how is this affecting your life? In other words, what are you *not doing* because you think you can't make a difference to the outcome?

Advanced: In and Out of Your Control

1. Take a blank sheet of paper. At the top, write down an issue that is on your mind and you want to address.

2. Draw a vertical line down the middle of the page. In the left column, write down all the aspects of this issue that are bothering you and

you cannot control. In the right column, write down all the things you could do that might have an impact.

3. Circle of few of the things you can do to have an impact and put a date next to each for when you will take action on it.

4. Take action!

Often when people complete this exercise, they are surprised by how much they can put in the right column. A long list will give you the confidence to take control of the situation and make useful things happen.

CHAPTER 4

Start a New Chapter

You're sitting in your rocking chair on the terrace of your beach home, overlooking the Pacific Ocean, and watching the sun set with a glass of wine by your side. With your 100th birthday only a few weeks away, you're reflecting on your life and recalling how the major decisions you made at different stages affected the course it followed. You remember the day you chose to move to California, the struggle to get a job as a writer, the naysayers who told you it was a waste of your time, your chance meeting with the woman who quickly became the love of your life. As you reflect, you realize that doing the things others told you were impossible became the most prized moments of your life.

A few weeks later, as your entire family gathers for your 100th birthday, one of your daughters asks you to give advice to all your grandchildren and great-grandchildren. And you decide to share the reflections.

"My advice to all of you is to understand that there is very little in life you can't do," you say to your family. "The choice we all have is between *will* and *won't*, instead of *can* and *can't*. Sure, people tend to say they can't do something or you can't do something. But that just disguises the fact that there is still a choice that can be made—in almost all situations. There is always a choice. What people actually mean is they *won't* do something or they *don't want* you to do something. You always have the option."

"Can't" Is a Four-Letter Word

This difference in attitude between "can't" and "won't" is a subtle but vital one, because it indicates whether you feel responsible for your actions and your future. In fact, the existentialist philosophers, led by Jean-Paul Sartre and Martin Heidegger, were the first significant body of thinkers to claim that humankind is totally free and totally responsible for its actions. This may sound less radical now than it did in the middle of the twentieth century. But it is much more radical than many of us allow when we consider how to improve our lives.

Today, our lives are full of rules, guidelines, and principles that we have invented, or have been invented for us, to help us make choices but also to provide us with excuses for poor decisions. And although they may masquerade as immutable laws, they are more like local bylaws, which are often outdated, irrelevant, and just plain wrong.

Here are a few you may have come across or live your life by:

• Job security is greater at larger, well-known companies.

• If you want a successful career, you must have a college degree.

• You are more likely to get divorced if there is a large age gap between you and your partner.

• People who finish at the top of their class get the best jobs.

Much of our upbringing is filled with threats about the horrible things that will happen if we don't stick to the rules. Santa Claus won't visit us if we're naughty. The bogeyman will get us if we're out past curfew. This carries into later life, when we are fearful that our friends or family won't approve of us or our motives will be misunderstood.

For those of you who tend to be swayed by irrational fear, your regrets are often based on the things you didn't do and the opportunities you didn't take: *Why didn't I leave the firm once I was qualified for a better job? Why didn't I take the chance to go to Memphis when I had it? How different would my life have been if I'd proposed to her that night on the boat?*

Others amongst us suffer from irrational exuberance. These people might be described—especially by those with irrational fears—as not having their feet firmly on the ground. The regrets they are most likely to have are along the lines of *Why did I rush into that?*

Some of the small businesses that collapse every year are started by people with irrational exuberance who didn't think through the decision they were making. Irrational exuberance is similar to undiluted optimism (which we described in chapter 2). We all know people who make quick and risky decisions at the drop of a hat.

The irony, of course, is that each type, whether fearful or exuberant, encourages the other. A megafailure for an irrational exuberant provides evidence to someone with irrational fear that their fear is well justified. *See what happens if you give up a good job?* Equally, to the irrational exuberant, the sight of someone unhappily stuck in a rut is evidence that they have nothing to fear but fear itself. *Oh, they may be secure financially, but look how unhappy they are.*

Irrational exuberants are, however, the exceptions in our society. Due to our upbringing,[1] most of us are much more likely to be worried about failing or letting someone down than we are to take risks and not worry about the consequences.

This chapter will help you get better at making life's big decisions. There are tips in here for those who are used to saying *I wish I hadn't,* but the majority of advice is for those who want to avoid looking back and saying *If only* or *I wish I had.*

The Ride of Your Life: How People Make Big Decisions

As we intentionally make changes in our lives, all humans go through psychological steps. A helpful way of illustrating these steps is with the grandly named "existential cycle," which has four stages: doing, contemplating, preparing, and experimenting.[2]

These four stages are much like exercises in risk management. No one wants to look back on his or her life at some point and say *I wish*

I would have or *If only I had*. The existential cycle helps you process life-changing decisions, such as getting a new job, getting married, or moving to a new city or country.

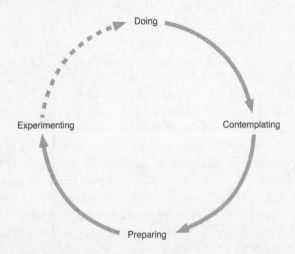

The first stage, "doing," is where you spend most of your life: It is your settled, equilibrium position. The doing may be all sorts of things—writing emails, riding horses, reading books, washing up, going to meetings, listening to lectures, cooking, dancing, running, sharing stories with friends, telling jokes, or making love. Of course, these are not done all at the same time (not unless you're really talented). Whatever the activity may be, and however enjoyable or dull it is, you are doing it and it tends to keep you occupied.

Sometimes you get around to the next stage in the cycle, "contemplating," and consider whether or how things could be different. *I wonder what life would be like if we moved to California or Florida? Do I really want to be an accountant for the rest of my life? Am I leading a "good" life?*

Occasionally you move on from contemplating to "preparing," the next stage in the cycle. You search on the web for real estate agents in San Diego or Key West, find out what property prices are, check weather patterns, possibly even visit your preferred destination on your next vacation. You have moved beyond imagining how things could be different to investigating the practical options for how to make them different.

The next stage is actually making the change. You leave your job, buy a house, and move all your possessions. This stage is called "experimenting." After you've settled in and started the beachside bar you'd dreamed about, this becomes your normal way of living, and you are once again in a state of doing. The cycle in itself is not complicated. The challenge is moving through it at the right pace and in the right way.

The Doing Magnet

As you travel around your cycle, you will have conversations with yourself that stop you from moving on to the next stage and instead take you back to doing.

Sometimes these thoughts can be very sensible and prevent you from wasting time or following the wrong path. But sometimes, unfortunately, they prevent you from both spotting and taking opportunities that could dramatically improve your life. The trick lies in recognizing the internal conversations and being able to make an informed decision about whether to listen to them or to ignore them and move on.

Conversation One: Dreamers Are Losers

Action produces results. Doesn't it? That's what most of us were led to believe. However, you might miss out on great things in life because an internal conversation has convinced you that all dreaming is bad, that it's a waste of time. Maybe, when you find yourself dreaming, you tell yourself something like this:

- *I must get on with things.*

- *No point in dreaming. I'll only be disappointed.*

- *I should be grateful for what I have.*

- *I have my feet on the ground.*

- *Let's deal with today.*

These are some of the internal conversations we all have that stop us from contemplating and bring us straight back to doing.

They struck a particular chord with a participant at one of Mind Gym's workouts, who, on seeing the cycle, realized that she had never really left the doing stage, or at least she had only ever reflected on the mundane issues of daily living rather than the big questions about her life.

Her cycle looked like this:

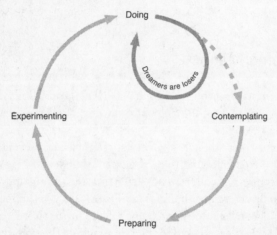

"I don't think I have ever asked myself how my life could be different or better," she explained. "I only thought about how to make sure it keeps going as it is. That's not to say I'm unhappy, only that I've never really thought about what I could do that would make me happier."

This woman—in her early forties, married, financially secure, and in a successful career—has a strong internal conversation that keeps her in a constant state of doing. When significant changes do occur in her life, they are likely just her responses to external events. And even then, her efforts would be geared toward getting her back to doing as quickly as possible.

A couple of years previously, for example, she had been laid off from her job. Instead of wondering what opportunities this opened up or how to use her severance package to possibly pursue a new career or learn new skills, she immediately rushed into looking for another job, one that would be almost identical to the one she had just left. Here's the kicker. It wasn't that she had loved her job and didn't want to do anything else, but she felt guilty for not just following the quickest and most obvious path back to staying busy.

Conversation Two: Get Real

Oftentimes, this conversation is the most confusing. It's that little voice in your head that tests reality. It's familiar if you're the person who dreams of being a filmmaker or an author or of starting your own business. You might not know any filmmakers or authors, therefore it doesn't seem real to dream of being one. You might know a person who started their own business but failed. So, you deem your dream impractical. Your internal voice might say something like this:

- *It would never work in practice.*

- *Nice idea, but I'd better get on with the day job.*

- *Someone else has probably already beaten me to the punch.*

- *There's no way I could do that.*

- *It's too much of a risk.*

Even when you get past the dreamers-are-losers conversation and reach the contemplating stage, the doing magnet is still very much there and just as powerful. At this stage, however, it works in a different way: You put up a string of practical objections to explain why your dream won't work in reality. *It's a shame, but it's just not practical,* you might decide, and then you get back to doing. As a result, your cycle looks like this:

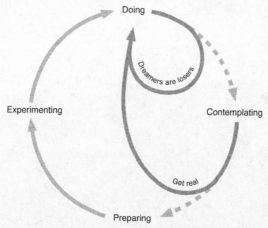

Conversation Three: Catastrophic Fantasies

The Rubicon is a river that marked the boundary of ancient Italy. Any army that crossed it was declaring war against the Roman Republic. So, when Julius Caesar—who at that time was still a general—crossed the Rubicon with a legion in 49 BC, there could be only one of two outcomes: he and his army would conquer or they would be destroyed.[3] This is the origin of the phrase "crossing the Rubicon," which has come to mean taking an irrevocable step.

In the existential cycle, an irrevocable step occurs when you move from preparing to experimenting. During this stage of the cycle, you might be telling yourself something like this:

- *Even though I don't know the result, I have to try.*

- *I hope it's worth the risk.*

- *I might fail, but I'm going for it.*

This is when you turn ideas into action, when you hand in your letter of resignation, tell your husband that you want a divorce, throw out all your old clothes, sign up for the Foreign Legion, or stop using contraceptives. It is the most difficult stage in the cycle and the one where the doing magnet is the strongest—because you know that once you move forward, there is no turning back.

You can see in the next illustration where the Rubicon lies within the cycle. You might also notice something else: a conversation that could stop everything.

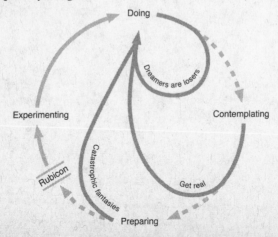

The most common reason why some of us don't cross the Rubicon is that we create what are called "catastrophic fantasies." A catastrophic fantasy is a bleak prediction of what would happen if we experiment with something new—if we do cross our own Rubicons.

We all create catastrophic fantasies, particularly when contemplating big decisions, and quite often they scare us into sticking with the status quo. Most men planning to propose marriage, before they do so, create catastrophic fantasies about married life. These may include a nagging wife, gorgeous women desperate for their attention whom they will have to resist, limits on being able to hang out with their buddies, the end of bachelor freedom, and so on. The men who do propose recognize the catastrophic fantasies as nonsense and appreciate that the likely outcome will be very different. The men who don't spot that they are creating catastrophic fantasies may miss out on the opportunity of a lifetime.

There is, of course, a third group: those who make a realistic assessment and decide that they do not want to commit to one person for the rest of their lives, or that the particular person they would be committing to is the wrong person. There is nothing wrong with that. Crossing the Rubicon is not always a good thing. In reality, some of our fears and worries may be accurate.

I dream about being able to swim an Ironman distance of 2.4 miles. However, I also believe that I'm not in good enough physical condition. I might get out there and end up too tired to make it the entire distance. Rather than risk drowning, I decide not to swim at all. The challenge we all have when venturing around the existential cycle is knowing whether our decision not to experiment with something new, and instead go back to doing, is realistic and sensible or ill-founded, damaging, and based largely on irrational fear.

While there is no definitive way of knowing for sure, there are some telltale signs to help you gauge whether your decision not to cross a particular Rubicon is based on rational concerns or irrational fears. Here are five signs that you are probably right not to cross the Rubicon and your decision is probably based in realism and sense:

1. You have considered the arguments for both sides and have decided that your decision makes the most sense. If pressed, however, you could make the case for the opposite view.

2. You are confident that you won't regret your decision later. You have thought about what the realistic best outcome is, and either it isn't

good enough or it isn't likely enough. Basically, the reward isn't worth the risk.

3. You have thought through the worst-case scenario (as opposed to the catastrophic fantasy) and it is something you want to avoid at all costs. (To cross the Rubicon you really need to have decided that the worst-case scenario is worth the risk.) Basically, the risk isn't worth the risk.

4. You can imagine advising someone else in your situation to do the same. We're all much more levelheaded when it comes to someone else's life—their pleasure or their pain.

5. You are relieved to have reached a conclusion and also pleased about the journey you have taken to get there.

Here are five signs that you should not leave the banks of your Rubicon yet, so that you can continue to explore your decision:

1. The worst outcome that you are imagining is extreme, verging on the absurd (you'll not just fail to swim 2.4 miles, but be eaten by sharks).

2. You feel nervous and unsure about your decision. You keep putting it off, and you aren't doing anything constructive to help make the best choice.

3. You can imagine circumstances in which, looking back, you would deeply regret your decision.

4. The decision to keep things roughly as they are doesn't fit with how you see yourself. Maybe it seems cautious, whereas you see yourself as courageous, or it feels contradictory to some of the values that you hold most dear.

5. Everyone else may disagree, but you are still excited by the prospect of the change.

When the Doing Magnet Is Weak

Irrational exuberants are those people who are forever saying things like *I wish I hadn't rushed into that* or *If only I'd thought about it first.* Rather than never crossing the Rubicon, they're happy to head over far too easily—without ever considering the size of the army on the other side. In terms of the existential cycle, their doing magnet is relatively weak—the centrifugal momentum of the next new thing is stronger than the gravitational force of the status quo.

If you find that you can't hold down a job, you can't keep a relationship, you spend money on a whim, or you haven't gotten around to making your home into a place you like living in, *and* you regret it, then you may be suffering from a form of irrational exuberance. The best advice in this situation is this: spend longer at the preparing stage before wading across your Rubicon.

For example, consider one of these choices:

- Think through all the possible disadvantages of taking this course of action as well as the advantages—really make an effort to present the case for caution on this occasion.

- Contrast the allure of the new situation with how your existing life might improve even if you don't make this big change. People who are always moving on to new jobs often fail to consider how their current jobs could get better. A new job may be attractive, but it is wrong to assume the old one will stay the same. New possibilities could open up. What happens when your boss moves on?

- Contemplate the bigger and better gains and pleasures you could have if you didn't always go for instant gratification. Could the gratification get more gratifying?

- Consider any decisions you made in the past that led to situations you later regretted. What can you learn from these that will help you make a wiser decision this time?

If You Want to Improve, You Have to Cross the Rubicon

You have a choice in how you run your life. There is no "can't," only "will" and "won't." The trick is knowing why you are, or aren't, moving around the existential cycle and, in particular, crossing your Rubicon. Like we've said, the right thing isn't to always cross or always not cross.

The right thing is to understand why you want to cross or don't want to cross, and then make your decision.

Nevertheless, none of us want to live our lives in a constant state of doing. I might not be in good enough shape today to swim 2.4 miles, but that doesn't mean I won't be in the future. Plus, our reasons for remaining in one state may not be strong. At some point, in certain aspects of our lives, if we want to progress, we must cross the Rubicon.

A decision to not cross the Rubicon based on the wrong reasons—when catastrophic fantasies rule our mind-sets—is what causes people to look back on their lives and think *If only.* . . . All of us who have looked back and been proud of what we have done have crossed the Rubicon at least once and maybe many times.

There's a famous Latin maxim, carpe diem, which translated means "seize the day." The question you have to ask yourself is, *When it comes to crossing Rubicons, just how much of a Caesar am I prepared to be?*

GIVE YOUR MIND A WORKOUT

Beginner: Find Where You Are in the Existential Cycle

1. Think about one of the main areas of your life—say, your career or your home.

2. Ask yourself which stage of the existential cycle you are at most of the time.

3. Analyze whether this is a good place to be. Or are you preventing yourself from moving around the cycle? Is there a danger that you might be saying *If only.* . . in a few years' time? If so, how can you change your internal conversations to help unblock yourself?

Advanced: Conquer Your Fears of Change

1. Think of an issue, something you've wanted to do for a while but are putting off because of fear.

2. Make an exhaustive list of all your fears about this issue and try to examine the root fears that underlie them all by asking *And then what?* after each fear. For example, "I've wanted to ask Sarah out for a long time, but I'm afraid she will say no." Now ask, *And then what?* "I'm afraid I'll lose the courage to ever ask anyone out again." *And then what?* "I'm afraid I'll always be alone." *And then what?* "I'm afraid I will never be happy." And continue in that way with each fear. Doing this will help you get closer to the root of your fears.

3. Now categorize your fears. Go through each one on your list and decide whether it is rational or irrational. (Hint: Irrational fears frequently include absolutist terms, such as "always" and "never.")

4. List some benefits of conquering each of your fears—not necessarily reaching the goal you want (e.g., Sarah says yes) but rather what conquering that fear will do for you.

5. After working through the previous steps, decide whether to address the issue you chose at the beginning. Maybe your fears are well founded and you'll continue to sit tight, or—more likely—you'll realize you're filled with irrational fears and catastrophic fantasies that you don't need to listen to any longer.

CHAPTER 5

End Procrastination Now

Waiting until later is one of life's guilty secrets: Everyone says they don't procrastinate, but everybody knows they do. Whether it's in work or in relationships, getting healthy or breaking bad habits, we all have the capacity to turn into an ostrich, put our heads in the sand, and hope that whatever it is we don't want to do will just disappear.

Sometimes it's the small things, like leaving a pile of laundry unfolded or not cleaning out the cat's litter box. Other times the issues are slightly bigger, like going to the dentist or knowing that it's time to lose some weight—things that might affect our lives in the longer run. And there are the more time-sensitive issues, like ending a relationship or asking for a promotion.

Let's face it, when we want to put off doing something, we can get pretty creative about coming up with a list of excuses: the student who wants to give up drinking coffee but "can't" until her exams are over; the single man who won't ask someone out because he doesn't feel strong enough to cope with a possible rejection; the office worker who knows she should write that report but is too stressed to even start; or the Scorpio who won't send off that proposal because his horoscope warned about an unpredictable disappointment.

While we all procrastinate from time to time, it's far too easy for an occasional lapse to turn into a destructive habit. It's as if life is a credit card: Just as you can treat yourself to some new clothes and decide *I'll worry about the cost next month,* you can catch a movie instead of sitting down on a Saturday afternoon to pay your bills. Of course, the problem is that at some point you still have to pay the credit card company—looks like in the near future a Saturday afternoon paying bills will be even less pleasant.

Like credit card bills, it's all too easy to build up debts in your "life bank," putting off one little thing after another. And paying back these time debts can take a long time and be painful—because in all areas of life those "bills" accumulate "interest." The weight-loss plan you wanted to start three months ago now has seven more pounds to contend with.

The good news is that procrastination, rather than being a characteristic you are born with, is actually more of a bad habit you pick up over years. And just like you can learn how to procrastinate, you can also unlearn it. You can teach yourself to earn money before you spend it. You can teach yourself to finish projects before you treat yourself to an entertaining afternoon at the movies. And you can teach yourself to get in shape so the guilty-pleasure foods are in fact a guilty pleasure. As a result, you will not only feel less stressed and more in control but also have a lot more time to spare.

The secret to overcoming procrastination is to find out how, in any given situation, you are procrastinating. Then it's just a short step to working out what you can do to teach yourself new habits.

Scientific and psychological research has shown that there are five main reasons why you put off doing things.

Complacency

It's not very difficult, so I can do it any time.
It won't take very long, so I'll fit it in later.
I know what I have to do, so I'm already halfway done.

Believe it or not, the first form of procrastination comes from an overly strong sense of self-confidence. It's the belief that you are on top of the situation and, therefore, you don't need to bother with it yet. This level of confidence can lead to complacency. It can appear as almost laziness or a general lack of concern—you're so certain of the outcome that any special effort is unnecessary. However, rather than a coasting ride to success, this form of procrastination quite often leads to the opposite result. In the fable of the tortoise and the hare, the hare is so sure of victory over the tortoise that he settles down for a quick nap, only for the tortoise to defeat him. Similarly, in almost every James Bond film, there is a scene where the arch-villain has Bond in his grasp, only to let the spy escape and thwart his plans for world domination. In these situations, evil cunning and overconfidence always seem to go hand in hand.

Dealing with Complacency

One way to deal with this form of procrastination is to imagine a great reward in the future. But you can only take advantage of this great reward if you've completed the task at hand. So, for example, if your passport needs renewing but you leave it until the day before you go on vacation because you think it'll be so easy to renew, you need to imagine a friend calling you in the middle of the night with a spare ticket for a weekend in paradise. The kicker is that the plane leaves at five A.M. If you don't have an up-to-date passport now, you can't go.

Alternatively, set more challenging goals for yourself. If you aren't motivated to finish an undesirable task, you need to change the situation. With the story of the hare and the tortoise, it clearly isn't enough incentive for the hare to just beat the tortoise: he feels (wrongly, as it turns out) that he can accomplish that in his sleep. But if the hare had challenged himself to not only beat the tortoise but also break the course record, he would have continued sprinting to the finish line and would never have lost the race.

Finally, if the task you face is relatively easy, just get it done. If you're an arch-villain in a James Bond film, just pull the trigger and carry on with taking over the world. Don't pause to gloat and show 007 the evil genius of your plan. While you're wrapped in your gloating, he'll be raising an eyebrow and delivering a sharp one-liner, and you'll be plunging to earth without a parachute. If you're not an arch-villain in a James Bond film, you won't be rewarded with a new world order, but your world will be a little more ordered, and that's a start.

Avoiding Discomfort

I'm not going to enjoy doing this at all.
This is going to take a really long time.
It's really unpleasant, so I'll start another time.

This sort of procrastination focuses on the unpleasantness of an activity, particularly compared with a far more enjoyable alternative.[1] When there are dishes to be washed, that television show about gardening can suddenly become fascinating. Perhaps the visit to the dentist can wait until next month, the telephone bill can be left until after payday, and that tax return can be filed tomorrow. Right now a great gardening show is on television.

There are more serious examples too. You might be unhappy in a long-term relationship but can't face the unpleasantness of ending it. You might know your health is at risk if you don't change your habits. You might worry that you could lose your job if the big, painfully long project isn't completed. In each case, the anticipated discomfort involved in taking action is enough to make you delay taking action.

Dealing with Avoiding Discomfort

When your discomfort stems from the size of a task (the tax return), break it down into bite-size tasks instead (get the bank statements, read the form, fill in section A, and so on). Doing one of these smaller activities makes the whole task feel easier. Once you get on a roll, the whole project may be completed before you know it.

A second idea comes from the Mary Poppins school of philosophy: a spoonful of sugar to help the medicine go down. Many of us don't enjoy household cleaning, but that doesn't mean we can't make it less of a chore. Pour yourself a cup of coffee or a glass of wine to sip while you scrub away (but only if you do it now); crank your favorite tunes—even create a playlist specifically designed for doing the dishes.

Here's a final challenge: Every day do one frustrating activity that you would normally put off until tomorrow. Not only will you be amazed by how much more you get done, but you'll soon run out of really frustrating things to do.

Fear of Failure[2]

I really won't be able to do this properly.
I've failed at this before, so I'm bound to fail again.
It's a big step, and I'm scared I may not be able to cope.

Sometimes the prospect of not succeeding is enough to halt any movement forward. Imagine there's someone you find attractive and want to ask out on a date, but you don't because you're afraid they'll say no. Or there's the possibility of a promotion at work, but you don't raise your hand because you're worried you might not get the job. Trying to get into a hip nightclub, making sales calls, signing up for salsa dancing classes—there are hundreds of things you may avoid doing for various reasons, but the real reason is a fear of failure.

You may even use this form of procrastination as a sort of escape clause.[3] By not doing work, not trying, not making an effort, you have an excuse for when things go wrong: *It's not that I'm not a good writer; it's just that I didn't bother with the revisions.* Or *I know I could give a better presentation than Phil, but I just don't want to put all my effort into it.* These excuses may dull the pain of failure, but you'll never taste the satisfaction of succeeding against the odds.

The problem here has nothing to do with failure; it has everything to do with fear. Mistakes, after all, are nothing to be afraid of. In fact, they are often the primary source of learning. Henry Ford may have said it best: "Failure is simply the opportunity to begin again, this time more intelligently."

Dealing with Fear of Failure

Confront your fear of failure head-on by considering what you have to lose and/or gain by taking action. Think, for example, about relationships. Which is worse: never dating anyone because they may not like you or occasionally being rejected? Think about it. All you really need is one person to say yes. And beyond that, if you can learn from the "No thanks, I'm not interested" rejections, you may be able to get a lot more yeses. *Is it my deodorant? Is it my language or manners? Am I trying too hard?* Likewise with jobs: It doesn't matter if you get turned down, so long as you learn from the experience; you'll keep improving, and sooner or later someone's going to say "You're hired." But no one's going to say this if you never apply in the first place.

Emotional Barriers

I'm too stressed/tired/excited to do this now.
I'm not in the right frame of mind.
I'm just not in the mood to do this right now.

Sometimes we use emotion as a reason to stop ourselves from taking action.[4] We convince ourselves, for whatever reason, that now isn't the time to do something and we're better off waiting for that "perfect moment."[5]

Imagine suffering a nightmarish journey into the office: a roadside accident leaves you stranded for an extra twenty-five minutes in bumper-to-bumper traffic. Then, when you finally get to the office, rather than answering an urgent email, you decide you need coffee and maybe a donut. But that's still not enough to release your tension before you tackle the email. So, you wander to the water cooler to chat with a coworker—to gripe about the traffic jam—before you can get in the right mood to work. And maybe you've already had some bad luck this week, so you're anxious about making any big decisions. *Today is not the day I should be responding to important emails. And I was going to start my diet today, but not after what I've been through.*

The problem with waiting for a perfect moment is that it never arrives. There will always be another good reason to put things off. Maybe you're trying to cut back on going out for drinks after work. But today isn't the day to stop because you are under too much stress. Or you've earned it because you are stressed and your buddy Tommy got a promotion. Wait a month. The chances are you'll wait another month, and then another—those stressful days and traffic jams and important emails will keep coming. And the excuses will come with them. Basically, there's never going to be a perfect moment to face the fire, start your diet, or answer an important email.

Dealing with Emotional Barriers

One way to overcome emotional barriers is to imagine the outcome of not doing something immediately. You might be the sort of person who thinks *I'm too stressed to start this project now,* but consider how much more stressed you'll feel if you leave the project until the last minute.

Action Illusion

I'm very busy, so I must be making some progress.
No one appreciates quite how much I've done.
There's so much to do, I just can't stop.

An action illusionist, as the name suggests, is the magician of the procrastinating world. But rather than waving a wand to make people or rabbits or the Statue of Liberty vanish, they use all their sleight of hand to make time disappear. They're the sort of people who, rather than studying for exams at school, will spend endless hours writing and rewriting their study schedule, and then say, "I just didn't have enough time." Or they'll pop onto the Internet to do some research and will still be there hours later, answering emails that have no correlation to their project. When challenged, these crafty people repeat their mantra: "I have done a lot with my time!" This, of course, is the biggest illusion of all, because they didn't accomplish the one thing they were supposed to do.

The most interesting thing about suffering from action illusion is that you can quite often spend more energy not doing work than it would take to get your task done.

Dealing with Action Illusion

If you're an action illusionist, the key to breaking this type of procrastination is to understand that you are not doing what needs to be done. You may technically be working: you keep checking your inbox; you have another look at the monthly data; you even reorganize your desk because the clutter is somehow imposing on your goal of completing your task. Yes, you are busy doing work-type tasks, only they're not the tasks that really need to be done.

Break this type of procrastination by deciding what would be a successful outcome from your effort. Decide what you can do first that would most help you achieve your goal. Do that one thing first, and then decide what would be the next step toward completing your task. Don't let anything come between you and your objective.

What's Your Excuse?

The secret to overcoming procrastination is to find out how, in any given situation, you are procrastinating. Then, it's just a short step toward working out what you can do to teach yourself new habits.

To find out what your excuse is, think about something you're putting off. Then, consider the following fifteen statements, and circle the number that represents how true you think each statement is for the situation you're thinking about.

Mark each statement in the following manner:

Circle 1 if the statement is *Not at all true.*
Circle 2 if the statement is *Rarely true.*
Circle 3 if the statement is *Sometimes true.*
Circle 4 if the statement is *Often true.*
Circle 5 if the statement is *Totally true.*

1. This doesn't concern me much.   1   2   3   4   5

2. I'm not going to enjoy doing this at all.   1   2   3   4   5

3. I really won't be able to do this properly.   1   2   3   4   5

4. I'm too stressed/tired/excited to do this now.   1   2   3   4   5

5. I'm very busy, so I must be making some progress.   1   2   3   4   5

6. It's not very difficult, I can do it anytime.   1   2   3   4   5

7. I'm not in the right frame of mind.   1   2   3   4   5

8. I'm very busy, so the results should follow soon.   1   2   3   4   5

9. It won't take very long, so I'll fit it in later.   1   2   3   4   5

10. I've failed at this before, so I'm bound to fail again.   1   2   3   4   5

11. This is going to take a really long time.   1   2   3   4   5

12. I'm just not in the mood to do this right now.   1   2   3   4   5

13. It's a big step, and I'm scared I may not be able to cope.   1   2   3   4   5

14. It's really unpleasant, so I'll start another time.   1   2   3   4   5

15. I know what I have to do, so I'm already halfway done.   1   2   3   4   5

Tally Your Numbers

Add up the numbers you chose for the statements as follows:

Statements #1 + #6 + #9 = _____ (Complacency)

Statements #2 + #11 + #14 = _____ (Avoiding discomfort)

Statements #3 + #10 + #13 = _____ (Fear of failure)

Statements #4 + #7 + #12 = _____ (Emotional barriers)

Statements #5 + #8 + #15 = _____ (Action illusion)

The total for each group of answers should be between 3 and 15. The nearer your total is to 15, the more you lean toward that form of procrastination. If any total is below 8, then you probably don't need to worry about it too much. But if your total is 12 or more, reconsider and reread the corresponding portion of this chapter. And please, don't wait to read it later!

General Tactics for Ending Procrastination

After learning about the five main reasons we procrastinate and taking the previous quiz, you may have found that you tend to procrastinate for one reason in one part of your life (e.g., at work) and another reason in another part of your life (doing chores at home). Or maybe you are inclined toward a mixture of two or more types. As important as it is to understand why and how you procrastinate, it is even more important to use some general tactics to try to remedy your type.

The following simple tactics will help you tackle the primary types of procrastination. Some tactics will work better for some people than others, so it is worth experimenting to find the right one that works for you.

Strive for Five: The Five-Minute Start

Five minutes is nothing—it's just three hundred seconds. It's the length of a song, the time it takes to boil an egg, and a commercial break on TV. Pick up a project you've been putting off and give it just three hundred seconds of your time. Once the five minutes are up, stop and reassess. Do you want to give it another five minutes? If so, carry on for another five. Stop and assess again. Continue in five-minute increments. And each time assess your progress. After a while, the momentum of beginning the task will carry you forward, and you'll forget about all those five-minute chunks.

Home Run: Set Goals and Rewards

During the day, or even portions of the day, set goals and rewards for yourself. Each time you hit a goal, you earn a reward—a short break, a hilarious YouTube video, a quick round of your favorite mobile phone game, or some other treat. It's important that the goals are realistic and the rewards are in proportion. Make sure you select a time to review your progress and adjust your targets accordingly.

Be Good to Yourself: You Today Versus You Tomorrow

Sometimes, if you find yourself buried in work, you might feel upset with yourself for not having started the work earlier. Try taking this one step further and imagine a conversation between "you today" and "you tomorrow." If "you tomorrow" (let's call him Saturday Tom) could chat with "you today" (let's call him Friday Tom), what would he have to say about your procrastination? If Friday Tom is leaving all the work for Saturday Tom, then Saturday Tom is not going to be a happy guy. So, be nice to Saturday Tom: make sure that Friday Tom does his fair share as well.

Set Creative Punishments: Negative Consequences

Another tactic is to make the consequences of inaction so unbearable that you have no choice but to get busy now. You could write a donation check to someone or something you really dislike: a rival team, if you're a football fan, or an opposing political party. Give the check to a friend with strict instructions to send it if you do not achieve your goal. Or be creative with your punishments: send flowers to a celebrity you despise or join the fan club of a pop group you think are awful. The more embarrassing and humiliating, the more incentive there is for you to get the task done.

I Was There: Witnessing Accountability

In the same way that weddings are public ceremonies, with friends and relatives there to celebrate but also to reinforce the vows the bride and groom are making, so is "going public" with your goal. If your goal is to go on a diet, do you feel more pressure when you don't tell a soul about it or when you announce it to all your friends, with strict instructions to refuse you if you ask for a french fry? It may seem an obvious way of making yourself feel guilty, but it can also be highly effective. Share your goal online as well. Post it on Facebook. Ask your connections to support you if you make your goal, or criticize you if you don't.

The Procrastination Nutshell

Procrastination is the unspoken slayer of dreams. We all have different reasons and excuses for why we procrastinate. We all suffer from the consequences of procrastination in some area of our lives. It may sound a bit ironic, but now is the time to deal with your procrastination. You won't be able to fix it easily or forever with one attempt. However, if you keep seeking to understand and fix your procrastination, you'll soon jump-start many areas of your life.

Beginner: Procrastination Mastery

If you are procrastinating over a situation, write down the task that you need to get done. Then work through the following questions to see if you can come up with a solution:

- Why is it important to get this done?
- How does the thought of starting to work on this issue make me feel?
- How does the thought of completing work on this issue make me feel?
- Which procrastination attitudes are getting in the way? Why?
- What tactics could I use to get over this?
- When will I get it done by?
- Who will be my witness?
- When will I review my progress?

Advanced: Change Your Habit

The beginner exercise was about a particular task; this exercise is about the whole picture—the procrastination habit itself.

Grab a paper and pen before starting.

1. Why do you procrastinate? Go back through the five main reasons for procrastination and figure out which you are most guilty of. Pick your top three reasons and list them in the order in which you use them.

2. Get specific. Write down exactly what sorts of things you procrastinate about and what you say to yourself to justify procrastinating.

3. Identify your beliefs. If you know what underlying beliefs you hold about the reasons you procrastinate, you can try to change them.

Use "The Six Steps of Arguing with Yourself" method beginning on page 40 (chapter 2) to help you change the root belief that is holding you back.

4. Change your language. Now that you've started changing your beliefs, write down a different way to talk to yourself about the tasks you habitually avoid. Imagine your most effective self. What would he or she say to your procrastinating self?

5. What is the first action step in changing your procrastination habit? Arguably, changing how you think and talk to yourself about this habit is the very first step. But take a moment here to decide on the first tangible action step you can take. This will vary depending on your core reason or justification for procrastinating. For instance, if your core reason is action illusion and you mostly procrastinate at work, then the first action step for you might be to regularly document at the start of every task what counts as real effort and what counts as procrastination.

6. What's the reward? Habit changing succeeds when rewards are built into it. Pick a reward that will motivate you to change your procrastination habit.

PART THREE

Deepen Connections

SHE WANTS to slow down. He wants to jump in.

He rolls his eyes. She crosses her arms.

We all know that relationships are complicated. But should we just resign ourselves to complications? Or should we really dig in to create stronger, more enriching, and rewarding relationships—that don't have so many complications? Can we create healthy relationships that are energizing instead of depleting? Can we build relationships that are fun to work on instead of something we feel obligated to work in?

Whether you want to deepen connections with friends, family, colleagues, or a significant other, this part offers you insights into your relationships and gives you the tools to improve them. When you improve your relationships, something else amazing happens: Your whole life feels more rewarding. You see the world differently and more positively. You feel more energized not only in those relationships but in everything else you do—your work, your hobbies, and your goals. But the process of improvement all starts with you. You're the person who is involved in every one of your relationships.

The first chapter in this part, "Get in the Right Relationship Mind-Set," will give you a greater understanding of how you perceive yourself and show you how you perceive others. You'll then take a look at how the people in your relationships might view you as well as others. When you understand the perceptions of yourself and others, you'll be able to quickly identify and remove false or misleading perceptions to strengthen your relationships.

Next, you'll learn something that can make or break any relationship: all the tiny clues that spotlight what went wrong, what could go wrong, and how to avoid going wrong altogether. For those of you struggling with a current relationship, "Bid for Attention" is a must read. In this chapter, you'll identify your verbal and nonverbal bids for attention. You'll be able to spot the cues you receive from your relationships; discover the messages you're sending to your partners, your friends, your coworkers, and the world; and learn how to change these cues to build deeper connections.

Finally, "Get the Best from People" dives into the concept of motivation. What motivates you to fix a relationship? What motivates you to enter a relationship or even to stay connected to someone at all? In this chapter, you'll learn how to spot other people's motivations and identify your own motives, so you can deepen your connections and have a greater impact in your relationships. This chapter will forever change the way you see yourself and the people around you. Even more important, it will teach you how to get the best from others and yourself.

Get ready to deepen your connections. If your romantic relationship is solid, this section will still help you better understand your interactions with coworkers, friends, someone you're forced to deal with, your child's teacher, your best friend's boyfriend or girlfriend—even your in-laws.

CHAPTER 6

Get in the Right Relationship Mind-Set

Do your clients irritate you, your suppliers let you down, or your romantic relationships wither after just a few months? If you find it difficult to keep old friends or make new ones, maintain your colleagues' loyalty or stay with the same employer, the chances are it's because of your relationship mind-set. Your relationship mind-set is the established set of thoughts and attitudes you hold that determine how you approach and respond to others. These thoughts and attitudes influence the quality of your relationships, how you interpret others' behavior, and how you connect with others. A healthy mind-set is likely to lead to positive, enduring relationships at both work and home.

No one knows for sure how we arrive at our relationship mind-set, although most psychologists suggest that we develop it in our early childhood. Psychologist John Bowlby, a pioneer of attachment theory, believes that a relationship mind-set is formed based on an infant's experiences with its caregivers—parents or family members.[1] As young children, we look to caregivers for protection, comfort, and support.

Based on a caregiver's responses to our needs, we paint a picture of how the world of relationships works—a template that we use to interpret any new relationships.[2] We start to make assumptions about what we can expect from other people and even what we deserve. Based on these early childhood expectations, we develop strategies and ways of responding and attaching to others.[3]

Are your relationships characterized by intimacy? For example, do old clients still invite you out to lunch? Are you close to your brothers or sisters? How independent are you? Do you flourish when you're left to your own devices and resent being given advice? How you behave in your relationships, Bowlby believes, is influenced by how well you experienced secure attachments when you were young.

Early childhood experiences may influence your current relationship mind-set, but it doesn't mean you have to be a slave to those experiences forever. If you feel your relationships are not as strong as they could be, then understanding your current mind-set is the first step toward improving them.

Understand Your Relationship Mind–Set

To understand your relationship mind-set and learn what you can do about changing it, start by considering the following statements. Don't spend too much time thinking about each one. Quickly decide whether you generally agree or disagree with the statement.

1. Most people seem to like me.   Agree / Disagree

2. I am comfortable about getting close to others.   Agree / Disagree

3. I worry about being alone.   Agree / Disagree

4. People are rarely there when you need them.   Agree / Disagree

5. Other people tend to respect me.   Agree / Disagree

6. I am comfortable depending on others.   Agree / Disagree

7. I tend to worry that romantic partners don't really love me.   Agree / Disagree

8. I find it difficult to trust others.   Agree / Disagree

9. I enjoy close relationships.   Agree / Disagree

10. I worry others don't value me as much as I value them.   Agree / Disagree

Are You Okay?

There are two factors that make up your relationship mind-set. The first factor relates to how you see yourself, which we'll call *I'm okay*.[4] The second factor relates to how you see others, which we'll call *You're okay*. To discover which factor is predominant in your mind-set, look at whether you answered "Agree" or "Disagree" to each specified statement earlier and then add up the corresponding number of points. For example, if you agreed with statements 1, 3, and 7, and you disagreed with statements 5 and 10, you will have a total of 2 points.

This table is for the *I'm okay* factor:

	Agree	Disagree
Statement 1	2	0
Statement 3	0	2
Statement 5	2	0
Statement 7	0	2
Statement 10	2	0

Write your total *I'm okay* points (it should be between 0 and 10) here:_____.

Now do the same for the next set of statements, which relate to the *You're okay* factor:

	Agree	Disagree
Statement 2	2	0
Statement 4	0	2
Statement 6	2	0
Statement 8	0	2
Statement 9	2	0

Write your total *You're okay* points (it should be between 0 and 10) here: _____.

These results reveal how you typically look at yourself and how you look at others. Of course, this is a simple evaluation with only ten responses, so the results you'll get are more suggestive than conclusive. Nevertheless, it can help you become more aware of how you relate to others.

If your *I'm okay* points are greater than 6, then you're likely to feel pretty good in your own skin. You value yourself and are likely to agree with the statement *I'm okay* and maybe even *I'm an all-around good person*.

If the *I'm okay* total is less than 4, then it suggests the opposite. You might not value yourself very highly. You might agree with the statement *I'm not okay* or *I'm not good enough* or maybe even *There's a lot that's not quite right with me*.

The same rules apply to the *You're okay* points, which are about how you see other people. Do you tend to assume that other people are good, worthy, and positive until they do something that proves otherwise? Or is it more often the other way around: they need to prove themselves before you are willing to be impressed. A positive total (especially more than 6) suggests you're in the *You're okay* camp. And a total of less than 4 suggests you're in the *You're not okay* camp.

Plot your results in the following grid to see what your relationship mind-set tends to be:

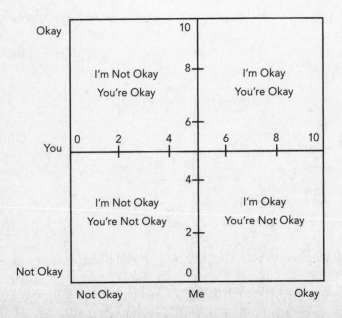

You should now have plotted where you are along the two axis lines, which will place you in a particular quadrant of the grid. This is where it gets interesting, because you can now consider the two factors together, which will give you a sense of your overall relationship mind-set. We'll go through each of the quadrants, explaining the meaning and impact of the variations in each relationship mind-set.

Quadrant 1: I'm Okay, You're Okay

People with this mind-set are in the best position to build positive relationships. They adopt the perspective that everyone—including them—is inherently good. They tend to be logical and understanding. They are influenced by emotion but not ruled by it. They're self-aware and tolerant, and they understand that people often behave irrationally. They also look for the positive motives behind other people's behavior. When things go wrong, they give people the benefit of the doubt and do their best to work collaboratively with them. People with an *I'm okay, you're okay* attitude are perceived by others as being open, direct, and honest.

If you are in this quadrant, you are likely to have a good sense of self-worth and be trusting of others. As a result, you're also likely to be at ease around other people and feel comfortable about having close relationships. If your relationships aren't working, it's not because of your relationship mind-set.

Quadrant 2: I'm Okay, You're Not Okay

When people have an *I'm okay, you're not okay* mind-set, they typically behave with a sense of superiority. They believe that they're better or smarter than everyone around them. In their opinion, people constantly fail and disappoint them, not delivering what they said they would or as they should. People with this mind-set criticize and reprimand others by focusing on their failings and shortcomings—usually while glossing over any errors or missteps they may have made themselves.

Being on the receiving end of people with the *I'm okay, you're not okay* mind-set is not pleasant. They come across as argumentative, crass, and dismissive (*I always know best*). As a result, other people may avoid them, leaving them feeling unsupported, which in turn reinforces their view that others are somehow wrong. Although people with this relationship mind-set often come across as having presence and importance, they also often feel threatened and isolated.

Points that land you in the *I'm okay, you're not okay* quadrant suggest that while you may feel good about yourself, you don't have a lot of faith in other people. You may have found that other people are unreliable, so you protect yourself by not allowing others to get too close. This mind-set can inhibit others from forming strong relationships with you.

Quadrant 3: I'm Not Okay, You're Okay

People with this mind-set tend to feel pretty rotten about themselves. They sense that when relationships fail, they are at fault or they are less competent, successful, or significant than others. They may lack confidence or feel that they don't fit in. They are often on the lookout for evidence of their own shortcomings, highlighting the areas where they compare unfavorably with others (e.g., *He is smarter / more stylish / in better shape than me*) while ignoring the fact that they themselves may be miles ahead of their counterparts in other areas.

People who get stuck in this mind-set often feel helpless and, as a result, tend to let opportunities pass them by. To those around them, these people can be exhausting. Compliant, lacking in confidence, and short on motivation, they seem dependent, vulnerable, and a bit weak. And while seemingly friendly, they can be hyper-negative complainers who never get enough support and encouragement. Basically, they behave like victims.

If your points place you in this quadrant, you're probably very hard on yourself while putting others on pedestals. You may think that you would feel happy if only you could get people around you to respond properly to you. But if you retain the particular *I'm not okay, you're okay* mind-set, you won't. And whatever support others do give you, it still won't be enough.

Quadrant 4: I'm Not Okay, You're Not Okay

The *I'm not okay, you're not okay* quadrant is not a nice place to be. People with this mind-set have usually been dragged here by others (such as uncaring parents, cruel lovers, or bullying employers). Certain life events or strings of events may have damaged these people's faith in humankind and left them feeling helpless. If you're familiar with the *Winnie-the-Pooh* characters, think Eeyore.

People with an *I'm not okay, you're not okay* mind-set expect the worst of themselves and others; they expect to fail and to be let down. This becomes a self-fulfilling prophecy (because they seek out the pitfalls) and a self-reinforcing prophecy (*See, I knew they'd let me down*).

People in this quadrant are low on confidence and high on negativity, pessimism, and cynicism. Being around them can be a demoralizing experience. If your point totals place you in this quadrant, you don't have high hopes of others and don't feel good about yourself either. As a result, you tend to reject others as a way of protecting yourself from being hurt. In fact, you've probably already stopped reading this book, because you believe it can't possibly help you.

A-Okay

When we are being kind to ourselves and generous-spirited with others, relationships are likely to flourish; we're much more likely to solve problems than apportion blame, take responsibility rather than play the victim, deal with an issue instead of giving up. Ideally, we'd spend all our time in the *I'm okay, you're okay* quadrant. In reality, most of us move between the quadrants as events, situations, and people smack us around in life. Equally, we all have an anchor quadrant, one where we spend most of our time.

But knowing where you are (and your current mind-set) is half the journey. Knowing what to do about it is the next challenge. What follows are practical ideas for making the change to an *I'm okay, you're okay* mind-set.

Five Tips for Acquiring an *I'm Okay* Mind-Set

Your new motto is "I see the best in me." Here are five practical ways to help you live that motto and restore faith in yourself.

Talk Yourself Up

Psychologist Christopher Peterson found that explicitly acknowledging our part in making good things happen helps shift us to more of an *I'm okay* way of thinking.[5] To do so, try these approaches:

Write down twenty things you've done well in the last month. Review the list. What does this tell you that you're good at (other than writing lists)? Try to find at least ten significant things that you can be proud of.

Every day write down in a journal five things you've done well—it doesn't matter if they were important or challenging tasks (working out hard at the gym, delivering a critical presentation at work) or mundane or routine tasks (mowing the lawn, completing a Sudoku puzzle, making a killer pot of chili). Once a week look at the list and identify ten more things that you're good at. Even better, write down the part you played in making these good things happen. So, if you've written "had a good workout at the gym," add a description of how you made it happen: "This happened because I set myself the goal to leave work at six-thirty P.M. I also avoided the strong temptation to crawl home to the sofa and drink beer. And I kept reminding myself of how good I would feel." Writing down these items may seem unnecessary. It isn't. Those who do the writing report a much bigger benefit, especially if they stick with it. If you want to move out of *I'm not okay,* get a notebook and start scribbling.

Focus on Solutions

When the problem seems big, it's easy to feel helpless. Consider what you can do that will make a positive difference to that problem, no matter how small the impact will be. Then do it. Concentrating on action (and then patting yourself on the back when you complete the task you set for yourself) is a productive way to appreciate your value a bit more.

Do What You Do Best

As one successful entrepreneur explained, "I figured out what I like doing and then found someone to pay me to do it." That's good advice. Maybe you're a rock star in the kitchen. Or you do stellar presentations at work. Or you're the envy of everyone at the gym or on the dance floor. Most of us shine at something. Your challenge is to spend more time doing those things. Write down the five things you do best. And then figure out how to reorganize your life so you can spend more time doing them.

Hear the Praise

There are people out there who like you, appreciate you, and look up to you. They may not be making their admiration completely obvious, so you may not be picking up their signals. From the smiling lady on the bus to the client who doesn't complain (which is rather out of character for him), pay attention to the small signs and signals that are large indicators of the good you're spreading. And if you don't know what signals to look for, pay attention to your own behavior around someone you like or admire.

Minimize the Trash

Things go wrong. It happens to all of us. The difference is in how you speak and think when things do go wrong. To get to *I'm okay,* put the trash talk and negative thinking in the garbage can. Learn to view negative experiences as temporary: one missed deadline doesn't mean you are always late with everything; the occasional memory lapse doesn't mean you can't be trusted to remember important information. You don't hold on to trash forever; you deal with it daily. Therefore, minimize your daily missteps. So what if you forgot to buy milk? So what if you forgot to call to schedule your nail appointment? Does it really matter in the bigger scheme?

Five Tips for Getting into You're Okay

You may not have a cheerleader to keep your thoughts positive and your spirits lifted—especially when other people can, and will, let you down. From time to time you'll have moments when you view others negatively. But if you start giving everyone the benefit of the doubt, you'll be on your way toward changing your relationship mind-set in a positive direction and moving to *You're okay.*

Alternative, Positive Explanation

Assume the best realistic motivation behind another person's behavior. What does that mean? It means be positive. Assume that person is hopeless rather than cunning, nervous rather than angry, shy rather than rude, and under pressure rather than vindictive.

Guessing someone's true intention based on imperceptible behaviors can get you into serious trouble. Instead, why not assume the positive as a default? If it's too difficult to assume the best, then simply don't attempt any interpretation at all. Note the person's behavior and move on.

Look for the Good

It's easy to concentrate on what's wrong with people. Try focusing on what's good about them. Everyone has great qualities, which are often the reasons why we like them in the first place. Consciously think of what's good about a person when you're talking with them (or communicating with them in any way—in correspondence or in conversation). By itself, this will help improve your relationship.

Be Patient

Two examples don't make a pattern. We all make mistakes, especially when we're trying to change. It's easy and tempting to size people up on a mistake or two and hold it up as proof (at least to yourself) that there's something wrong with them. Watch out for a person's positive behaviors too, before making up your mind about what kind of person you think they are.

Lower Your Expectations

Do people often let you down? Maybe your expectations are so high that they always will. This doesn't mean that you have to accept poorly executed work or friends who don't show up when they said they would. It does, however, suggest that your consistently high standards may be damaging your relationships. Lower them.

Forgive

If you can't lower your expectations, at least forgive quickly and easily. Otherwise, you will spend much of your energy feeling angry or upset about people letting you down, which isn't much fun. Forgiveness doesn't mean excusing what happened in the past; instead, it means allowing the relationship to move forward.

When They Don't Want You to Change

Your friends, family, and coworkers are accustomed to how you are and have expectations of how you will behave toward them and around them. In fact, there may be some kind of positive payoff for them in you remaining how you are. If you decide to change your behavior, it will change things for them too. And they might not like that.

For example, perhaps you've always had a negative perception of yourself and a positive view of others (i.e., you operate from an *I'm not okay, you're okay* mind-set). You have probably been very attentive to the people around you, and they have gotten used to that. They may believe that your incredibly attentive behavior is your way of demonstrating love for them. Imagine then what happens when your behavior changes and you stop being so clingy. The people around you may experience a sense of loss. Your attentiveness may have actually made their lives easier. As a result, even while they are glad that you are feeling better about yourself, they may resist the changes. So, be prepared to encounter resistance and to offer reassurance to those around you.

Enough About Me

The *I'm okay, you're okay* perspective provides you with insight into how you think about relationships. This means you can choose to think differently in order to have better, longer-lasting relationships. Understanding these perspectives also has a surprise benefit: it tells you how others want to be treated.

While you were reading this chapter thinking about your relationship mind-set, you probably pinpointed a lot of other people's mind-sets. If you know how others view relationships and themselves, then you know exactly how to treat them—and how to form a deeper relationship.

Finally, from Woody Allen, for those of you who are still thinking *It's them, not me* . . .

"Doc, my brother's crazy. He thinks he's a chicken."

"Well, why don't you turn him in?"

"I would, but I need the eggs."

GIVE YOUR MIND A WORKOUT

Beginner: I'm Okay

If you're not already in the *I'm okay* mind-set, these two tools will help get you there:

1. Remind yourself of your positive attributes. Pick a few people that love, respect, and/or admire you and write a list of what they might see in you that you don't see in yourself. For example, this might be what made your romantic partner fall in love with you, your boss hire you, or your younger sibling look up to you. Keep this piece of paper somewhere safe so you can refer to it whenever you're feeling bad about yourself.

2. Kill the negative internal voice. On a separate piece of paper, write down all the negative things you say to yourself, all the reasons why you fall into the *I'm not okay* category. Once you've listed them, say good-bye to these negative, false, and unhelpful beliefs and burn the piece of paper. Watch it go up in flames as you very consciously decide to be more forgiving of yourself.

Advanced: You're Okay

Think of a category of people you know, such as colleagues, clients, or college friends. On a sheet of paper divided into three columns, write down everyone you know in this category (don't miss anyone significant), and place each person's name beneath one of the following three column headings: "People I Think Are Great," "People I Think Are Okay," and "People I Don't Like."

Which column is the longest? This is a good indication of how you see relationships. If you have a *You're okay* mind-set, the longest lists will likely be in the first two columns, ideally with the "People I Think Are Great" being the longest. But if the "People I Think Are Okay" and "People I Don't Like" columns are longer, it suggests your relationship mind-set is not as conducive to having great relationships as it could be. Try these two steps to change that:

1. Consider the strengths of the people listed in the second and third columns (maybe even write those strengths down), and see how many names you can genuinely shift to the "People I Think Are Great" column.

2. Looking at the people listed in the second and third columns, where do you think they would place themselves in the *I'm okay, you're okay* quadrants? Does that help you think about them differently?

CHAPTER 7

Bid for Attention

Have you ever tried to trace the events of a broken relationship to figure out when it started to go wrong? Was it the time you scratched your partner's car (honestly, you could barely see it) and didn't tell her for weeks? Or when you went away for the weekend even though you knew your brother was going into the hospital? Or when you had that awkward conversation with your boss about her not giving you feedback before a big presentation?

Whatever you came up with, you're probably wrong. How can we be so sure? Because it's not the high drama or grand passions that make or break a relationship; it's the small stuff, the almost imperceptible micro signals that you send constantly throughout the day.[1] The relationship likely started to go wrong months earlier, when you were asked a simple question like "Would you like a cup of coffee?"

Surprising as it may sound, how you replied to this question may have sealed your relationship's fate. Because how you respond to the thousands of apparently inconsequential comments people make every day determines what happens to your relationships far more than a big blowout argument. Indeed, so vital are these tiny signals to the health of a relationship that observing them in the arguments of a married couple for just fifteen minutes can provide a prediction of future divorce with over 90 percent accuracy.

In the early 1980s psychologist John Gottman was wondering why some married couples stayed together while others broke apart. Obviously he wasn't the first person to ponder that question. However, he is the only one who raised millions of dollars to build an apartment in Chicago filled with hidden cameras and microphones in an attempt to answer it. In his *Big Brother*–style house, Professor Gottman watched closely as a series of couples went about their daily interactions. He didn't know what he was looking for, but he was expecting something more than the routine chitchat of everyday life. Here is an example of what he saw and heard:

She asks, "Anything interesting in the paper?"

He responds, "Nope, just the usual old stuff. Some old lady got mugged on her way out the door . . ."

After a while of watching this so-called everyday life, Professor Gottman was reaching the point of calling it quits—and calling the experiment a failure. But that's when something interesting happened. Before throwing in the towel, he took one last closer look and, like a forensic detective, found the answer he was seeking. It was buried in the tiny details of those seemingly meaningless and inconsequential exchanges between people. As meaningless as they seemed on the surface, at a deeper level, the exchanges were highly nuanced, emotional signals, or what Gottman called "bids."

A bid is something that invites a response. Often we are not actively aware of the micro signals we send, and even less aware of the effect these signals have in our interactions with others, until it is too late. By then, the relationship—with our spouse, boss, friend, coworker—is unraveling.

The impact of Gottman's work was enormous. Based on his insights, a whole new approach to marriage counseling was developed. His findings about how we respond to bids apply to more than just spousal relationships, though, and provide the psychology behind the advice in this chapter.

The good news is that bids are very easy to spot and pretty easy to change. So, if you know where to look and are willing to make a little effort, you'll never again need to go in search of the origin of a broken relationship.

Sweat the Small Stuff

Picture this scene: Your boss is sitting in front of her computer. She's working. Or perhaps she's pretending to work when in fact she's updating her Facebook page or reading her emails—you know her better than we do, so you choose.

Now imagine yourself entering her office and asking her "Do you want a cup of coffee?" Your boss could choose to respond in one of three ways:

1. She could acknowledge your offer in a positive way: "That's really nice of you. I'll have cream and sugar." Or "Thanks, but I'm okay right now." In psychologists' speak, this is called a "turning-toward response" or a "toward bid."

2. She could acknowledge your offer in a negative way: "Your coffee is disgusting. I'll get it myself." Or "You want to get me a cup of coffee? What do you want in return?" This is called an "against bid."

3. She could just stay silent or change the subject: "There's this new film out about the life of the flamingo." This is called a "turning-away bid." By replying, she acknowledges that you've spoken, but she doesn't engage with what you've said. In effect, she ignores your bid.

Whatever response she chooses determines what you do next. Consider this for a second. Only the first, the "toward bid," is likely to encourage you to make another of your own bids. Faced with an "against bid" or a "turning-away bid," you're more likely to make an unconscious mental note not to bother offering her a cup of coffee next time.

Positive bids create a virtuous cycle. When you respond to someone with a toward bid, the person feels good about him- or herself. As a result, that person is more likely to make more positive bids, which, in turn, lead to more positive interactions (and more offers of coffee). The research shows that when you use plenty of toward bids, the effect on your closest relationships is enormous:

- You laugh more, feel greater affection, and are more likely to be interested in other people's discussions.[2]

- Siblings (in particular those of different genders) are more likely to have a close, supportive, and satisfying relationship with one another.[3]

- Your children benefit. When parents are in a relationship full of positive bids, there is less conflict, and the children in these families are more attentive and likely to perform better in school.[4]

- You're less likely to get divorced. In other words, you're more likely to stay with your partner.[5]

- You get more sex. Okay, there's no research to prove this yet, but given everything else, it makes sense. That alone makes this chapter worth reading, right?

Overall, the research is unequivocal: people who respond positively to others' bids have healthier, happier, and much more successful relationships.

Let's look at the research that says couples who make more bids toward each other, rather than against or turning away, are more likely to stay together. Gottman discovered that there is a magic ratio: Couples who manage a ratio of five positive (toward) responses to one negative (turning away or against) response are more likely to have a healthy, long-lasting partnership.[6]

In 1992, Gottman teamed up with two mathematicians to test this model.[7] They recruited seven hundred couples who had just received their marriage certificates. The researchers then videotaped a fifteen-minute conversation between the husband and wife of each couple and counted the number of positive and negative bids. Then, based on the five-to-one ratio, they predicted whether each couple would stay together or divorce.

Ten years later, Gottman and his colleagues got in touch with each of the couples to determine the accuracy of their original predictions. The results were stunning. They had predicted divorce with 94 percent accuracy—based on scoring the couples' interactions for just fifteen minutes.[8] The research also revealed a gender difference. The men who ended up divorced had generally turned away from their wives' bids 82 percent of the time, whereas the men in ultimately stable relationships only ignored their wives' bids 19 percent of the time. Women use turning-away responses slightly less often. The women who ended up divorced had ignored their husbands' bids 50 percent of the time, as opposed to those in ultimately stable relationships, who had ignored their husbands' bids 14 percent of the time.

The impact of bids is present in all relationships, not just in the most intimate ones. At work, the ratio of positive to negative bids will affect the quality of your relationship with your boss, your peers, and those you manage. The bid ratio is likely to reflect the difference between those customers or suppliers you look forward to seeing and those you don't. If you've ever had a customer who didn't seem to care, you know exactly the feeling of a turning-away bid.

It's now time to turn your attention to making the best bids.

Toward Bids

In improvised comedy there is only one rule: however outlandish the suggestion, the players never contradict one another. For example, one player might open with, "Maggie got up on Monday morning and went out to her car." The next player could add to that with, "And she drove to the airport, where she caught a plane to Morocco" or "And on her car seat she found a briefcase full of hundred-dollar bills." These are positive responses that build on the opening bid. The second player cannot instead say, "Actually, it was Sunday and Maggie didn't own a car." That's a negative, or against, bid. It doesn't develop the story. It also feels like a slap in the face to the person who made the initial bid.

The same rule applies to healthy relationships. A positive bid may be as simple as a laugh or a knowing smile. It may be a phrase or question. But whatever form it takes, this positive response reassures the initial bidder that you have heard and accepted what they say (even if you don't necessarily agree with it).

Psychologists have identified four types of positive, or toward, bids. A healthy relationship will have a mix of all of them:

Nearly Passive

A friendly grunt, an affirming "uh-huh," or a gesture of acknowledgment: a nod or a smile. (Note: This is a friendly grunt, not the "Go away and leave me alone" grunt favored by moody teenagers.)

Low Energy

A few words of acknowledgment—"okay" or "sure"—or a question to clarify the bid: "Sorry, what did you say?"

Attentive

Now you're getting involved. These responses indicate sharing opinions, thoughts, and feelings. They include an offer of empathy, insight, a joke, or a question. Actions like a good-night kiss or a handshake are also attentive responses.

High Energy

Attentive responses, but even bigger—with more energy, complete attention, and full eye contact. These are usually enthusiastic responses ("Wow, congratulations!"). High-energy responses are often physical (big hugs, sloppy kisses) and loud (hearty laughs, giggles). They also have the most positive impact—when you get this kind of reaction, you really know you've been heard. But remember the experience of being greeted by a sloppy dog: too much of this kind of positive attention can be exhausting, particularly if the recipient is a rather shy person.

Now that you understand the various types of toward bids, consider if you are likely to use one of these types more often. Given that most healthy relationships have a ratio of five positive responses to one negative response, it's important that you keep your bids going toward. Here are three ways to do so:

1. Always respond by showing that you've heard what has been said, even if you want to change the subject: "I'm so glad that you've found a flat that you like. That must be a weight off your mind. I've just finished a new draft of the report, so if you have a moment . . ."

2. Open every conversation with a positive bid. In his research, remember, Gottman found that he could predict, with over 90 percent accuracy, the outcome of a relationship based on what he heard in the first fifteen minutes of a conversation. In many cases, the first three minutes gave a strong sense of whether the relationship was going to survive. If those first minutes are full of negativity, blame, and criticism, the outcome will be negative as well.

3. Even when you vehemently disagree with a person's suggestions, say what you like about those suggestions first. Establish common ground (e.g., "I like the fact you're being totally up front"; "I appreciate how passionately you feel about this issue") before presenting your case.

Against Bids

An against bid is always unpleasant. Yes, you have received a response to your own bid, but you wish you hadn't. Mocking, ridiculing, belittling, and making sarcastic comments about a bid or the bidder are all against responses. And they always make the other person feel bad. There is little of positive value in an against bid except a short and very temporary release of anger, frustration, or denial. It's like racking up charges on a particularly expensive credit card, where you get a brief "thrill" from what you've purchased but then you endure months or years of pain as you try to pay off the debt.

Well, okay. There is one more benefit from against bids: if you want a person to feel bad (and annoyed with you) as part of some complex negotiation or because you're hoping to get that person out of your life no matter what, then against responses may be just the ticket.

Here are six familiar against responses. Unless you're more angelic than most, prepare to wince:

Contemptuous

A contemptuous response to "Shall we ask for directions?" would be "We wouldn't need to if you could just read the map." Ouch.

Belligerent

Someone is spoiling for a fight. If a person asks "Do you want to see a film?" and the response is "Do you really think I have time for a movie? Don't you realize how busy I am?" it's pretty obvious where the conversation is going.

Contradictory

These responses are designed to get a reaction—ideally "I'm sorry; you're right" but usually something rather less savory. The following are all contradictory responses: "I think you'll find there's a better way to tie a garbage bag," "Leave it alone; let me do it," or the supremely irritating "Actually, I think you'll find it's pronounced . . ."

Domineering

These responses assert authority and attempt to force the other person to withdraw, retreat, or submit. For example, a daughter might say, "My dream is to be on *America's Got Talent*." A mother might respond, "Don't be ridiculous. You're not nearly talented enough."

Character Attack

"I didn't quite understand what Michael meant in the meeting today" gets the against response "Of course not. You weren't paying attention, as usual." "You always," "you shouldn't have," or "you never" are early warning signals that a load of negative bids is on its way.

Defensive

Me: "I can't find my book." My spouse: "Well, don't look at me!" Here, the respondent—even though no blame was being apportioned—is on the defensive.

When someone responds against you, you feel undervalued. If you do hang in there, you'll probably stop making further bids. That'll effectively put an end to the interaction and damage the relationship. If the other person is in a position of power (like an aggressive boss), you may suppress your emotions to avoid conflict, and the relationship will become one based on fear. But if you are the one responding against others, understand that these negative bids seriously undermine your relationships. It's critical that you change your bids to positive ones.

Here are three ways to avoid against bids:

1. Pause. Count to five in your head. Slowly. If that doesn't work, explain to whomever you are with that you want to take a breather to calm down. And, no, storming out and slamming the door doesn't count.

2. Repeat what the other person has said. Or summarize it favorably and check that you've understood it correctly. Often we respond against when we have misinterpreted what someone has said.

3. Report on what is going on. "I notice that we are both raising our voices in this discussion about who is cooking dinner. How can we answer this question calmly?" Psychologists call this "reported observation." It is based on the principle that if we name what is going on, we have a better chance of choosing to do things differently to prevent a bad outcome.

In all cases, think of using negative bids much as using a credit card: the short-term gain is rarely going to be greater than the long-term pain.

Turning-Away Bids

Turning away is when you ignore someone's bid or act preoccupied or uninterested. There may be a reason why you are being unresponsive; you might feel irritated or your attention may be elsewhere. But whatever your conscious motivation, turning away from a bid indicates that you have disengaged from the relationship. The outcome is not going to be good.

Research shows that when people repeatedly ignore or dismiss one another's bids, they become hostile and defensive. And the sad fact is that most people turn away without even knowing they are doing it. So, what do turning-away responses look like? They tend to occur in three different forms:

Silence

Let's say you're searching the Internet or cooking or driving. You're engrossed and, to be honest, you're not really interested in whatever's going on around you. So, you zone out and try to ignore any bids coming your way. No one wants the "silent treatment"; if someone is with you, that person may feel this is a snub. The trouble is that if this person keeps trying to interact with you, you're just as likely to respond against

("Can't you see I'm busy?") as toward ("Sorry, I was completely away there; what did you say?").

Dismissiveness

You ignore the substance of what the other person is saying and either focus on some incidental detail ("She had nice fingernails"), reframe the issue ("Yes, yes, but the real issue is . . ."), or minimize the importance of what's being said ("Does it matter?").

Changing Lanes

In the middle of a conversation, you change the subject, either by announcing a new and irrelevant piece of information ("It says here that penguins can do elementary algebra"; "I feel like going for a walk") or with a deliberate non sequitur (Dad: "Did you finish your home-work?" Son: "What are you cooking for supper?").

In Gottman's research, turning-away bids were more common than against bids, but the effects are frighteningly similar. For example, he found that during a conversation at dinner, stable couples engaged each other as many as a hundred times in ten minutes, whereas those headed for divorce engaged each other only sixty-five times. And when one of the partners was met with a turning-away response, those in stable marriages rebid 20 percent of the time, whereas those headed for divorce rarely even attempted to rebid. Instead, they disconnected from their partners. But even among those who rebid, 20 percent is a very low figure. It suggests that, even in a stable relationship, a turning-away bid has the effect of closing down communication between people.

Turning-away bids also increase conflict. If a bidder is repeat-edly ignored, he or she is likely to become angry and critical of the respondent. As a result, the emotional temperature goes up and small incidents become big issues. A small dismissal today can lead to a relationship meltdown next year. From little acorns . . .

Stonewalling is a deliberate attempt to turn away. You might argue that you're buying space and time from the demands of others by doing this, but stonewalling is not the best way to handle a situation. You'll get a much better response if you accept the bid and then explain to the other person that you feel the need for space.

Here are three ways to help you avoid turning away:

1. Observe yourself for a day and find out how many bids you ignore—accidentally or deliberately. Most of us turn away more than we think (though we are much better at judging how many times others turn away from us). Once you've learned to spot your turning-away behavior, you'll almost certainly reduce it.

2. Are you turning away to avoid an argument? It's often the case. We don't want to attack (in effect, to turn against), so we avoid or deny the situation by turning away instead. Unfortunately, the impact is not so very different. You might try to discuss the issue or even just acknowledge the issue and delay a deep conversation until later, so you eventually understand more about the other person's underlying concerns. Simply say, "I know this is on your mind, but I'm worried it's going to lead to an argument now. Can we discuss it another time?"

3. Fill the silence. A good proportion of our bids that involve turning away happen when we feel we can't be bothered to make the effort to listen fully. A genuine "uh-huh" will usually be enough to do the trick.

Change Your Bid Patterns

Just like health is either attained or destroyed by one more salad as opposed to one more french fry, relationships are built and destroyed via small signals that add up over time. The trick, of course, is learning how to recognize the small gestures and change them. So, next time a friendship, a relationship with a coworker, or your marriage starts to feel shaky, don't panic. Instead, identify how you are responding to the other person's bids and increase your effort toward positive responses. With a little mindfulness and attention, you can change your patterns and get the relationship back on track, usually without the other person even noticing.

GIVE YOUR MIND A WORKOUT

Beginner: Learn the Language

Learning the language of bids gives you a great tool to take control of your relationships. Here is a swift way to become fluent in the language of bidding:

1. Pay attention to the bids other people make. Soap operas, for example, often crank up the conflict by including lots of turning-away and against bids. The exchanges between close friends, on the other hand, demonstrate how toward bids create warmth and affection in lasting relationships. Small talk is usually made up of a series of toward bids.

2. Keep a notebook with three sections, one for each kind of bid. Write down examples as you hear them. You should be able to list up to a hundred of each type within a week.

Advanced: Focus Your Bids

Think of someone you see quite often and with whom you want to improve your relationship, then follow the next steps over the course of a month:

Day One

Write down how you feel about this person and describe your relationship with them.

Day Two

Think about the number of positive and negative bids you make to this person. Give yourself a score from one to ten for how well you think you balance positive and negative bids. A ten would be the top score, and it would mean a balance that matches Gottman's ratio of five positive bids to one negative bid, or better. Scoring a one means that your relationship is full of turning-away and against bids.

Day Three

Think about what you need to do to move two points closer to that top score of ten. It will probably involve halving the number of turning-away or against bids.

From Day Four On

Keep cutting the total number of turning-away and against bids in half until you reach a ratio of five positive to one negative. Maintain this ratio for the remaining days of this month.

One Month Later

Write down your feelings about this other person and about your relationship. Only after you have done this, compare today's views with what you wrote a month ago, and repeat the steps until you feel you've got the right balance of bids.

CHAPTER 8

Get the Best from People

He's such a handsome boy. He takes after his father. He's big and strong—a natural sportsman. He'll have to fight the girls off, you know." This gushing mother's description of her son isn't exactly wrong. It's just a little bit different from how other people might see him: a scrawny, odd-looking kid whose only sporting skill is the speed with which he changes channels when a football game is on TV.

The writer Anaïs Nin once observed, "We don't see things as they are, we see them as we are." When it comes to people, this couldn't be more accurate. Two people might perceive the same person totally differently. This is partly because we typically change our behavior depending on the company we keep. For example, even if you usually use colorful language, you probably wouldn't swear or talk about sex in front of your parents. Or you may act differently around your boss than you do around your coworkers. We all do this, and it's normal.

But it's critical to understand that the different impressions people have of us are due to both how we adapt our behavior to different circumstances and how other people see the world and us. Imagine two colleagues walking out of a meeting in which their new boss made some staffing decisions on the fly for a new project. One of the colleagues might be thinking, *What a relief to have a leader who makes decisions on the team,* while the other might be thinking, *We're going to have to be careful with a leader who is so impulsive.*

The fact that people see the world from different perspectives probably isn't news to you. But what you might find interesting is that the way someone interprets *your* behavior probably tells you more about him or her than it does about yourself. And you might be even more interested to know that when you understand how the people around you see the world, you can adapt your behavior to get the best from them and help them get the best from you.

So, what's the driving force behind how people see the world? Their motivations.

Understanding Other People's Motivations

When we go to the supermarket, we have our own individual ways of shopping. Some people like to do their grocery shopping as quickly as possible. They consider it a successful shopping experience when they found the items they needed in as little time as possible.

Other people carefully plan their grocery shopping: they make lists, they visit each aisle of the supermarket in a specific order, and they organize their coupons by product category to ensure they don't miss any deals. For these people, a successful shopping experience means they found the items and brands they wanted at the right price, even if shopping took a little bit longer.

Another group of people see the supermarket as a treasure trove to be explored. They show up without a list and meander up and down the aisles, checking out new products and choosing items on impulse. For these folks, a successful shopping trip is not so much about whether they found the right things to buy but whether they discovered something new and exciting.

If these various shoppers went to the store together, there would more than likely be some conflict. The first shopper would be halfway around the supermarket before the second shopper even finished making their list, while the third shopper would be chatting with the clerk passing out samples of cheese.

We do many of the same things but we choose to do them in very different ways, depending on what is most important to us. In the supermarket scenario, the first shopper's motive is speed, the second shopper's motive is accuracy, and the third's motive is discovery. While behavior can easily change depending on a situation, our motivations are much more constant. People tend to have an idea of what matters most to them, and unless something major happens in their lives, they stick to that point of view. So, if you understand what motivates other people, you can adapt your behavior to fit with their personal priorities.

How do you find out what motivates someone else? Although science may never come up with a definitive conclusion on how to analyze people's motivations, you can get close enough by analyzing four basic motivational styles—recognizing that even though we all show stronger areas of motivation, no one is motivated by just one thing. Now let's introduce the four different motivational styles.

The Carer

A carer likes nothing better than everyone getting along. If there is any conflict, their instinct is to help solve it. A carer's foremost desire is for harmony with whatever group of people they are in, be it their family, their team at work, or a group of friends. They see themselves as "people" people. They are naturally social and friendly, and they make a real effort to get to know someone. They are also often very effective networkers. Strong relationships are of paramount importance to carers. As a result, they are quick to express how they feel (with the hope others will reciprocate). They are loyal, and they will typically surrender in a disagreement for the sake of harmony. Carers also like to involve other people in making decisions, though while still wanting to be involved themselves. They have a strong desire to nurture other people, looking after them in times of trouble and being eager to explain or teach to help them flourish. They also want to be liked and appreciated themselves—a few words of praise go a long way.

Here are some classic signs of a carer:

- Stuck with a problem? "Let's ask someone" is a carer's natural response.

- At their best, carers are honest, sincere, supportive, friendly, and sociable.

- At their worst, carers are simple-minded, naïve, smothering, demanding, and snoopy.

- Carers hate deliberate unpleasantness, insensitivity, bullying, rudeness, being ignored or left out, and social isolation.

- They are the perfect person if you want something done sensitively.

The Driver

In many ways, drivers couldn't be more different from carers. Adventurous and easily bored, drivers are constantly pushing forward. If carers are motivated by being liked, then drivers aim for respect. They are motivated by challenge, excitement, and getting things done. They want to get to the point fast and, ideally, first. And then they're on to the next thing, and then the next. They like to have demanding goals with clear outcomes and, preferably, a competitive element. If a situation doesn't have direction, a driver can become frustrated, but given a suitable challenge and left to their own devices, they will make things happen and quickly. They consider it generally better to make a decision, even if it turns out to be the wrong one, than to put things off. They are more likely to initiate something than complete it—they like to get the ball rolling but will avoid organizing and implementing if they can.

Here are some classic signs of a driver:

- Stuck with a problem? "I'll sort it out. In fact, I'm almost done" is a driver's natural response.

- At their best, drivers are direct, competitive, excitable, fast, decisive, and challenging.

- At their worst, drivers are harsh, aggressive, superficial, inflexible, and argumentative.

- Drivers hate boredom, delays, chat rather than action, analysis paralysis, committees (only slow things down), people (or anything else) who get in the way of making things happen.

- They are the perfect person if you want something done quickly.

The Professional

Professionals believe that attention to detail is everything. Whereas drivers are eager to move on to the next challenge, professionals like to tackle their challenges and finish their tasks properly. They are driven by a desire to do something very well—they want the best possible solution, and once they commit, they will be inclined to do whatever it takes to get that best solution. They might accomplish this by thinking differently about a problem or being very thorough in the way they do something, or both. The professional's mantra is the saying "If a job's worth doing, it's worth doing properly." The professional's desire for things to be "right" means that they are often the first to spot gaps or errors and to challenge assumptions about the way things are done. They value being given the freedom and independence to think things through by themselves. Their desire for self-sufficiency, however, means they can also be hard to get to know.

Here are some classic signs of a professional:

- Stuck with a problem? "Let me think about it" is a professional's natural response.

- At their best, professionals are independent, original, rigorous, self-contained, thorough, and accurate.

- At their worst, professionals are aloof, nitpicky, cold, long-winded, and fussy.

- Professionals hate slapdash behavior, delivering something that isn't finished, being rushed into things, being told how to do something, constant disruptions, personal questions, big egos, and group hugs.

- They are the perfect person if you want something done "right."

The Adapter

Adapters are people who are a combination of all the other three styles. They see the merits of focusing on people, getting things done, and doing things right. They value flexibility and take a balanced approach to any situation. They often take the role of peacekeeper in a disagreement, because they quickly empathize with each of the different perspectives. Adapters like to experiment, be open to change, and make sure all the bases are covered and all the options are considered. They sometimes feel pulled in many directions by their different motivations.

Here are some classic signs of an adapter:

- Stuck with a problem? "I'll work out a way to find a solution" is their natural response.

- At their best, adapters are flexible, adaptable, collaborative, good mediators, and jacks of all trades.

- At their worst, adapters are weak, political, all-pleasing, without conviction, and masters of none.

- Adapters hate people who are stuck in their ways, obstinacy, and extreme behaviors.

- They are the perfect person if you want someone to manage all possible eventualities.

What Do They Think of Each Other?

Now that you know the four basic motivational styles, the next step is to understand how people with different styles interact with one another. This is where it gets interesting—and problematic—in relationships. You might be on a team or in a relationship in which one person is motivated by doing something thoroughly and another person is motivated by getting results as quickly as possible and moving on. When these different motivations collide, the result is often conflict.

What a Carer Thinks of . . .

- *Drivers:* They are a bit egotistic. They might mean well, but they can plow over other people. I would like to get to know drivers better, but I'm not sure I would like what I found. If drivers took a little more time to get to know people, and be more sensitive, they would be a lot more effective.

- *Professionals:* They are a bit like a cold fish. They're very good at making sure we do things properly, but they can take it to extremes—even when it's obvious everyone else is bored or wants to get on with things, they just keep going.

- *Adapters:* They are open to new ideas. They appreciate that people matter. I like their flexibility, but I'm never quite sure where they stand.

What a Driver Thinks of . . .

- *Carers:* They're soft and easy to get around. They deal with the people stuff, which doesn't really interest me. They can be overly sensitive. However, they're good people to go to when I need support and need to get others on board with me.

- *Professionals:* They're painfully slow. Don't they care about results? I wish they'd live in the real world. They're always finding fault with things. On a good day, I guess they stop us from errors and can get us to come up with better ideas, but there is always a price.

- *Adapters:* They seem to understand the importance of getting things done, but they change their views and are hard to pin down.

What a Professional Thinks of . . .

- *Carers:* They often ask me how I feel rather than what I need—and this misses the point. They're quite needy, although they are friendly and mean well. And they always seem interested in what I have to say—they'll listen even if they don't always understand.

- *Drivers:* They are adrenaline junkies—always looking for change rather than following things through. I admire their energy but get frustrated by their lack of staying power. If you want something left half finished, then they are the right people to ask.

- *Adapters:* They need to get their priorities straight. They're thinking is often muddled, although they are more sympathetic to making sure things are done properly than the others.

What an Adapter Thinks of . . .

- *Carers:* They have a sensitive side, which I appreciate. It's good to have someone who cares and keeps the group together. However, they can fail to understand that other people's priorities are different.

- *Drivers:* They have lots of drive and energy to make things happen, but they need to listen more and be open to different approaches.

- *Professionals:* They have an excellent eye for detail and quality, but they can be very set in their ways and sticklers for process. This means that they don't always know when to let go and when to stand firm.

All the reactions to motivational styles that are different from our own are very common. While each type of person may admire the qualities of the other, it's easy to see how these types of people can, unintentionally, rub one another the wrong way. For example, imagine if four people with different motivational styles had to choose a restaurant for dinner together. The carer would be eagerly asking everyone what type of food or ambience they wanted, the professional would be checking restaurant ratings and prices online, the driver might listen to them for a few moments before getting fed up and announcing where they should go ("Let's just go; otherwise, we'll still be discussing it when all the restaurants are closed"), and the adapter would be tempted to agree with the last person speaking or suggest a process to make a decision.

All these different approaches are not conducive to a great evening out. So, if you were in this group and wanted to get the best outcome for you and the group, you would need to adapt your behavior to fit with other people's motivations.

Making a Good Impression

The way you choose to make a good impression on people will depend on that individual's motivational style. All of us are likely to be a mix of more than one type. However, if you can spot a person's dominant or strongest motivation, then there are things you can do to create a positive relationship that will give both of you what you need. Below are some clues on how to spot each motivational style.

How to Spot a Carer

Carers will ask how you are. They will remember your birthday, the names of your family members, and your various pets. They will be thrilled to connect one person with another. They make great hosts of parties and will always make sure people are comfortable.

Carers will also stand up for others. Just because they like harmony, that doesn't mean they shy away from conflict; if there is an underdog, a carer is more than likely to support them and help them take on an opponent. However, if there is a way of solving a problem without becoming too competitive, that's what they'd prefer.

How to Get the Best from Carers

Involve them, ask their advice, and make them feel appreciated and included. Carers love being involved in the emotional and personal aspects of any situation. Remember that they feel frustrated when they feel powerless to help. If you go to a carer with a problem, help them to help you solve it; otherwise, they may feel as though you are simply dumping on them. A carer's desire to keep everyone happy can sometimes backfire because they find it difficult juggling conflicting interests.

How to Spot a Driver

Drivers see themselves as people who do things and make stuff happen. Ask them what they did on the weekend and you'll probably hear about the seven things they managed to squeeze into an action-packed forty-eight hours. Drivers are drawn to competitive activities, so a "friendly" afternoon has all the competitive hallmarks of a Boston Marathon. Often because drivers want to achieve, they are in a hurry or anxious about doing something. Drivers don't mind a bit of an argument (and may even stir the pot sometimes). They will always stand up for their point of view. Of course, drivers will relax, but even that might be done ferociously, with just enough time to chill out before the next event makes an appearance.

How to Get the Best from Drivers

Drivers like activity and action. To get the best from a driver you need to present a situation in an energetic manner. What is challenging about the situation? What is exciting about it? What is the ultimate goal? A driver's threshold for boredom can be quite low, so challenges need to be appealing. Bear with a driver if they respond competitively to challenges, and allow them to enjoy their moment if they succeed. Like carers, drivers like appreciation. But rather than being appreciated for their support, they like appreciation for having met a goal or challenge. When possible, avoid overexplaining or holdups in processes. Drivers just want to race forward.

How to Spot a Professional

For professionals, quality is the best policy. Professionals believe that there is a "right" way of doing something. Given that, a professional may well tell you that your apostrophe is in the wrong place. They'll give you details about things, like how the best restaurant in the area is just around the corner (they'll also provide the address), and they'll tell you what to avoid ("The kung pao chicken is horrible").

You can also spot a professional by the fact that they will have an opinion, and while it may not always be stated, it will certainly be held. The thing about professionals is that whether their opinion is wildly unorthodox or traditional in the extreme, they are sure it is the right opinion.

How to Get the Best from Professionals

Professionals like independence and self-sufficiency, so give them plenty of opportunity to think things through. They appreciate exploring how to improve or change what currently exists, and they want the opportunity to do something original. They will not be pleased to have to provide a poorly thought-out or overly hurried answer, so give them ample time to arrive at a great solution. Patience with professionals often pays off because they offer interesting and improved solutions.

How to Spot an Adapter

Adapters can adopt any of the other motivational styles. They may focus on people, challenges, or finding the "right" solution. You can spot an adapter because he or she will probably understand all the other motivations and think of the one that isn't being represented at the time. As well as taking account of everyone's opinions, an adapter will be extremely flexible and creative about coming up with alternatives and different solutions.

How to Get the Best from Adapters

Let them work through the contingencies and allow them to explain the differences between the others. Give them the opportunity to be flexible and change their minds about how to do something. By doing so, they may well come up with something you'd never have thought of yourself. And if they are behaving like one of the other motivational types, then adapt your own behavior accordingly.

What Is Your Motivation?

You may have made a good guess at what your dominant motivational style is after reading this chapter. The following quiz will give you a basic understanding or affirmation of what you probably already know.

Keep in mind as you take this quiz that it's best to think about the results in context. Rather than thinking about your life as a whole, try focusing during the quiz on a particular part of your life, like your work or your role as a parent.

For each statement in this quiz, you have 10 points to allocate between the three alternatives (*a, b,* and *c*), depending on how much you think each applies to you. This could be a combination of 3, 3, 4 or 10, 0, 0 or 7, 2, 1—you can assign as many or as few points as you like to each statement option, as long as the total equals 10. Your response might look something like this:

Example:

0. I really like it when . . .

　　a. things are done correctly.　 *5*

　　b. the other people involved feel good as well.　 *2*

　　c. I've achieved something difficult.　 *3*

Don't worry or think too much about the points; just assign the value that seems right to you about the area of your life you're currently focused on. Ready? Go.

1. I really like it when . . .

   a. things are done correctly. _____

   b. the other people involved feel good as well. _____

   c. I've achieved something difficult. _____

2. I really dislike it when I feel that I am doing something . . .

   a. unprofessional. _____

   b. unpopular. _____

   c. boring. _____

3. It would really bother me if I lost . . .

   a. my independence. _____

   b. my allies or friends. _____

   c. my get up and go. _____

4. I love having time to . . .

   a. do something properly. _____

   b. get to know people better (or get to know new people). _____

   c. take on new challenges. _____

5. I like . . .

   a. being allowed to get on with things. _____

   b. being in the thick of things. _____

   c. being in charge. _____

6. I most appreciate praise when it . . .

   a. comes from an expert. _____

   b. comes from the heart. _____

   c. comes from results. _____

7. I am at my best when . . .

   a. I'm working out the solution to a difficult problem. _____

   b. I'm helping others. _____

   c. I'm under pressure to deliver. _____

8. I value . . .

   a. freedom. _____

   b. friendship. _____

   c. excitement. _____

9. The best decisions are made . . .

   a. based on the facts. _____

   b. collaboratively. _____

   c. quickly. _____

10. My motto is . . .

    a. "If a job's worth doing, it's worth doing properly." _____

    b. "Treat others as you would like to be treated." _____

    c. "Just do it." _____

Ready to find out if your guess was right? Add up your points from each option, *a, b,* and *c,* and enter the totals here:

Totals

   a: Professional = _____   *b:* Carer = _____   *c:* Driver = _____

Why aren't adapters included? Because they are an even mix, which you'll know by looking at your totals for *a, b,* and *c.* Consider it this way: If your point totals for *a, b,* and *c* are each between 22 and 44, then you are an adapter. (For example, if your totals are *a* = 37, *b* = 35, and *c* = 28.)

However, if your points in any one category total more than 45, then you are most likely that type. (For example, totals of *a* = 23, *b* = 24, and *c* = 53 would indicate that you are a driver.)

If no category has a total over 45 but one category is under 22, then you are a mixture of two types. (For example, if your points are a = 41, b = 41, and c = 18, then you are a mix of professional and carer.)

Are You Motivated?

Now that you've learned why and how your motivational style can connect or clash with others' motivational styles, you can start to approach your interactions with others keeping their motivations in mind, as opposed to assuming they need to adapt to yours. Approaching people in this way will lead to longer lasting, more productive, and more fulfilling relationships.

GIVE YOUR MIND A WORKOUT

Beginner: When Your Motivational Style Works Against You

We do what we do based on our motivations. We get better at the things we do often. In this way, our motivations quickly become our strengths. But here's a twist. Some psychologists believe that weaknesses are often strengths taken to the extreme. Your motivation toward action becomes the strength of directness. But taken to an extreme, you turn out to be dictatorial. Your motivation to care becomes the strength of supportiveness, which taken to an extreme becomes smothering. Your motivation to be thorough becomes the strength of analysis, which taken to an extreme becomes nitpicky. So, if you understand your strengths, you can also understand your weaknesses, at least how others perceive them.

1. Divide a sheet of paper into four columns.

2. Reflect on your strengths. In the first column, list your greatest strengths, those that you demonstrate both at work and at home. If you're finding this hard, ask others how they would describe what you're best at.

3. In the second column, identify your weaknesses by writing what each of your strengths would look like if it were taken to the extreme. For example, confidence could become arrogance.

4. Now, anticipate extremism. In the third column, write down when you are most likely to take a strength to the extreme and make it a weakness. Is it during conflict? During times of stress? When you're in charge of something? Learn to anticipate the situations when this is most likely to happen so you can avoid it.

5. Write in the fourth column what you can do when you feel a strength might become a weakness.

Advanced: Working with All Motivational Styles

1. Try to spot the various motivational styles. Choose two people in your life. The first choice should be someone you have a close personal relationship with and whom you think doesn't share the same motivational style as you. Your second choice should be someone at work, whom you don't see eye to eye with.

2. On a sheet of paper, write down two things that you dislike about the styles of each of the two people you chose. Follow that with two things you value about their styles. Then, put yourself in their shoes and do this step again, this time thinking about what they would dislike and value about your style. (This will help you understand that there is no "best" style.)

3. Now, flex your style. Go back into this chapter, where we discussed "How to Get the Best from . . ." and intentionally approach your two choices of people in a manner suitable to their motivational styles. Pay special attention to how they respond to you, then write down the differences you notice from how they responded to you previously. You'll be shocked at how quickly this exercise can elevate your relationship.

PART FOUR

Persuade Others

YOU KNOW you're the right person for the promotion. Now you need to convince your boss.

Your sister is in an unhealthy relationship. You'd like to urge her to move on, but are your arguments compelling enough?

You have an idea that could help your company gain a new customer base, which could bring the company big bucks. Do you know how to communicate your idea?

There's a simple truth about the human species that most of us tend to forget. Basically, we all believe we're right. As self-serving as that may sound, the power of persuasion isn't simply about personal gain or manipulation. How do you persuade a loved one to avoid dangerous behaviors? How do you persuade a friend to reach their potential? And even though persuasion can be used for personal gain, it's also necessary for survival—to get jobs, keep customers, and steer your life in the direction you want it to go.

In jobs, in friendships, with family, and in love, it seems that while some of us are very good at persuading, others are not. What makes one politician so likable while the other grinds at your patience? What makes one salesperson so good at making you believe you need a product you'll never use? Why is it that some people always seem to be the most beloved person in the room—they're charming and overflowing with charisma wherever they go? Do you want the person you like to like you back? Persuasion is the key. It's a powerful tool you can use to get what you want out of life, and to help others get what they want out of life.

This part explores the power of persuasion. It offers insights and tools that will teach you how to persuade others on three levels.

First, you're going to learn about influence. In "Win Hearts and Minds," you'll read about the nine tactics of influence and how to use them. You'll discover which tactics you are already good at and how to improve your use of the tactics you're not so good at. These can help you win at work, strengthen relationships, and get more out of what you want in life.

Second, in "Impress Everyone," you'll find out about impact words that can change the way people receive you. You'll learn about storytelling, the power of asking the right questions, and how to increase your charisma in the real world, to make more friends, create closer bonds, and instill and communicate trust.

Finally, the last chapter in this part, "Give Great Feedback," will take you even further into the realm of your persuasive potential. You'll learn how to remain likable and charming even if the information you need to communicate isn't the most positive. You'll find out how to properly and effectively praise and recognize people—a powerful tool in motivating friends, children, and team members. And you'll discover how to handle some of life's stickier situations, like how to be honest without being brutal.

We all want and need people to like us and respect our opinions. This is the go-to part of the book if you want more friends, want more respect, or simply want to be heard.

Persuasion is powerful. Use it wisely. Those who master it often change the world around them.

CHAPTER 9

Win Hearts and Minds

Most of us have heard that a cat is supposed to have nine lives, and we know a pregnancy lasts approximately nine months. But we are largely unaware that there are nine primary tactics used to influence other people. Why, then—like a tourist who repeats the same words louder each time a local doesn't understand—do we try to influence others with just a few ineffective methods? Sure, we make small tweaks or cosmetic changes to these approaches, but our underlying strategies for influencing others remain frighteningly similar, even when they continue not to work. And when they don't work, we blame everything else—the other person is just being difficult, the situation was wrong, or something else.

In order to change your strategies, you need to understand the first principle of influencing others. To illustrate this principle, imagine you are in a fine restaurant. It's full. And even though you're celebrating your recent job promotion, you wonder why everyone chose this fancy place to dine. In the restaurant are many other diners: A group of business colleagues—four men and one woman—are with a client whom they want to impress. A young couple is on a second date and the man is pretending to be wealthy (which is why he left his old car at home and took a taxi). A mature couple is celebrating the wife's birthday (but she won't say which one). A German family is on vacation and had read in a guidebook that this is the best restaurant in the area. What is significant about this situation, and so many others like it, is that everyone has made the same decision: to have dinner in the same restaurant on the same night. Yet each person has also made this decision for a different reason—*their* reason. This is the number one principle for understanding influence: people make decisions for *their* reasons, not yours.

When you try to influence others, it is essential that you understand the other person's reasons so you can use tactics that will work to persuade *them,* as opposed to tactics that would work on you. With this in mind, you are ready to learn about each of the nine primary tactics. Whether you want to teach the world to sing, your daughter to clean her room, your company to give you a promotion, or your friends to come on vacation with you to Miami, mastering these tactics for influencing can make the difference between defeat and delight.

Reasoning

What Is It?

"There are three excellent reasons why contemporary art is a worthwhile investment. First . . ."

The tactic we call reasoning, at its best, is the process of using facts, logic, and argument to make a case.

Give Me an Example

"You should run the marathon next year. The training will make you fitter and healthier; it will give you something to focus on outside work, which you said you wanted; and you will raise money for a good cause, maybe that hospice you gave all your old clothes to for their fund-raising sale. It just makes sense."

When Is It Useful?

This tactic is useful most of the time. Reasoning is the bread and butter of influencing. The challenge is to support your views with relevant information and a coherent argument. Although reasoning requires more effort than some of the other tactics, it is much more likely to create your desired effect.

Warning

When you present a view or position as if it is a fact (e.g., "This problem is going to take a long time to solve") but without any evidence to back it up, then the reasoning is weak. Weak reasoning is the most common influencing tactic people use,[1] but without the evidence to back up your view, it is far less effective.[2]

Inspiring

What Is It?

"Imagine a world where . . ."

Almost the exact opposite of reasoning, the inspiring tactic focuses on the heart rather than the head. It appeals to emotions and suggests what could be possible, if only the other person were persuaded.

Give Me an Example

Some of the most well-known uses of the inspiring tactic can be seen in political leaders' speeches. Great examples are Martin Luther King Jr.'s "I Have a Dream" speech and Shakespeare's "Once more unto the breach, dear friends" speech given by Henry V. These speeches don't just ignore logical argument but defy it. Take this excerpt from John F. Kennedy's speech about putting a man on the moon, with commentary from a skeptic in brackets.

We choose to go to the moon in this decade and do the other things, not because they are easy, but because they are hard [Yeah, like that's a good reason for doing something; hey, I reckon we should paint the garden fences with a toothbrush and nail varnish because it's really hard], because that goal will serve to organize and measure the best of our energies and skills [How so? Why wouldn't feeding the starving in Africa or increasing world literacy do it just as well if not better?] . . .

For all the skeptic's heckling, this speech helped mobilize a nation. The magic about inspirational appeal is that it touches our hearts by appealing to our values and our identity. Like falling in love, when the inspiring tactic works, nothing can beat it (certainly not a cynic).

When Is It Useful?

This tactic is especially useful when your rational argument is weak or unclear and you want a high level of emotional commitment. The inspiring tactic doesn't tend to be used much in daily life, especially in the workplace, which is a shame because it's a powerful way to persuade and excite.

Most of us have been seduced by this tactic as children (e.g., "It'll make you big and strong when you grow up"), when watching TV (e.g., advertisements with young, sexy people having wild times drinking a particular brand of soda), or when we're with friends who are hooked on a new craze (e.g., "You have to check out dune bashing: the surge, the speed, the heat, the views").

Warning

It is not just what you say but also how you say it; the inspiring tactic demands conviction, energy, and passion. When deploying this tactic, a dreary demeanor will leave you floundering. Deliver inspiration like it matters more than life itself and you'll be pretty much invincible.

Asking Questions

What Is It?

"Would you like to be rich?"

Asking questions encourages the other person to make their own discovery of your conclusion (or something similar).

Give Me an Example

I am walking through the airport when a woman with a clipboard approaches me from in front of a large advertising board and asks, "Do you have a credit card?"

I utter a dismissive "Yes" and keep walking.

"Do you get airline miles with your card?" she persists.

"Yes, I do," I reply, slightly irritated, and carry on walking.

"Do you use your airline miles?" The truth is I don't, but I'm not going to get caught up in this conversation.

"A bit," I reply, but my walking slows.

"Would you rather have cash?"

I stop, turn, and look at her for the first time.

"Do you have five minutes to fill in a form to get a credit card that gives you cash?" she asks.

In five questions I have been persuaded to do something I haven't done in over a decade: switch to a new credit card.

When Is It Useful?

This is a great tactic when it is important that the other person feels responsible for the outcome. In coaching and counseling, for example, a course of action or therapy is much more effective when the other person believes it was their idea rather than when they grudgingly give in.

Asking questions is also useful when you're trying to persuade someone who has more power than you—maybe your boss ("Do you think I'm overdoing it?" "Do you struggle with work–life balance? How do you deal with it?") or your client ("Are you happy with the gold service? Or do you ever wish you had the platinum?").

Warning

This is one of the hardest tactics to use because it is impossible to know how the other person will respond. If the questions are too broad, then you are likely to veer off course; if they are too narrow, the other person will spot what you are up to and may refuse to cooperate. But while most of the other tactics get weaker if they're used too much, asking questions is a tactic that has an extended battery life—it's effective time after time.

Cozying Up

What Is It?

"You're a smart guy."

If you feel positive toward someone, you are much more likely to agree with them, and you almost always feel positive toward someone who makes you feel good about yourself. This is the cozying up tactic.

Give Me an Example

"Hi, Sandra. You're looking well. I heard from Mark that you did a great job on the Johnson case. Not an easy situation—well done. I have a challenging case coming up in October and am pulling together a top-level team to work on it. Would you be interested?"

When Is It Useful?

Cozying up is a particularly good tactic to use when you're trying to influence people with less or the same level of power as you, because they are likely to value your views. Many of us use it on our partners ("Darling, you look like a million bucks"), our friends ("I know you are someone I can trust"), and our clients ("You're the sort of person who will really appreciate this—because you're smart").

The danger with cozying up is that if you're too obvious when using this tactic, you'll have the opposite effect ("You're only saying that because you want me to do something for you"). As a result, some people avoid it altogether. They are missing out. A less risky approach is to leave time—sometimes even several days—between making someone feel good about themselves and trying to persuade them.

Warning

Using cozying up on someone who clearly has more power than you can look like sucking up. So, unless you know what you are doing, be mindful about how much kudos you're sending out into the world.

Deal Making

What Is It?

"If you pick me up from the airport, I will . . ."

Deal making is when you offer or give another person something in return for their agreement with you. It may be explicit, but it doesn't have to be.

Give Me an Example

"I promised a friend I would walk his dog while he was on vacation. Then tonight I was offered Beyoncé tickets at the last minute. I'll buy you dinner if you come over and watch the dog while I'm at the concert."

When Is It Useful?

Deal making is useful when you want to increase the odds in your favor and don't mind giving something away in return. Sometimes it is necessary to be up front ("If you help me paint the bathroom, I'll cook dinner every night next week"). At the same time, the deal can work better when the connection is only implied ("Sure, I'll introduce you to my sister," and then twenty minutes later, "Can you really get me into the VIP section at the golf tournament?"). Often deal making is most effective when the connection is all but invisible, like it's something you would have done for one another without a deal.[3]

Warning

This tactic works by appealing to a desire for fairness. Some people can "take, take, take" without feeling any remorse or indebtedness (or they may just think you're a generous fool). Deal making won't work with this type of person unless you are very up front about the terms of the exchange.

Favor Asking[4]

What Is It?

"Can you help me out?"
Favor asking is simply asking for something because you want or need it, but you're not offering anything in return.

Give Me an Example

"My guest speaker has just pulled out of the event I'm organizing next week. All I can say is that I'd be eternally grateful if you'd be willing to step in and give a speech to my group."

When Is It Useful?

This tactic works well only when the other person cares about you or their relationship with you. If used sparingly, it is hard to resist.

Warning

The person you ask for a favor might feel that you owe them one in the future. If you think they do, make sure you "pay back" that favor or you won't get such a positive response next time.

Using Silent Allies

What Is It?

"Everyone who has read this book so far . . ."

The use of silent allies invokes other people, who are generally similar to the person you are trying to persuade, to make your case ("All professional runners train this way, so you should too").

Give Me an Example

The advertising slogans "Nine out of ten dentists recommend . . ." and "America runs on Dunkin'" are classic examples of this tactic. Movie reviews and quotes from satisfied customers are also common examples. Outside of advertising and marketing, the silent allies approach is often used in the workplace, where you might hear comments like "All the best graphic designers use a Mac." In social situations, you might hear "All the cool kids are wearing these jeans, and they're the top-selling brand." The best silent allies are those whom the person you are trying to persuade naturally associates with, such as professionals in their own industry or people with similar interests or beliefs.

When Is It Useful?

One of the most powerful ways to persuade teenagers to do anything is to show them that their peers, especially the cool ones, are doing it already. The silent allies tactic also works in business by, for example, referring to best practice models or a list of past clients. If the person you are trying to influence is concerned about risk (and most people are, deep down) or is anxious to fit in, then this can be your winning tactic.

Warning

Some people actually prefer to be contrary ("I only like underground bands"). Entrepreneurs, for example, are rarely dissuaded from trying something because no one has done it before. They actually see it as a potential benefit.

Invoking Authority

What Is It?

"It's our policy not to refund cash."

The invoking authority tactic is used from a position of power or by appealing to a rule or principle. It doesn't matter whether the authority invoked is formal or implicit, so long as it is recognized by the person you are trying to influence.

Give Me an Example

"I won't work for you unless we sign a contract" is an explicit approach to influence that not only appeals to the rules but also creates them.

"I won't take business calls between the hours of five P.M. and seven P.M. because that is dinnertime with my family" is an approach to influence that creates boundaries based on principles.

When Is It Useful?

The advantage of invoking authority is that the tactic is quick and straightforward. The downside is that it is more likely to lead to compliance than commitment. It's better to invoke authority as a last resort rather than use it as your opening gambit, unless you are in a rush. Authority can, however, make a positive impression on someone who abides by similar rules or lives by similar principles.

Warning

If you try to persuade using this tactic and don't succeed, then you don't have many other options left (mainly the forcing tactic, detailed next). You are also likely to have damaged a relationship. And like using silent allies, this tactic can have the opposite effect from the intended one. Think of Dirty Harry being told he is being pulled off a case, only to carry on his investigations anyway. Or Julia Roberts in the movie *Erin Brockovich* refusing to bow down. If the person you're trying to influence doesn't agree with your rules or principles, using authority can have a quick and extreme impact on your relationship. Be warned, this tactic is a bit like drawing a line in the sand.

Forcing

What Is It?

"Do it or else."

The forcing tactic involves engaging in assertive behavior, such as threats and warnings.

Give Me an Example

"Eat your vegetables or you'll be going straight to bed."

"Love me or leave me."

"The last person in your job didn't last very long; we wouldn't want you to make the same mistake."

"The more time you spend arguing about it, the less time you'll have left to do it."

When Is It Useful?

Forcing is used when you want something done fast. Therefore, it's ideal in emergencies.

Warning

Because forcing is relatively easy to adopt and usually delivers short-term results, like compliance, it gets used a fair bit, especially when combined with using authority. However, relationship breakdowns can often be traced back to uses of the forcing tactic. Almost like smoking cigarettes, the immediate damage appears minimal, but the long-term effects can be terminal; and even if you give up using this tactic, it could be too late, so it's probably best not to start.

Using the forcing tactic can also be quite addictive, because it gives the user a sense of power when it gets results. Only employ forcing when everything else has failed.

How to Use the Nine Tactics

Just because you know about the different types of golf clubs, that doesn't make you a golf champion. However, without knowing all the types of clubs, it would be almost impossible to improve your game. Similarly, becoming familiar with the nine tactics is a great start, but you need to learn when, how, and where to use them in order to influence others effectively. Once you are fluent in the language of influencing, you can become a lot more mindful about how you influence (and how others try to influence you).

Here are four ways you can use your newfound knowledge of the tactics to improve your influencing form.

Know Yourself

There are no right or wrong influencing tactics. Which are most effective will depend largely on the situation and the person you are trying to influence. Consider which tactics you tend to use most and which least. This is likely to vary in different areas of your life. For example, at home you might use the cozying-up tactic, whereas at work you might use the reasoning and deal-making tactics. Once you've figured out which tactics you use most and least, consider whether you should try some of the other tactics you rarely use.

Get Strategic

People rarely use one tactic by itself. The skill of employing tactics lies in combining them in the right way for any particular situation. So, before starting, it can help to develop an influencing strategy. Here are two examples of influencing strategies:

Situation: Your husband can't swim and you have recently moved to a house on the edge of a lake.	
Objective: To persuade your husband to learn to swim	

Influencing Tactic	How to Use It
Inspiring	"Imagine how great it would be if on long, hot summer days we could both take the children into the lake, help them to swim better, and play games together as a family."
Favor asking	"I lose sleep worrying about you having an accident near the lake. If only for my peace of mind, please learn to swim."
Deal making	"If you learn to swim, I will organize and pay for a beach vacation in Florida."
Forcing	"If you don't learn to swim, I won't let you play with the children outdoors."

Situation: You are the president of the local hockey club and you are short of funds because people aren't paying their club dues.	
Objective: To persuade the club members to pay their dues	

Influencing Tactic	How to Use It
Asking questions	"The club cannot afford to buy any more shirts. This means we cannot all play in the same colors, which makes us ineligible for any of our tournaments. What do you think we should do about this?" (Potential follow-up: "What would convince you to pay your dues?")
Reasoning	"If dues are paid, then we will have enough funds to prevent an overdraft and be able to buy enough new shirts for the next tournament."
Using silent allies	"A number of people have paid up their dues. It would be great if everyone did."

Invoking authority	"As president, I insist all members must pay their dues immediately."
Forcing	"Anyone who has not paid their dues by the end of the month will no longer be considered a member of the club and will need to pay another joining fee if they want to rejoin."

As you will discover, there are some sequences that work better than others. For example, the asking questions tactic usually needs to be used early in the sequence, as does the cozying-up tactic. Once you have used the invoking authority or forcing tactics it is difficult to move to any of the other tactics, so those are usually best as last resorts. Favor asking and deal making are often used after other tactics have been tried.

Be Flexible

Even the best plans can go wrong. If your attempt at influencing doesn't seem to be working, then think about which tactics you haven't used and try them out. It's much easier to change your approach when you have easy access to alternatives.

Keep Improving

No one influences effectively 100 percent of the time (no matter what they tell you). The best way to improve your skills is to observe what is going on and figure out what you could do differently. Here are some ideas:

- For each of the tactics, give yourself a score, from 1 to 10, for how good you are at it. Once you have identified the tactics you are less good at, you can work on improvement.

- Reflect on your influencing strategies. Which ones are effective? Why did the successful ones deliver good results? What can you learn from the strategies that haven't worked so you can develop a better strategy to use in the future?

- Which influencing approaches seem to work best *on* you? How are other people using them and what can you copy or adapt from them to make you more effective?

- How do other people influence someone you find difficult to persuade?

What Lessons Can You Learn from Watching Master Influencers at Work?

If you're finding that you're still not as good at influencing as you want to be, remember the point presented at the beginning of this chapter: People make decisions for their reasons, not yours. The most common reason why you aren't effective is that you are looking through your own eyes rather than seeing things from the other person's perspective.

GIVE YOUR MIND A WORKOUT

Beginner: Find a Role Model

1. Think of someone you find very persuasive. This could be a friend, coworker, celebrity, politician, or anyone else.

2. Write down what their influencing approach is and which of the nine tactics they rely on. What is it about how they use their particular tactics that works so well?

3. Consider how you could adopt some of their persuasive techniques— and if you'll need to learn or develop certain skills to do so (e.g., Are they truly inspirational because they are a great public speaker? Could you take a public speaking class to also become more inspirational?).

Advanced: Blocks and Releases

1. Divide a sheet of paper into two columns.

2. In the first column, write down what blocks you from using certain influencing tactics. Are you afraid of failure or rejection? Or is it harder to influence someone more senior to you? Or does the technique feel unnatural and awkward?

3. In the second column, write down the practical ways you think you can overcome each block. Some ideas include planning your influencing approach, anticipating responses, practicing with a partner, and considering the benefits to you and to the other person. Work through these ways and be specific. For example, if you plan to get over your block by practicing with a partner, decide which partner you'll practice with and when.

4. Take action. Follow through on the various ways in which you plan to overcome your blocks.

5. Practice in real life. Pick a situation where you'd like to influence someone and test out just how persuasive you can be.

CHAPTER 10

Impress Everyone

What makes someone influential? Over the years, we've asked this question to thousands of people. And the most common response we hear is charisma—being able to connect, charm, and win over others with one's personality. The thing is, charisma is not something you're born with. It's something you learn.[1] If you want to be the person everyone wants more of, welcome to Mind Gym's version of charm school. The following ten lessons will help you impress anyone.

Lesson One: Hope

Billboard's Hot 100 list of the biggest singles is dominated by optimism. In the top ten you'll find "Hey Jude" by the Beatles, "You Light Up My Life" by Debby Boone, and "I Gotta Feeling" by The Black Eyed Peas. Of course, the list makes sense. We all want to feel that the future can be better. These songs radiate hope. Optimists outperform pessimists in political elections, sales, and social connections (for more on the power of optimism, see chapter 2), because hope tends to attract other people and is, quite simply, attractive.[2]

Louis Armstrong's "When You're Smiling (The Whole World Smiles With You)" is a song and a sentiment that obviously runs through the blood of most charismatic people. It's not that they don't have dark days. Charismatic people just don't advertise them. Instead, they emulate hope by

- speaking optimistically about the future,
- sharing believable steps to attain that future, and
- expressing confidence in the ability of others to take those steps.

Lesson Two: Passion

When you're passionate, people are drawn to you. It's hard to fake passion. Whether they're passionate about saving the planet, rising to the top of an organization, the latest fashion, freshwater fishing, or fine art, charismatic people talk about subjects they care about. Which people do you think are really interesting? Now, why do you think they're really interesting? It's because they're all passionate about something—they passionately work toward a goal and they take part in something they care about. Even if you're not interested in the thing they are passionate about, you're drawn to that person because they exude passion. You may not be a skier but you may know a guy who spends every waking moment on the ski slopes—and his excitement is contagious. Perhaps you work with a woman who provides foster care for the local Humane Society and her caring for wayward animals is enviable. There's no way you would take on three homeless dogs at one time, yet you truly appreciate that she loves to do it. This is passion, and charismatic people ooze it. Charismatic people express their passion by

- articulating a strong, informed point of view;
- speaking with energy and vigor; and
- demonstrating single-mindedness and focus in what they want to achieve.

Lesson Three: Connection

Have you ever felt in sync with a group of people? Chances are you're experiencing what psychologists call "entrainment."[3] It's that feeling you get when you're in flow or when you feel a very strong sense of connection. My movements match your movements, my rhythm is in harmony with yours, we laugh together at the same volume, we use similar words, and we even make hand gestures at the same time.[4] You might experience entrainment when you see an old friend and you find yourselves finishing each other's stories. Or you might meet someone for the first time and feel like you automatically "click." It's a fantastic feeling when it happens naturally. Usually, however, it doesn't happen without a nudge. And you can give it a nudge by matching the other person in some of the following ways:

- Speak at the same volume, pace, tempo, and rhythm.

- Reflect or mirror similar body language, like crossing your legs.

- Share similar beliefs and values.

- Make statements or offer views that the other person is sure to agree with.

It's apparent that you've made a strong connection with someone when you gesture, move, or giggle and they do too. Or when you sit up, so do they. Once they begin to emulate you, you know you've made a connection. Charismatic people connect in this way deliberately. So, if you want to see charisma in action, pay attention to the most charismatic person in the room and you'll see that they are matching the behavior of those around them.

Lesson Four: Congruence

Have you ever met someone who says something but it's hard to believe they really mean what they're saying? Charismatic people's words always align with their actions and body language. Whether it's a tired salesperson making the same pitch for the fifth time that day or a child showing confusion when you ask if they ate the last cookie, inconsistencies between spoken language and body language can be spotted pretty quickly, and from a mile away. Congruence occurs when all the nonverbal signs are aligned with what is being said. To achieve congruence,

- concentrate on the conversation;
- speak about subjects you actually care about;
- believe in what you're saying;
- relax your body;
- enjoy the truth; and
- maintain a low, natural breathing rate.

Charismatic people are trusted because of their words and actions. They are not trusted because they know everything there is to know about their subject matter. They admit when they don't know the answers, which makes them believable when they do have answers or insights. Their verbal and nonverbal communication is aligned. And just like inconsistencies can be spotted a mile away, so can congruence.

Lesson Five: Impact Words

The power of charismatic communication comes not from changing the way people think but from changing the way they feel. Just as a cup of coffee might make the person you're speaking to excitable, the right words will make them excited about what you have to say. Charismatic communication is dominated by three types of words. You'll notice these words tend to be absent in typical conversation. So, if you are trying to amp your charisma level, use these types of words more frequently:

1. Words that express a specific emotion: upset, determined, excited, concerned, happy, passionate, nervous, thrilled

2. Words that evoke the senses, such as sounds and smells, and other physical sensations: smack, blossom, clunk, grate, crash, whoop, chill

3. Descriptive words that create a picture in the listener's mind: immense, slender, towering, shimmering[5]

Of course, impact words can be overdone, as we often see in the media. They are used heavily in celebrity tabloid shows to shock the viewers, in political talk shows to fuel anger toward the opposing party, and in talk radio, such as Howard Stern's show, to push the envelope of acceptability.

Obviously you don't want to overuse impact words in a budget meeting or even on a second date. The phrase "Choose your words carefully" has never been so resonant.

Lesson Six: Generosity with Answers

Notice the difference between these three conversations.

Conversation One:

"How was your weekend?"

"Good, thanks."

Conversation Two:

"How was your weekend?"

"I had to work."

Conversation Three:

"How was your weekend?"

"On Saturday, we went to the park, which was just at that perfect moment when the leaves are turning a beautiful orange and the wind is cool enough to make you glad you have a scarf. On Sunday, we took a brisk walk and discovered this quaint little craft coffee shop. The ambiance was cozy. The coffee was piping hot, and the pancakes were among the best I've ever eaten."

It's easy to imagine that the three responses above were from people who had different weekends, but that isn't necessarily so. Many of us can reduce the gamut of our emotions to "fine" or "okay."

A charismatic person offers anything but a simple "It was good." Instead, they are generous with their answers, sharing specifics, giving color and flavor with incidental detail ("beautiful orange"). They also share how they felt to some extent. The next time someone asks "How was your weekend?" what will you say?

Lesson Seven: Remember When

Can you think of a time when you couldn't stop yourself from smiling? You were so happy that you were beaming with joy and everyone could see it. When was that? Why were you so happy? Or can you think of a time when you had to make a very difficult decision, and it was really tricky, but you made a call and it was the right one? Can you remember what you considered? What made you finally know you'd done the right thing? Or can you think of a time when you delighted a customer with the work you'd done? What did they say? What had you done that so impressed them?

These are examples of elicitation questions—questions designed to elicit an emotion, usually a positive one. If you answered each of the questions, you probably brought back into your conscious mind a scene in which you felt pretty good. As you recalled the scene, chances are you felt more positive, right here, right now, as you're reading this book. Questions can also be used to elicit emotions, as well as things that you view as positive: Whom do you most admire? What do you enjoy doing most on weekends? What's your favorite food?

You can also guide other people's feelings by referring to positive situations most of your listeners have experienced. For example, in a speech given at a charity event you might say, "Do you remember the feeling of fear and excitement you had when you started college? My mother cared deeply about my education. I remember her working very hard to get me there. Do you remember that moment when you realized you were on your own? I remember that, after my mother dropped me off and drove away, I appreciated how much I needed to learn and discover, how much I needed to repay the faith she had placed in me. But I also knew that I was surrounded by people who were friendly, smart, and supportive. That's how I feel now, standing before you at this inaugural meeting of our charity."

Whether elicitation questions evoke curiosity, pride, desire, hope, or determination, they are a reliable way to stimulate the emotions of others. Charismatic people ask these questions often to engage and connect with others.

Lesson Eight: Story Time

When it comes to charisma, nothing can be as powerful as a story. Stories capture the hearts and minds of an audience. They personalize information, teach lessons, and provide an example that can help people connect to or understand a larger message. Charismatic people are often brilliant storytellers. Consider Walt Disney, who created an empire that allows people to enter a fictional story (even though there is always a greater meaning). Or consider Bruce Springsteen, who has told his American story through lyrics.

Water cooler chitchat at the office is rarely two colleagues offering prescriptive advice or insight. Instead, it's stories about what someone did and what happened as a result. Politicians also tell stories about people. They gain support by sharing stories they've picked up from voters while on the campaign trail—the farmer who's trying to support his family, the mother who hopes her children live a better life than her, or the senior citizen who is terrified about his future retirement.

All of us have stories. And this is why we all find stories so relatable. The problem is that we all don't leverage the power of storytelling to win friends and influence others. So, to help you get going in the right direction, here is a summary of the four vital elements in any story:

- *A protagonist.* This is the lead character, the hero. Throughout a story, a protagonist goes on a journey. It may be a literal journey—such as Dorothy's journey from Kansas to the land of Oz in *The Wizard of Oz.* Or it may be a symbolic journey, which leads the protagonist to a new understanding or teaches something profound. The journey to Oz teaches Dorothy, who was dissatisfied with her life in Kansas, that "there's no place like home."

• *A predicament.* To generate intrigue, a protagonist needs to be faced with a challenging situation that forces them to take action or make a choice. Something that will get our audience wondering, *What's going to happen next?* The more unpredictable the outcome, the more engrossed the audience will be. The mother mentioned in a politician's story might have overcome tremendous odds to get where she is today—and now that her personal predicament has been managed, her predicament shifts to changing the future for her children.

• *A plot.* This is an account of what happened and how it happened. A storyteller adds details and emotions to enrich the story. The writer E. M. Forster put it like this: "'The king died, and then the queen died' is a story. 'The king died, and then the queen died of grief' is a plot."[6]

• *An outcome.* All the elements of a story come together in a way that resolves a protagonist's predicament and ends the journey. Fairy tales often end with the message "and they all lived happily ever after." Politicians' stories often end with a legislative solution that could solve a problem.

If you want to be more charismatic, you'd do well to pepper your conversations with great stories—making sure that you include a protagonist, a predicament, a plot, and an outcome.

Lesson Nine: Surprise

In the movie *Dead Poets Society,* Robin Williams's character, John Keating, gets his students' attention by making a dramatic entrance. The first time he enters the classroom, he walks straight through without saying a word and exits by the door at the back of the room. The students are confused and intrigued. Then, almost as an afterthought, Keating sticks his head back into the room and invites them to follow him. They're hooked. The surprise was irresistible. Charismatic people often go beyond the obvious by suggesting or doing the unexpected. They excite people around them, leaving people wondering what they will do next.

Unconventional responses to familiar situations grab your attention and stay in your memory. Think of the most charismatic people you know. Most likely, you can tell a story about the time they surprised you or someone else.

Lesson Ten: Put Me at the Center

Children are often enchanted when a storyteller gives a hero or heroine their name and plenty of other similar characteristics. "He had brown hair and blue eyes, much like you do" will leave a child begging to hear more of the story. Of course, the adult version of this tactic is slightly more subtle, but only slightly. Here are a few tips that will help you gain charisma by putting others at the center of the story:

- When telling a story, give your protagonist some of the positive characteristics of the person with whom you want to build a relationship. It usually pays to sprinkle in a little flattery: "Just like you, Sarah was always open to new ideas."

- Draw comparisons between the details of your story and episodes in the person's personal history: "It was just like the time you took Jan kayaking on the lake and you saw the storm coming and . . ."

- Use expansive body language that includes and engages the listener. Perhaps you touch the person on the arm, make direct eye contact, or raise an eyebrow to show that this conversation is all about them.

- At key junctures of a story, ask people what they think happened next. Or ask them to consider what they would do in this situation. Listen generously and point out how their suggestions fit with the next stage in the story.

- Animate the scene you are describing by making it concrete. Act it out with whatever items you have to hand: "The coffee pot represents the farmer and the cards in your wallet are all his dogs, then take this sugar bowl—that represents . . ."

- Use your listener's name. It sounds so obvious, but it makes us feel good to be acknowledged by name: "The challenge, Justine, is how to get all the delegates there on time . . ." Don't overdo it, though. Keep it real. All these techniques can have the opposite effect when they're overdone.

Graduating Charm School

Charisma is a great tool of influence. In fact, it's one of the primary tools. Some of us are born with charisma or are socialized to be more naturally charismatic than others. Nevertheless, the most charismatic people have been taught or have trained themselves in the seemingly fine art of being charming. You might find that some of the tactics in this chapter come more easily to you than others. But more than anything else, if you want to learn to influence others, it's important that you practice and become aware of all these tactics. Becoming a master at one tactic is great—unless of course that tactic happens to be a turnoff to the person you are trying to influence. Practice, practice, practice. Charisma is learned.

Oh, and here's one last piece of advice to keep in mind: listen to your gut instinct.

On the evening of August 27, 1963, staff writers for Dr. Martin Luther King Jr. scrambled to draft a speech. Dr. King, upon arriving in Washington, D.C., to address a crowd of more than two hundred and fifty thousand people at the March on Washington for Jobs and Freedom, had already planned a speech for the following day. It was a message he had delivered two months before. But his staff thought they could create something better.

When Dr. King stood on the stage the next day, his speech was to be the one written by his advisers and titled "Normalcy, Never Again." He began with this prepared speech, but after a while he felt that something wasn't quite working. He observed the mood of the crowd. He listened to a colleague, Mahalia Jackson, urging him to improvise. King listened to his instincts. And then, the words he really wanted to say poured out: ". . . I have a dream."

Beginner: Introduce Yourself with Impact

A moment many people dread is when they're asked to introduce them-selves, particularly in front of others. But it is a great opportunity to demonstrate your charisma.

1. Assess how you currently introduce yourself to new people. What is your approach? Are you as impactful as you'd like to be? How do people react to your introduction? Do they ask questions to learn more about you or nod and change the subject?

2. Write a couple practice introductions on a piece of paper, and in each include one or more of the tactics in this chapter.

3. Plan the way you will introduce yourself. How will you find congru-ence with another person? How will you sound? What will your body language look like?

4. Try it out. Test your new introductions the next time you are at a networking function or a party. Which introduction worked best, and how will you remember to keep using it?

Advanced: Weave a Story

Come up with a few different stories to keep in the back of your mind and pull out whenever you need to have greater impact.

1. The best stories come from personal experience, so think back through your life and jot down some of the defining moments of your childhood, young adulthood, adulthood, career, and parent-hood, if that's applicable. Make a list of these moments.

2. Pick three to four of the moments you just jotted down and write what you learned from them or how they changed you. Perhaps you overcame adversity and grew as a result. Or perhaps something surprising happened that changed how you thought about yourself or the world. Use "Lesson Eight: Story Time," in particular.

3. Practice delivering your stories out loud. Time yourself and aim for a maximum of two minutes. Use impact words and passion. Practice telling your stories to someone you are close to who will give you candid feedback.

4. When you're ready, test your stories at work or in a social setting and see how people react. Be sure to have powerful body language when you do this so you make a connection with your listener(s).

CHAPTER 11

Give Great Feedback

You know who they are. They're the people who are always late for everything. They're the people who smack their gum at the office. And they're the people who test all their different cell phone ringtones on a packed flight. They're the people who annoy you.

Changing the way other people behave may be immensely desirable, but it is also notoriously difficult. We want to give them our honest opinion about how we feel about their behavior, but for all sorts of reasons we don't. Why not? Because quite often telling people what they could do differently to improve their lives backfires: "Are you saying I smell? Who do you think you are? And while we're on the subject, I have a thing or two to say about your personal habits as well." Rather than improving their lives, they make yours more difficult.

The decision not to tell people when they annoy us or when their behavior affects us in a negative way has wide-reaching consequences. When relationships break down, a person gets passed over for a promotion, friends drift apart, or teams turn in on themselves, the root cause is often something relatively insignificant that could have been dealt with ages ago with an honest exchange. Instead, it was left to fester.

Fortunately, there are two techniques for expressing our opinions to someone that have very impressive success rates when it comes to changing the way that person behaves. These are techniques that have been around since the beginning of time, that we all use occasionally (although not always effectively) and that everyone can master. An abundance of scientific research supports their potency.[1] The techniques are praise and wise counsel.

Praise

Praise is the act of showing recognition and appreciation for someone and/or their actions. It could be something simple like thanking your spouse for taking out the trash or buying your top salesperson a gold watch or giving someone an award for outstanding achievement.

How Much Do You Praise?

Should you be praised for the amount of praise you give out? Look at the following questions and consider your answers to them:

- When was the last time you congratulated someone for something they did well? In the last hour? Today? Yesterday? In the last week? More than a week ago?

- In a normal day, how often do you praise someone (not necessarily the same person) for something they did? Once at best? Two to three times? Five to ten times? Ten to twenty times? More than twenty times a day?

- When you last praised someone, did you say "Well done" and leave it at that? Or did you tell them what they did that was good and outline the impact of what they did?

- Think about someone close to you (colleague, partner, etc.). For every ten times you've given that person praise, how often have you criticized? Never? Once? Five times? Ten times? Twenty times? Fifty times? One hundred or more times?

There's no correct answer to the question of how much praise we should be giving. In most situations, we don't communicate enough praise. If any of your answers have given you pause, then, like most of us, you could be in need of a bit of praise appraisal.

Why Don't People Offer Praise?

A vice president of an investment bank (let's call her Valerie) admitted that she never told people when they had done something well. Her reason? "That is what they're paid for," she explained. If they were doing a satisfactory job, Valerie's argument suggested, it seemed unnecessary to praise them. Perhaps the word "vice" in Valerie's job title referred to her bad habit of not praising, because the view from the people who worked for her was likely to be quite different. They don't know when they've done a good job because no one tells them. In search of approval, they keep trying new approaches, often ignoring successful ideas for others that have less chance of working.

The number one reason why we don't praise people is that if someone is doing something well, we assume they already know how we perceive their work; therefore, there is no point in telling them.

A second significant reason is we somehow imagine that praise undermines us. Valerie imagined her team would think less of her if she congratulated them. She felt expressing praise would suggest that she had low standards and was easily impressed. In fact, many highly respected people are very generous with their praise, largely because they don't feel threatened by the people around them. Praising is a sign of confidence, not weakness.

The third significant reason is perhaps the silliest. Basically, we feel praising people can be embarrassing. We worry about making someone feel embarrassed. And if a person feels embarrassed, so do we. Certainly praising people can be awkward if handled badly. For example, it's best not to shout "You were a tiger last night!" when your significant other drops by the office to join you for lunch. So, what you really need to do is learn how to give praise effectively.

The rest of this chapter is devoted to how to offer praise effectively and includes some techniques for using praise's alter ego: counsel (which is also known as constructive criticism). If you can master praise, you are less likely to offend and more likely to make a helpful difference.

When Should You Praise?

Choosing the right moment to praise someone makes a significant difference to the impact that praise has on the recipient. Ideal times to give praise are ...

At the Time or Soon After the Activity Being Praised Is Completed[2]

In the broadest sense, when you praise minor achievements, you should do it immediately; otherwise, it will look like a bigger deal than it is (e.g., "Thanks so much for making me that delicious cup of tea a week ago last Thursday"). With more significant matters, praise carries more weight when you convey the praise a few hours or days later. This suggests that you have thought about what the person has done and aren't just giving an automatic response.

When You Aren't Asking for Something in Return

If you are expecting something in return, then the praise is greatly devalued and may even have a negative effect.

When You Have the Recipient's Attention

A passing remark that a person can't hear or can pretend to ignore is a waste of effort when it comes to praise (for example, when they are watching their favorite TV show or leaving the house in a hurry).

When the Recipient Is Alone

This isn't essential but it does reduce the chance that they—and you—will be embarrassed. Equally, if the praise would be increased by the approval of others, then a more public setting is absolutely appropriate—a meeting at work, a group lunch, or a team get-together might be better (e.g., "You might not have noticed her efforts, but Zoe is our unsung hero"). Consider the activity being praised and where the praise is best suited.

How Powerful Is Praise?

You might be wondering why all this praise is necessary. Other than the fact that it makes you feel good to say nice things about your teammates, employees, or friends, does praise actually benefit you? Here are four reasons why you should praise more people, and more often:

1. *It works.*[3] There is a strong correlation between telling people that they have done something well and them repeating that behavior. Nothing else you can do has such a predictable impact on how someone will behave in the future. Not only that, but telling that person what *not* to do can have all sorts of unpredictable consequences. So, if you want to change someone's behavior, this is by far the best way to begin.

2. *Absence makes the heart grow weaker.* Some people have enough confidence to know when they've done something good without anyone telling them. The rest of us need guidance on how well, or badly, we are performing; otherwise, we become confused about what we should and shouldn't be doing. In some areas (such as athletics), our performance can be easily measured, but in real life (as a parent or as a good friend), it's more difficult to assess. Praise is a powerful way of letting others understand how they are doing.

3. *Love is in the air.* An environment where people give one another appropriate and authentic praise is usually a good one to live and work in. People tend to feel warmly toward one another, and when things go wrong, they are more likely to help out than to criticize.

4. *Give and you shall receive.* When you give praise, you are more likely to be liked. We tend to think well of people who are positive about others and even more so if they appreciate our strengths. Plus, praise is infectious. If you give it, you will probably find that other people start praising too, and some of their positive comments will be directed at you. What goes around, with praise, tends to come around.

Five-Star Praise

There are times when a quick "Nicely done" is sufficient. However, if you want the impact of praise to last and you want a good chance at changing how a person does things in the future, then you would do well to follow the five-star praise model.

Give yourself one star for each of the following that you typically do when communicating your praise:

Provide Context

If the praise isn't given immediately, then it will help the person if you describe a bit about the incident you are talking about. For example, "That dinner we had in your home—when was it? Last Thursday? Yes, that's the one."

Be Specific

The more specific the praise, the more effective it is.[4] By just saying "Thanks for the report; it was great," you are not giving the person anything they can use and apply in the future. Was the report great because it was long, had pictures, started with a succinct summary, included questions for the reader to answer, or what? The best praise focuses on specifics. Again, find a balance. Simply telling the host of that dinner (in the previous example) "Great food" might not be enough. But telling her "I particularly liked the infusion of rosemary that seeped through the succulent lamb like the soft scent of early dusk in the savanna of my adolescence" is clearly over the top.

Describe the Impact

This is the part that motivates. When people understand the positive consequences of their behavior, it's a big incentive for them to repeat the good things they did. Again, a balance needs to be struck. Overstating the impact (e.g., "You saved my life by preparing such a wonderful meal") will sound fake, and your praise will have significantly less impact—if any—because it almost sounds like you're mocking the situation.

Reinforce Their Identity

This makes the person feel really good about themselves and/or their actions. You might say, "I have to compliment you. Not only was dinner delicious but to get that many interesting people together and make sure they were all served at the same time, as well as engage in conversation as the host, is simply impressive. That's organization and attention to detail at its finest."

Congratulate

This is usually the beginning, middle, and end of praising. It has a role but if it's all you do, you get only one star.

When your praise earns five stars, you know you've done it right. It takes practice. But it's not like we all don't have a bunch of people in our lives who deserve some praise right now.

Think of a couple of situations in which you might praise someone, and think about how to give them the full five-star praise effect. Jot down the suggestions and confirm: Does the praise seem real? If it feels fake, think about another way of making your points.

What If There Is Nothing to Praise?

If you can't find anything to praise, then of course it's possible that there isn't anything the other person is doing well. However, it's far more likely that you simply aren't looking hard enough. If someone is usually late, then praise them on the one occasion when they arrive on time, or if they deliver something when they said they would, or even, possibly, when they are less late than usual. And don't forget to mention the beneficial impact this punctuality has.

Counsel

If you want to positively change someone's behavior, praise is more likely to work than criticism.[5] Nevertheless, some situations require you point out when someone is not doing a job well and what you want that person to change. For this, you'll need to turn to praise's constructively critical alter ego: counsel.

Consider this conversation:

"I think I've done enough on this project and I should move on to something new."

"You know, I wonder if you're resilient."

"Of course I'm resilient. What are you saying?"

"Only that you've been on this project for less than a month. If you can't stick with a client, you'll find it much harder to build the relationships and revenue needed to get promoted."

"Yes, I know that. Obviously."

This example is a high-risk approach to constructive criticism. On this occasion the criticism worked (the restless person did stay on the project and changed his behavior, and he was promoted as a result). The criticism succeeded only because the person whose resilience was in question had a strong relationship with, and respect for, the person giving the counsel. If the counselor's relationship was less strong, then they may have received a response like "I have staying power when I think a project is worthwhile and this one sucks," which would, of course, have sent things spinning off in the wrong direction. Giving good counsel can greatly help by allowing you to share your concerns and the other person to do something about them, but it can also backfire with disastrous consequences. The challenge is to criticize effectively. Here is how:

Start in the Right Frame of Mind

It is painful receiving criticism. The only time it feels acceptable is if you believe that the person giving it has your best interests in mind. So, if you want to prove a point, put the other person firmly in their place or criticize for any reason other than wanting to help the other person improve, the chances are the conversation will turn ugly. Don't think they won't notice your motives, because they will. If you're lucky, they'll surrender; if you're unlucky, they'll bite back. So, before you offer unsolicited advice, make sure you know that you are doing it first and foremost to help the other person. Sure, there may be a benefit for you too, but for the duration of the conversation, any thoughts of your personal gain must go on the back burner.

Five-Star Counsel

Similar to the five-star praise approach, the five-star counsel system is the best way to offer help and support, and keep the risk of true conflict to a minimum.

Provide Context

The first thing to do is set up the scenario you want to talk about. If you are confident the other person has a good idea what you are about to say, you may choose to start with a question: "What do you think the other guests thought of you at last night's dinner?" It is better if you can get the other person to acknowledge the issue because it will make the conversation feel more like collaboration than an attack. The risk, of course, is that rather than replying, "You're right; I think I got a bit tipsy and may have overstepped the mark," they might say, "They loved me; I was tremendously funny, the life and soul of the party." If you think the latter response is more likely, it's better to provide the context up front: "I want to talk about what happened last night at dinner."

Specifically and Objectively State What Went Wrong

Giving someone unsolicited advice on what they need to do differently means challenging their identity. Self-perception is something we all protect vigorously. Telling someone she missed the turn is specific and not up for argument: Either she missed the turn or she didn't. Telling her she's a bad driver, however, is general and will most likely provoke a confrontational response. The second star you can give yourself is for being specific in your criticism. The more specific and objective you make your argument, the better. Saying "As Molly told us about her trip to Egypt, you tapped your spoon repeatedly against your glass" is more likely to create a conversation, whereas "You rudely interrupted Molly's story by shouting and banging on your glass like a crazed chimpanzee" is more likely to start an argument.

Describe the Impact and the Significance

For your counsel to have the right effect, you need to be clear about the impact of the behavior. For example, one person might consider showing up at work ten minutes late as being pretty much "on time." It's only when the possible impact of this is explained (e.g., irritated clients or appearing lazy in front of the boss) that the point about lateness may be appreciated and treated more seriously in the future. In a social—instead of a work—context, a counselor's statement might look like this: "The danger in being late is that it might turn people off. They won't invite us to dinner anymore. Then you'll be stuck with me every night."

Reinforce Their Identity

However delicately your counsel is expressed, it can feel like a personal attack to the other person. So, it is important to make sure you encourage them to think positively about themselves to bolster their identity, maybe even stroke their ego a bit: "You are a great host," "You are loved by your friends," "You do tell the best stories of anyone I know," "You are usually so entertaining at dinner."

Seek Solutions Together

Discuss what to do to recover the situation and reduce the chances of it happening again: "It only goes wrong when you have been drinking on an empty stomach, and we did have to wait forever to get our food. What if, next time, you don't drink anything until after we eat?"

If you can get the other person to come up with solutions themselves, then there is a greater chance they will follow up and behave differently the next time. Of course, a few well-versed suggestions may ease the path. If the conversation goes well, it may be worth praising them for coming up with a great plan for next time.

Click, Don't Clunk: How to Avoid Insincerity

If you focus on following the five-star counsel sequence in this order, there is a risk that you may come across as awkward and not all that sincere. It's better to think of the five points as a list to cover during a conversation instead of a step-by-step guide. This will help reduce any awkwardness. To make your counseling "click," you need to make it feel like you and the person to whom you are offering the constructive criticism are on the same team. This requires empathy. If the other person feels that you empathize with their situation, then they are much more likely to listen and agree with everything else you have to say.

Mastering the Art of Feedback

Understanding the different aspects of praise and counsel is the foundation for success—but like so many things in life, these aspects are not as simple as they first appear. Further techniques and situations need deeper exploration.

Be Implicit: How to Subtly Praise and Counsel

Explicitly giving praise or counsel greatly reduces the chances of a misunderstanding. Sometimes, however, it can feel like you're making a big deal out of a situation. You want to say something that will make an impact, but you also want to be subtle. On these occasions, share your views implicitly. The predictability of this approach is less certain and the risk of it going wrong is much higher, but when a gentle nudge is all that is needed, a low-key technique, deftly applied, can have the right effect. Here are four ways to give implicit praise and counsel.

Tell a Story

Nursery rhymes are a traditional way of warning children about what to avoid or how not to behave. Aesop's Fables are designed to do the same thing for adults. Stories are an underused communication tool and a singularly powerful way of making a truth acceptable without having to address it head-on: "I remember when a new recruit arrived, fresh from college, all full of enthusiasm and determination to make a good impression and get promoted fast. However, this guy—Bill—became really frustrated when he didn't get promoted right away. But you know what? He stuck with it and ended up getting a far more interesting, and better, job because of his tenacity."

Get an Endorsement

Third-party endorsements are a great way of praising someone with less risk of embarrassment for both that person and you: "Anne told me that she's really impressed with how your work has improved." By sharing the endorsement, everyone's a winner. It's easier for the person in question to accept the comment, the third party (Anne) looks great, and, as the messenger of the compliment, you look good too.

Play the Joker

Humor can be a gentle way of letting people know what you think. It lightens the mood and can deflect a too-earnest conversation. Nevertheless, humor is one of the most high-risk techniques for praise and counsel, because it can go horribly wrong. What you may have intended to be funny can sound, on the receiving end, deliberately mean or nasty.

Use Nonverbal Communication

We all use nonverbal communication to give counsel implicitly. A raised eyebrow, silence in response to a question, and a roll of the eyes are all ways you can implicitly convey that someone would be better off behaving differently. To the same extent, a thumbs-up, wink, or nod can implicitly deliver praise. The danger with communicating nonverbally is that it can be overinterpreted: "I could tell from her expression that she really hates me." It also doesn't give the other person much to work with: "He gave me a thumbs-up, but I don't know if it's because I did a great job or he simply likes my new haircut."

The Sandwich: Using Praise and Counsel at the Same Time

A technique commonly referred to is the feedback "sandwich." What this means is giving praise ("You've done a great job with the project plan"), then counsel ("You have upset several people in the team who feel that you are not listening to them"), and then more praise ("I think you're going to have a stellar third quarter due to your organizational skills and your ability to get your team back on board"). The idea is to cushion the blow of counsel with praise so the counsel is more likely to be well received and acted upon.

In reality, however, the feedback sandwich will probably have the opposite effect.[6] The praise is either devalued, because the other person believes you were giving it only to dilute the counsel, or ignored, because all the person hears is the criticism. In performance reviews at work, people will often overlook a list of things they are doing well and only pay attention to the things they should improve on. If praise and counsel are given at different times, each is more likely to resonate and be remembered. If you're concerned that a counsel conversation will end up falling flat, put more energy into the solution-seeking section of the conversation. It's here that you can be upbeat and positive and rebuild a person's confidence.

Stamina: Keep Praising

The challenge with praise (as with so many things) is keeping it up. If you give someone lots of praise and then suddenly stop, they are likely to assume that they aren't doing so well, when it may just be that you have forgotten to continue with praise or your attention is elsewhere. A little praise regularly is better than a lot of praise and then silence.

Comparisons: Do You Dislike One Person More than Another?

There is a story of a middle brother who felt throughout his childhood that his parents preferred his elder and younger brothers. The brothers, as well as all the boy's friends, assured him that he was being overly sensitive, but he still felt he was the least loved.

When an aunt died and left the boys some family heirlooms, the parents had to divide the objects up between the three of them. The middle brother, even though he had received the same value of inheritance as the other two, shouted at his parents, "You always preferred both of them to me," and burst into tears. The mother looked in shock to the father and then turned back to her son and said, "Oh, darling, has it really been that obvious?"

The mother's reaction, of course, is shocking. How could she say such a horrible thing? Did she mean it? Sadly, she did. The middle brother had discerned that he was the least favorite son despite his parents' efforts to hide it. How and how often his parents praised their sons and how and when his parents criticized them sent messages that were impossible to dispute.

These comparisons happen all the time within groups. With a group of peers, be it your children or members of your team at work, it is vital to treat them on equal terms. It is not enough to give praise and counsel effectively to each member of the group; you also need to be consistent across the group.

Hot and Cold: Consistency Is Key

As mentioned earlier, for praise and counsel to have a positive impact, the number one condition is to do it for the benefit of the other person rather than yourself. The more you keep this condition in the forefront of your mind, the greater your chances of being consistent and predictable with your praise.

When it comes to telling people what you think of them, predictability is critical. Many managers believe that by behaving hot and cold toward their employees, they keep the team on their toes. But when feedback is dependent on the mood of the person giving it, people stop trying to improve and focus instead on anticipating the unpredictable person's reactions. Soon, the praise and counsel are meaningless, because the employees believe "He's only saying that because he's in a good mood."

The Nutshell on Praise and Counsel

Different folks, as the saying goes, require different strokes. Although this might be partially true, it doesn't mean you should give up on figuring out the right ratio of praise to counsel. Some people need more praise, while others may actually seek constructive feedback. As a rough guide, the lowest ratio you should offer is one to one—one praise to one counsel—but in most cases, praise should be significantly more frequent.

You can get the best out of people by learning how, when, and how frequently to praise and counsel. And it's something you can start doing right now.

GIVE YOUR MIND A WORKOUT

Beginner: Noticing Praise and Counsel

1. Every day for the next week listen for someone praising you or praising someone else, either in your life, on the radio, or on TV.

2. Each time you hear praise, rank it based on the five-star approach. For example, which of the elements did the praise include? And how

did the recipient respond? By the end of the week, you will find it much easier to tell why some praise is more effective than others.

3. Repeat the ranking exercise for counsel, allocating up to five stars for each constructive criticism you hear someone giving, based on the steps outlined earlier.

Advanced: Taking Action with Praise and Counsel

Part One: Using Praise

1. Every day for a week commit to praising someone when you wouldn't normally have bothered. On the first day of that week, one-star praise is good enough. But each day after that add an extra star to the praise you give, so by the end of the week you should have given someone five-star praise.

2. In week two, give four- or five-star praise to someone every day. You will quickly create a habit of praise by doing this. Enjoy it, and watch how people repeat the great things you are praising them for.

Part Two: Using Counsel

1. Write down all the things you've wanted to say to a person (or several people) but haven't. Commit to at least once a week telling that person what you want to say but doing so only when you think it will help them. It's probably wise to start with things that aren't too tightly linked to their self-perception and identity (it's easier to get someone to put dishes into the dishwasher, for example, than to make a mean person generous).

2. Before you give your (unsolicited) counsel, answer the following questions:

- What do I want to tell this person?

- How will this person be better off as a result?

- When am I going to tell him/her?

- Where?

- Who else, if anyone, will be around?

- Am I likely to be interrupted?

3. Finally, prepare for your conversation by answering a few more questions:

   - What am I going to say to set the context for this person?

   - What specifically went wrong?

   - How can I express this objectively?

   - What were the implications?

   - How can I explain these implications without appearing to put my own slant on things?

   - What are some of the things this person could do to recover the situation and/or prevent repeating the same unhelpful behavior?

   - What questions am I going to ask to help the person decide on their own solutions?

If you still feel unsure about the outcome of offering counsel, find someone with whom you can practice. Tell your practice partner to respond in a variety of ways so you can prepare for a full range of possible reactions.

PART FIVE

Resolve Conflict

IT'S UNAVOIDABLE. It's not comfortable. And it's something all of us could learn to handle better: conflict.

Let's face it. You might have experienced tough conversations in the past, with either someone you really care about or someone you can't stand, and the tension gets to a point where you wish the ground would simply open up and swallow you whole (or at least the person you're arguing with). And since this isn't likely, you need to find other ways to resolve the conflict.

Of course, conflict is something most of us would prefer to avoid. However, after reading this part of the book, you'll understand just how much of a positive influence conflict has, and can have, on your life, on your relationships, and at the office. Yes, it's true. You need conflict in order to progress in life. You need to share and hear different viewpoints. You need to disagree in order to learn other people's points of view as well as where we each draw the line.

Conflict exposes your boundaries. It helps relationships move forward. It creates better solutions at work—many innovations are the derivatives of disagreements.

Yet an unresolved conflict can create turmoil in your life. This part examines conflict on three different levels, all of which can help you manage and actually benefit from one of life's most common stressors.

In "Detox Your Relationships," you'll discover how to better handle situations and what language to use, so you can have positive discussions instead of nasty arguments. You'll get to know the right words to say, the words to avoid, and the words to listen for in any disagreement. You'll find out how not to generalize, interrupt, play the blame game, and other common nasty tactics we all fall victim to during conflict. And you'll learn how to transform your disagreements into positive steps forward—where both parties actually feel happy about the outcome of your discussion and disagreement.

Okay, so maybe you are not dealing with a disagreement, but instead you have to relate some bad news—you're breaking up with someone, firing someone, or sharing other challenging news. In "Navigate Difficult Conversations," you'll read about the secrets of dialogue, how to frame your conversations, and the two principles of keeping your dialogue out of the argument zone.

Even before you begin this next part, you've probably already thought about the one person who drives you crazy and with whom you are always in conflict. Guess what? You are playing a psychological game with that person. In "Take the Drama Out of Relationships," you'll find out about the markers of common conflict behavior and how to recognize and transform all those arguments that seem to repeat themselves over and over again. You'll understand the role you play in the conflict game and the role your "opponent" plays. Plus, you'll finally learn how to remove yourself from the game—coincidentally, without too much conflict.

This is a tough section. It's the one you'll want to turn to when you're facing that nasty little thing called conflict. You can't avoid it, so you might as well learn how to deal with it.

CHAPTER 12

Detox Your Relationships

It was a massive argument. It was a battle of epic proportion. It was ugly. But what was it all about?

When it comes to arguments, big things often come in small packages. The most trivial difference (e.g., where to put the frying pan) turns into accusation (e.g., "You don't do anything around the house"), personal affront ("or care about me"), and in extreme situations, action ("I'm out of this relationship; my mother always said you were a selfish jerk"). And it all happens in seconds.

Whether you're on the receiving end of the venom or you're the one dishing it out, the trick to stopping arguments from escalating is to separate form from content. And that's what this chapter is about: identifying the poisons you regularly reach for and recognizing the poisons favored by the people around you. While this knowledge may not be enough to stop tempers from flaring, it will help you prevent the spark from turning into a fire.

Here's a brief toxicology of six nasty argument poisons. We identify their symptoms (so you'll be able to see them coming), how to prevent them (in case you feel tempted to use them), and some antidotes (for when someone uses the poison against you).

Poison One: Assuming (aka "I Know You")

Symptoms

"You're being pedantic," "You're overreacting," "You're being ridiculous and unreasonable," or "You're angry/unhappy/insecure/flaky."

There aren't many things more irritating than people assuming they have a superior knowledge of your feelings. If you weren't annoyed before, being told you're angry is sure to push you over the edge. Even worse is being told what you should do: "You need to listen to other people," "You need to get your facts straight before you make claims like that," "I suggest you stop shouting."

Prevention

Unless the other person has shared their feelings, don't presume to know—or tell them—how they feel in that moment. Assuming you know what others are experiencing makes them react badly, because there's a good chance your assumption is wrong. After all, there can be a variety of interpretations for someone's behavior. A man is screaming. Is he upset, angry, physically hurt, or overwhelmed with joy? Until he tells you why he's screaming, you don't know for sure.

To avoid inadvertently using this poison, separate the observable facts from your interpretation of the other person. Keep your voice neutral and tell the other person what you are observing. Give them a chance to correct any mistakes in the facts or your interpretation. For example, "This conversation is getting louder. How are you feeling?" Compare that to "You're shouting" or "I know you're angry." The word "shouting" is a strongly nuanced word, suggesting the other person is out of control. Using "I know" suggests you can read the other person's mind. It's likely to elevate the argument into an explosion: "Oh no I am not," "Oh yes you are . . ."

Consider another example: If someone is repeatedly making the same point over and over, rather than telling them "You keep repeating yourself," which is loaded with negative connotations and inevitably makes the other person feel patronized, try saying "I have heard the same thing three times, and I'm still not getting it. Can you explain what you mean in a different way?" This approach helps the other person confirm that you've read their feelings correctly: "You bet I'm angry."

Once the other person confirms you've read their feelings correctly (i.e., that you understand they are angry), you are in a position to empathize with them: "I too would be angry in your situation," "I completely understand why you don't feel heard." Empathy gets you on the same side, rather than encouraging the other person to feel hostile toward you.

Here are some simple phrases that can turn the "I know you" attitude to "I am responsible."

I Know You	I Am Responsible
You are very confusing.	I haven't understood.
You obviously don't understand.	Have I been clear?
You're wrong.	I have a different recollection.
You don't love me.	I don't feel loved.
You aren't listening to me.	I don't feel listened to.
You're overreacting.	I imagine you feel strongly.
You're wrong about . . .	When I experienced . . .
I didn't say that.	What I meant to say was . . .
You're touchy/neurotic/flaky.	I imagine this is sensitive.
You're being aggressive.	I feel uncomfortable about this conversation.

Antidote

When someone uses this poison against you, assume the best intentions. It's tough to do so when someone is telling you they know how you feel or what you should do about something. But try to consider why the other person is saying these things. What's the most generous explanation? Are they frightened rather than angry, careless rather than malicious, stressed rather than rude? Put on an "armchair psychiatrist" hat and try to figure out what's really bothering them. A few words of support or a hug (if they are someone you know well) may be all that's needed to stop the poison from spreading.

Another way to respond to someone who is delivering this kind of poisonous statement is to agree with them. If someone tells you you're angry, agree: "Yes, I am angry. I feel that my effort has been wasted." Then pause. Allow the other person to respond. You'll probably find that you've taken the wind out of their sails. At the very least, showing your vulnerability will change the tone of the conversation.

Finally, if the person who is using this conflict poison is someone you love, you might employ what psychologists call "positive senti-ment override," which entails recognizing that the person who's upset with you is still the person you love; they're just making it tough right now. For example, a young man named Cody described to us the relationship he was having with his newly pregnant girlfriend. She was suffering from morning sickness, and when she wasn't vomiting, she was getting annoyed with him. Cody could have lashed back at her (after all, she was being totally unreasonable, shouting at him for doing things she'd asked him to do only moments earlier). But instead, he considered what was driving her behavior (e.g., she's tired and feeling lousy). Positive sentiment override requires you to look for the positive explanation of the other person's behavior rather than assume they are being difficult. When you love, admire, or respect that person, this response can become a natural habit and a very healthy one for robust relationships.

Poison Two: Generalizing (aka "You Always")

Symptoms

Under the influence of this particular venom, you become all-knowing. Without pausing for breath, you generalize everything from the spe-cific to the universal. So, not only do you feel the other person is not listening, you insist they *never* listen. Not only is your team member late with his report, you tell him he is *always* late, and while you are on the subject, you shout, "Nothing ever gets done on time around here!"

"Nothing." "Ever." Really?

DO YOU SEE BLACK AND WHITE OR SHADES OF GRAY?

People who are generalizers (otherwise referred to as "absolutists") pride themselves on 'knowing what I think.' They have clear rules they apply every time they encounter a similar situation. They see things in black and white. Gray, in their opinion, is for flaky wimps. What they don't realize is that the people who see things in shades of gray are much more likely to be open to new ideas, solve problems, and have strong relationships.

It appears, too, that absolutism is inversely correlated with wisdom. In a study by Alistair Ostell and Susan Oakland, eighty teachers were classified as "absolutist" or "non-absolutist" in the way they handled two work problems.[1] When the teachers were interviewed, results showed that the absolutist teachers perceived themselves as less effective at managing their emotions and handling problems, and they experienced their jobs as less pleasant than the open-minded and more flexible non-absolutist teachers. They also had poorer mental and physical health. The non-absolutist teachers—those who saw things in shades of gray rather than black and white—also reported finding problem solving easier and experienced better health.

It's untrue, of course. There are always exceptions. Even the employee who is often late will meet a deadline occasionally. If you are using the generalizing poison, the minute someone corrects you (e.g., "Actually, my presentation was on time last week"), your temperature rises and—bingo—you're in the middle of a full-on battle.

Under the influence of this poison, certain words elbow their way to the front: "always," "never," "every," "forever," "anything," "anyone," "everyone," "typical." They are often combined with "you," and they sound like this:

- "You always know best."

- "You never take my advice."

- "You never give any thought to me / the children / the cat / the future."

- "Nothing ever gets done properly."

- "Typical of you to forget something."

- "Every time it ends in disaster."

- "This always happens."

- "You never listen to anyone else's view." (Double whammy: "never" and "anyone.")

Prevention

In a court of law, the jury comes to a decision based on the evidence of the case in question. Previous convictions are not taken into consideration. In this way, the jury is encouraged to arrive at an unbiased judgment about the specific offense. This approach—judging the specific offense—is a discipline you should adopt if you're trying to avoid this particular poison.

When ascribing a cause to someone's behavior, keep to the specifics. If your partner arrives home late one night, be angry about that night. Resist the urge to bundle it up with all the other times they've been late or forgetful (e.g., "You never do anything that you say you will"). They'll just get defensive. Instead, keep focused on the details by using these antidote phrases:

- "On this occasion"

- "It tends to be"

- "With this particular (client, event, product, etc.)"

- "Right now"

- "During the (quarter, month, full moon, etc.)"

- "When you are (tired, excited, stressed, busy, etc.)"

With this particular poison, the secret lies in controlling the borders.

Antidote

If someone uses this poison against you, don't rise to the bait. Recognize their sweeping statements for what they are: a single incidence of anger. Ignore the inflammatory comments; picture them as arrows and see them falling short of their target, dropping harmlessly to the ground a couple of feet in front of you. Then steer the conversation back to the matter at hand: "There may well be wider implications to what you are saying. For the moment, can we focus on resolving this particular issue?" or "I understand. On this particular occasion, what do you think we should do next?"

Poison Three: Attacking (aka "That's You, All Right")

Symptoms

Name calling, character assassination, and mudslinging are all forms of this nasty poison we call attacking. Someone attacking you for what you say or do is one thing. But when someone launches an attack on your identity, it takes real restraint to keep cool.

The explicit version of this poison is pure name calling and labeling (e.g., "You're lazy, cunning, cruel, insensitive, and stupid, and you've lost your touch"). There are other variations of the poison that are more cunning and subtle, such as accusations made by association: "Only a fool would think like that," "A child could do better." Still other varieties of attacking invite us to work out the insult for ourselves: "Is this the first report you've ever written?" And let's not forget this particularly nasty insinuation: "What happened to your sense of humor?" To boost the venom, other people may also be brought in to hammer home the message: "Everyone thinks you're out of your league," "All our friends believe you're a fool." Or if that's too factual for your attacker, they might try hypothesizing: "I bet if you asked your family, they'd say you are a fool," "Any sane person would agree that you are wrong."

Prevention

When you feel yourself reaching for this particular poison, you need to make a swift mental turnaround to redefine those negative characteristics as positive ones. So, instead of using the word "lazy," consider her "unmotivated." Instead of denigrating his "stubbornness," admire his "determination." Don't worry that she's "passive"; just be pleased that she's "calm and relaxed." And don't wait until things get tense; take preemptive action.

Start your turnaround by reinforcing the positive aspects of the other person's character:

- "I appreciate how much you care about this."

- "You have been incredibly generous with your time."

- "I really admire your persistence/patience/application."

- "You deserve more appreciation than you've had."

You may ask, "What if my partner truly is passive?" Well, is anybody "truly" anything? Character judgments are always going to be subjective. Opting for a positive interpretation will prevent the argument from turning toxic; it will also help to weatherproof your relationship. Focusing on positive attributions is one of the signs of a healthy, resilient relationship. By using this approach, you'll quickly shift your mind-set from negative to positive.

Antidote

In the heat of the moment, we all say things we don't mean. The challenge is to remember that the person who is yelling at you, right here, right now, is going to say things they don't mean. Indeed, the more forcefully they hurl abuse at you, the less likely they are to actually mean it. So, imagine yourself wrapped in a protective shield. Nothing can get through it. Watch the insults bounce off it. For the poker players among you, opt to "stick"—you don't have to raise the stakes to stay in the game.

Some psychotherapists suggest that when we find a particular fault in someone else, it is in fact a fault we are aware of in ourselves. So, when someone accuses you of something, imagine they are describing themselves. Feel sympathy rather than anger. (Similarly, when you reach for an insult to throw at someone, pause and ask yourself, *Why has this matter agitated me so much? Who am I really criticizing?*)

It is often better to not acknowledge an insult than it is to avenge it. That said, the other person obviously wants to be heard, so offer the odd token acknowledgment: "Uh-huh," "Okay." Keep your voice neutral and then steer the conversation back to the core issue. Use a question ("Whose advice would you trust on this subject?") or a statement ("I am unclear how you would like me to rate the options").

Poison Four: Rejecting (aka "No, but . . .")

Symptoms

"Sticks and stones will break my bones, but words will never harm me," we are told. This may be true, but words can certainly turbocharge an argument—particularly these two words: "no" and "but." We don't even have to say them; we can roll our eyes, turn away, laugh dismissively, or just storm out and slam the door behind us. They all get the "no" message—our rejection—across loud and clear.

"No" brings the barriers down at the same time as it raises the temperature. The word "but" is just "no" in smarter clothes. They are both powerful poisons.

Prevention

When things start to get heated, lock the word "no" away in a box and bury it in a deep hole. Think of yourself as a mediator rather than a prosecutor and deliberately opt for moderate language. Aim to build and open up the conversation.

The quickest and easiest way is to use the words "yes . . . and" rather than "no . . . but." When you hear an idea you don't like, it's easy to shut it down immediately with a swift "no." "Yes" forces you to take a constructive attitude. For example, "Yes, the client might be wrong, and we should get all the facts before we respond" or "Yes, it is an original idea, and we should check whether more of the budget could be available to fund it."

Once you've replaced "no . . . but" with "yes . . . and," follow up with three things you like about the other person's suggestion. Then, and only then, address the things you don't like about their suggestion. To the person on the receiving end, that will sound very different from "three things I don't like."

For example, if someone suggests that you sell your car and buy a motorcycle, rather than saying "No, that won't work for me," first list three things you like about their suggestion: your commute would be cheaper, a motorcycle would be easier to park, and it would be easier to maneuver through city traffic. Then share the three things you wish were different about their suggestion: "I wish that I could find an alternative that would allow me to carry luggage and stay out of the rain, and that wouldn't prompt my friends to suggest I was having a midlife crisis."

This is a powerful strategy on many fronts. Your antagonist side feels listened to; you show that you're open to finding a solution, and you let the other person know what matters to you, which makes it easier for them to suggest acceptable alternatives. You may even find yourself modifying your position as you explore the pros and cons.

Antidote

When someone uses this poison with you, all you hear are variations of "no . . . but," and the discussion grinds to a halt. To get it moving again, reach for questions and suggestions. For example, "What would make you rethink your view on this?" Such a statement is bound to cause your antagonist to pause. They may answer "Nothing," in which case you can bring the discussion to a polite close. More likely, though, they will offer an olive branch: "If the boss came down here now and said she was sorry." Whatever their response, you have a chance to discover what lies at the heart of their anger and move toward a solution. Making suggestions will also move the discussion forward. "We can call the client directly; we can set up a conference call with the whole team; we can keep quiet and hope the issue blows over. What other options are there?"

But keep the alternatives genuine. Throwing in an option that is clearly unacceptable is just as toxic as any aggravating phrase. "So, are we all getting on the bus or standing around doing nothing for the rest of the day?" is just plain sarcasm.

Poison Five: Defending (aka "It's Not Me")

Symptoms

When you're attacked, you obviously want to protect yourself. But taken too far, self-defense can turn into a self-righteous tantrum.[2] It'll probably sound something like this:

- "I'm not trying to be difficult, but . . ."
- "I'm not disagreeing . . . I'm not shouting . . ."
- "It's not my fault."
- "I told you so."
- "I can't take any more of this."

Prevention

Forget the blame game. Turn your attention elsewhere. When you feel defensive and you hear yourself overusing the word "I," try to deliberately focus on finding a solution to the disagreement rather than just identifying the cause. Remember, this problem is probably bigger than the both of you.

Antidote

If you suspect you're likely to meet with this particular poison (meaning someone is pointing a finger at you), avoid aggravating the person's defensiveness by steering clear of the word "you." If the person is agitated, they'll hear an implicit criticism every time you use it.

Instead—and this time it's all right—use the word "I" to take ownership and talk from your personal experience. Keep your statements positive: "I am trying to find the best solution," "I do appreciate that there is a wide range of opinion." In this way, you'll avoid making provocative accusations.

If, however, it's too late and you're already in the thick of an argument, empathize. You may feel the other person is practicing self-pity; however, they may simply be looking for acknowledgment. Use statements such as "I know it's not your fault" and "I can see why you feel that you've had enough." Try offering partial acceptance of their position: "You are often proved right." Or just gently smile (but be careful with this, because it's easy to look condescending). Staying calm is the most effective way to a quick apology.

Poison Six: Interrupting (aka "Can I Just . . .")

Symptoms

When you're angry, you probably get impatient. You want to speak your piece, and you don't want to hear what the other person has to say. So, you interrupt and talk over them. In response, they shout over you. You yell back over them; they bellow over you. The volume goes up but neither person actually hears a word being said.

Prevention

However desperate you are to have your say, you're almost always better off letting the other person finish having *their* say. If you're itching to interrupt, try the following tactics:

- Swallow or take a deep breath to avoid speaking.

- Nod to show you are listening.

- Take notes to show you are listening (and to distract yourself from what you're feeling).

- Keep eye contact (if they think you're not listening, that will raise the temperature further).

Antidote

If someone interrupts you once while you are talking, stop. Let them have their say before you start again. If they continue to interrupt, ask them, "What's the best way for me to respond so that you will listen to my point of view?" or "Can I share my thoughts without interruption?" Note the wording there: "without interruption," not "without you interrupting me."

Conflict Can Be Detoxified

Conflict will happen. Your goal isn't to become agreeable. Your goal is to not get ugly and to turn arguments into discussions. As you become more skilled at recognizing the signs of each poison and applying the appropriate antidote, you may find the exchange of views frank but rarely ferocious.

What a relief!

GIVE YOUR MIND A WORKOUT

Beginner: Control Your Reactions

1. Identify the poison you are most familiar with and consider when it is most likely to be used.

2. Employ the advice in this chapter to prevent the poison's use, but also review the alternative responses in the antidote prescribed for that poison.

3. Fill in this "If . . . then . . ." statement to put your plan into writing and ensure you take action on it, with the "if" as the thing that triggers the conflict and the "then" as your ideal response.

   If _____, then _____.

Advanced: Change Your Ways

1. Be honest with yourself and reflect on the poison(s) you're most guilty of using in your interactions with others. We are all guilty of using at least one, so the more honest you are, the easier it will be to change your ways.

2. Pick someone with whom you'd like a stronger relationship and with whom you've used your poison of choice in the past.

3. Start an honest and open conversation with that person about the poison you use and how you're trying to change.

4. Ask the person how the poison affects them and your relationship. Give them time and space to talk about this (without interruption).

5. Finally, ask for the person's help in increasing your self-awareness by *gently* pointing out to you the moments when you reach for the poison.

CHAPTER 13

Navigate Difficult Conversations

think I'm pretty good at my job; my manager's always finding faults."

"I want a baby; my wife doesn't."

"I need to focus on my career; you want me to spend more time at home."

"I find you controlling; you find me incompetent."

"I want to commit; she wants to be free."

In some relationship dilemmas, there's a solution that meets everyone's needs. Others, like the ones just listed, are trickier: The stakes are high, the consequences are terrifying, and the topics are emotionally charged. The answer to these dilemmas isn't simply to generate more potential solutions. At the heart of these dilemmas are the big problems that cause real relationship damage.

One study found that when couples talk about problems in their relationships, 69 percent of the time the discussion is about an ongoing issue that has been a problem for many years, and 31 percent of the time the issue is related to a specific situation.[1] Resolution comes about after having the right kind of conversations, which psychologists call "dialogue."

Dialogue is conversation in which both participants are really listening to each other and actively seeking to resolve an issue, even if they can't do so immediately. To engage in dialogue you need to understand each other's perspectives and build upon what each other says. But listening isn't easy, particularly if the other person is aggressive or a little reluctant to share.[2]

The Principles of Dialogue

When you feel in some way slighted or wronged, it's very easy either to avoid the situation or to attack it. When you feel you want some sort of resolution, dialogue is critical. Tom and Susie are working parents and find themselves in a situation that seems impossible to overcome. But their dialogue, which illustrates the six main principles of a successful conversation, shows how they can resolve their issue by asking some important questions.

See how the six principles of successful conversations play out in Tom and Susie's dialogue, which takes place as they are getting ready for bed.

Principle One: Focus on What You Want for Yourself and the Other Person

The first question to ask when engaging in a dialogue is *What do I really want?* Having clarity on the answer helps you understand what you should aim for in the conversation. Typically the goal of the dialogue should be to get what you want and maintain a positive relationship. It's important, then, to uncover your real motivations and desires. Pay attention to how Tom and Susie sort out principle one.

> Susie: *We need to fire Jane and get a new babysitter. I really don't think things are working with her at all. It's sad because it was working so well at the beginning, but I can't believe how careless she's been lately.*
>
> Tom: *Like what?*

Susie: *Well, the thing that's really bothering me is that she's avoiding talking to me. When I got home from work the other day, all she said was "The children have had their dinner and are ready for their bath." And then she left with a quiet "Good-bye." She couldn't have left any faster.*

Tom: *Maybe she had somewhere to go?*

Susie: *No, it's really not working. Some of the things she has done have been unbelievable. She put bleach in the washing machine and then put the children's clothes into the next load without rinsing the machine. She spilled coffee all over the carpet on the stairs and didn't clean it up properly. I went into the boys' room the other day and the furniture had been rearranged, but she put one of the beds right against a radiator, which could have been dangerous. I'm really at my wit's end, constantly checking up and asking her to do things differently.*

Tom: *What do you think we should do?*

Susie: *Well, I think you should call her and tell her not to come back. I don't really want to talk to her anymore.*

Tom: *I suppose the question is,* What do we really want? *I don't think either of us wants the hassle of finding a new person who gets along well with our children. I mean Jane has done a great job for us in the past. Should we see if we can work it out?*

Susie: *It would be a pain finding someone new. And you're right. The children do love her. I suppose it's worth one last try. Should I ask her to stay a little later tomorrow so we can talk to her? I think it's important we're both there.*

Principle Two: Get Yourself in the Right Frame of Mind

Dialogue needs an attitude of empathy, openness, and honesty. It can be tempting to play down a situation, but the gravity of it needs to be shared, along with the desire to find a resolution.

Around a kitchen table cluttered with children's toys, finger paintings, and three cups of coffee, Susie and Tom are sitting side by side. Jane sits facing them with her arms crossed. Let's see how they deal with principle two.

Tom: *How was your day?*

Jane: *It was okay. We went to the park this afternoon and it rained a bit. We got a little wet.*

Susie: *Did you go to the café in the park? That's where we usually go when it rains.*

Jane: *Yes, of course.*

Tom: *Jane, Susie asked you to stay a bit later today to talk with us because we can all feel there's tension between us at the moment. When you first started working for us, we agreed that the most important thing is we keep talking. It feels like we've stopped doing that. I know it's been a bit tricky recently, but we really want to clear the air. So, let's start talking and listening again. We'd both really like to hear what you're thinking and feeling.*

Principle Three: Share Your Story and Ask for Theirs

In any situation, there are facts and surrounding stories. In a good dialogue, you need to share the facts, tell your story, and listen to the other person's story. You also need to understand that the other person's story is as valid as your own.

Tom: *We'd like to share our story. I'm sure there are things we've done that have upset you and there are things that have upset us. We're both confident that with the right conversation we can sort this out.*

Jane: *Definitely. I think it's important we talk. I'm not sure if that will help though. I really like your children. They're great fun, spirited, and sparky, but I find everything else pretty tough at the moment.*

Susie: *We definitely want to change things. We think you've looked after the children really well over the last few months, but I think we'd all say that something has to change if it is going to continue. We've had some really good times, like the trip to the zoo we did a couple of months ago. I'd love it if we could work this out, and I really mean that, but if we can't, it's probably better for us to part company. I know that would make Tom, the children, and me very sad though.*

Tom: *Susie, why don't you tell us a little bit about what you think is going wrong.*

Principle Four: Help Them Avoid Retreats and Attacks

The other person may very well go into retreat or attack mode. If they retreat, dig deeper by asking questions and check whether you understand the situation by paraphrasing or remarking on their reaction (e.g., "I get the impression you're not very comfortable with this. Can you share what you're thinking or feeling?"). If they attack, acknowledge their concerns and reconfirm what you're trying to achieve.

> Susie: *Okay. I feel there's been tension recently. It feels like it's stemmed from the fact that I've been asking you to do quite a few things differently. I was upset that you had put bleach in our washing machine, spilled coffee on the stairs, and changed the furniture around in the boys' room.*

> Jane: *I agree about the tension. To be honest, I've been wondering recently whether this is the right job for me.*

> Tom: *Is it your job as a babysitter in general or working with us specifically?*

> Jane: *I'm not sure. Probably a bit of both.*

> Tom: *I understand that Susie has asked you to do quite a few things differently recently. I can imagine that must be slightly demoralizing.*

Principle Five: Control Your Own Retreats and Attacks

Like a battle, there is a temptation for both parties to retreat and attack over the course of the conversation. Remaining even-tempered can be very hard, particularly if you feel wronged or attacked yourself. If you feel yourself going into a retreat or an attack, ask yourself how you'd behave if you really wanted the situation resolved and try to see why the other person might be saying what they are saying.

> Jane: *Yes, it is demoralizing. I find it difficult to be constantly told what I'm doing wrong. For example, the other day when I was going out you asked me three times whether I had the right stuff in the*

children's bags, and then you checked them yourself anyway. I find the rule about not having anyone else in the house while you're out over the top. I have friends who take care of children, and it would be good to have them over for a playdate, rather than always having to go out. I get told everything, from the temperature setting to use on the washing machine to when I should and shouldn't use bleach, plus you ask questions about coffee stains on the carpet—which I don't think was me, by the way. It all amounts to me feeling pretty worn down. I know how to take care of kids, and sometimes it feels like you don't recognize that fact. I feel like I'm not trusted and I'm not doing a good job. And that's hard. I shouldn't have put bleach in the washing machine or moved the furniture in the boys' bedroom, and I understand that you have very high standards, and I like that. But I feel we should keep these things in perspective, particularly when I'm doing lots of other things really well.

Susie: *I can understand why you feel this way. I understand that the frequent requests and reprimands are irritating, particularly because you're well qualified. I know I have high standards and I want the best for my family. I take great care with everything I do at home, so when I think something has been done without much care, I get really frustrated.*

Jane: *I do really understand that. And I want to make the best of it. I really like looking after your children and working with you both.*

Principle Six: Create a Plan of Action

In some situations, a solution may emerge. In others, it won't. What is possible, as in this scenario, is that people can find a way to talk about the situation and what to do if it happens again. It may take some time for all the parties involved to come up with something that works, but the only way a solution can emerge is if everyone is able to talk, listen, and understand one another.

Tom: *Okay, so what do we do about this?*

Susie: *Well, for a start, why don't we say that you can have your friends here during the day, if they are looking after other children? Our origi-*

nal thought was not to have people over whom we didn't know, but if it's to see other babysitters for playdates, that makes sense.

Jane: *That'd be great. I'll also make an effort to be even more careful, and if you tell me that I'm doing something wrong, I'll do my best to see it as you being careful about your home as opposed to criticizing my professional competence.*

Susie: *And I'll make an effort to be less picky. Would it be better for me to save my feedback and talk once a week or would you prefer that I give you feedback there and then?*

Jane: *Probably there and then. But if you see something good, it'd be nice to hear that too.*

Tom: *Great. I'm really pleased we've sorted that out.*

Susie: *Me too.*

The Final Say

It's true: tough conversations can be some of the most intimidating challenges in your life. But they don't need to be. Next time you have to navigate a difficult discussion, remember the six principles described in this chapter:

1. Focus on what you want for yourself and the other person.

2. Get yourself in the right frame of mind.

3. Share your story and ask for theirs.

4. Help them avoid retreats and attacks.

5. Control your own retreats and attacks.

6. Create a plan of action.

Many of us will avoid difficult conversations at any cost—often ruining a relationship and building up resentment. Don't. These conversations can, if handled correctly, add the most value and trust to your relationships.

GIVE YOUR MIND A WORKOUT

Beginner: Mental Practice

1. Listen for when other people attack or retreat; this can be done anywhere. See how skilled you can get at hearing these reactions. Sometimes it's obvious (e.g., shouting, walking away), but most of the time it's more subtle. Aim to increase your awareness of these subtle cues.

2. Think about how you would create a dialogue that turns things around. Some ideas to get you started:

   • If you spot an attack, empathize, summarize, acknowledge that what the person is saying is valid, and remain calm.

   • For a retreat, ask prompting questions, such as, "Are you finding this difficult?" Or state how you'd feel: "If I was in your position, I think I'd feel frustrated. Is that something you feel?"

Advanced: Use the Power of Dialogue

1. Think about someone you've had a recurring problem with where dialogue might help.

2. Plan your dialogue strategy using the steps in this chapter and the following questions:

   • When and where will you initiate a dialogue?

   • What will be your approach?

   • What is your plan for avoiding retreats/attacks?

   • How will you know if you've succeeded?

3. After you've had the dialogue, answer these questions:

   • What did you do well?

   • What could you have done better?

   • What will you do differently next time?

CHAPTER 14

Take the Drama Out of Relationships

Your partner arrives home late one evening. The first thing you hear out of their mouth is "I've had a very, very bad day." Of course, you listen sympathetically while they unload their frustration. You offer them a drink to calm their nerves. They don't want one. You make some suggestions as to how they might resolve their situation. Your ideas are dismissed as impossible, ill informed, or just plain wrong. Still trying to make things better, you offer them food. They're not hungry. You ask if they want to watch a light-hearted movie. How could they possibly laugh at a time like this? Finally, you suggest that things might seem better in the morning—and you propose going to bed early. Wrong move. Don't you realize that they are going to be up half the night sorting out this mess? In fact, don't you understand anything? Obviously you don't. So, they decide to go for a walk, taking the opportunity to slam the door on their way out.

Now it's you who needs a drink. You feel dejected and annoyed.

As you sip your extra-strong drink, you ask yourself, *How did that happen—again?* Something similar happened yesterday when you tried to help your friend who's going through a divorce. It also happened last week when you struggled to cheer up your coworker after his book was rejected by yet another publisher. Come to think of it, this seems to be happening all too frequently. The subject changes with each conversation, but the routine is depressingly familiar: You want to help someone and end up feeling rejected. You end up being the bad guy.

Are you unlucky or is this something you're doing? Are you to blame? Surprisingly, the answer is yes. It's you. But that is good news—because it means you can change.

Groundhog Day: Recognizing Recurrent Conflicts in Your Life

In the film *Groundhog Day,* Phil Connors (played by actor Bill Murray) repeats the same day again and again. Even when he commits suicide, it makes no difference—he still wakes up the next morning and has to live through the same day, which he knows is a repeat but everyone else is living for the first time. The only way out, he finally discovers, is to love someone else more than himself.

Most of us have *Groundhog Day*–like arguments, or at least patterns of behavior that repeat, regardless of what we do to stop them. What's so frustrating is that often you don't realize you're back in the old routine until it's too late—until he storms out or she slams the phone down or you find yourself skulking in the boss's office and feeling angry and foolish. Again.

So, why do you repeat these dreary and painful routines? There are two main reasons. First, you don't recognize what's going on; it's just never crossed your mind that you're engaging in the same argument over and over. Second, these patterns, in a slightly perverse way, provide you with the stimulus you need: they're familiar, they confirm your worldview (*No one appreciates me; See, I knew it would end like this*), and they give you an emotional "fix" (even though it's a negative one), which proves you still matter. For example, when a friend of ours told her father that she was pregnant, her father simply responded by saying, "I should've guessed by your weight gain." This insensitive response is probably driven by the father's need to prove to himself that, even with the arrival of a new generation, his daughter is still concerned with his opinion. On a subconscious level, the father wasn't sure that he could get a positive emotional response, but he knew he could get a negative one. So he did.

American psychotherapist Eric Berne wrote a seminal book about these *Groundhog Day*–like moments called *Games People Play*.[1] Berne calls these toxic routines "transactions" or "games." After extensive research, he concluded that we play these games in an attempt to get attention (which he calls "strokes") from another person. Basically, we're looking to confirm our role in a given relationship. That role might be negative, and even painful, but it's one we feel comfortable with. It's the role that confirms our beliefs about ourselves and the other person. When we find a game that delivers the goods, we keep on playing it, over and over.

This game playing isn't always obvious. The motivations are hidden in your subconscious. To a casual observer, you may be having a rather dull disagreement about how to load the dishwasher. Indeed that's probably what you think you are doing too. It's only when the ordinary argument leaves you feeling utterly wretched that you get an inkling you're playing for much higher stakes.

The Roles in the Game: What Are You Playing?

Great relationships are based on a sense of security. When you feel a lack of security, toxic transactions begin. Feeling insecure makes you want to adopt positions, or "roles." This is a temporary response to a situation, like an actor playing a part, and not necessarily a reflection of your true character. The difference between you and an actor is that you're not necessarily aware that you're doing it.

There are three roles people tend to adopt: persecutor, rescuer, and victim. Each is looking for security in a different way:

- The persecutor asks the other person to "agree with me." He or she, at that moment, sees him- or herself as "correct" or in some way superior and will persist in trying to get you to agree.

- The rescuer says "value me" or "appreciate how I can help." This person sees their role as providing valuable support or rescue. They want you to follow their advice.

- The victim says "protect me." He or she believes they are worse off or in some way below the other person. They look for a persecutor to mistreat them or a rescuer to confirm that they can't cope.

What happens in the "game" is that you take on a role (the rescuer, for instance) and the other person takes on a different role (let's say the victim). Then at some stage you switch and take on one of the other roles. Perhaps you switch to the persecutor and the other person, as a result, switches to the victim. The game concludes only when one person switches roles, forcing the other to switch roles too. Psychiatrist Stephen Karpman describes this as the "drama triangle."[2] In all psychological games, one person takes on one of these roles and the other person another, different role.

Charlie offers Tim a glass of red wine, and as he does so, he accidentally spills it on the new carpet. Charlie freezes. He's in shock by what just happened.

"So, are you just going to stand there staring at it?" asks Tim, slipping seamlessly into the persecutor role.

"Okay, okay, I'll clean it up," says Charlie, swiftly sliding into the victim role.

"I would hope so!" exclaims Tim.

Charlie returns from the kitchen with a cloth, but the game is still not over.

"Not that cloth, you idiot. Can't you see it's filthy? You'll ruin the carpet!" shouts Tim.

Charlie, now thoroughly ensconced in the victim role, murmurs an apology, gets a different cloth, and starts attacking the stain.

"You're rubbing it!" yells Tim. "Don't you know you should be dabbing it?" And with that, he shoves Charlie out of the way and takes over, complaining that he'll have to fix it—as he has to fix everything. "I suppose you're just going to stand there watching," he sneers.

And that's when the switch happens. Charlie has had enough: "It's only a tiny stain for heaven's sake. This is just typical of you—obsessing over trivia. Don't you have anything better to worry about? You're pathetic," he says, and then he marches out.

Now Charlie's playing the persecutor and a very effective one. Tim, sitting on the floor with a cloth in his hand, suddenly feels small, stupid, and unhappy. He's now become the victim. Game over.

This is unlikely to be a one-time game. Tim and Charlie probably play out variations on this theme repeatedly. Tim berates Charlie for being stupid until Charlie turns on him. Or, in the game's language, Tim plays the persecutor until Charlie the victim moves into being

Charlie the persecutor and Tim becomes the victim.

If the game is repeated, that's evidence it works. It's painful, yes, but it's effective. A game may be so efficient at delivering the desired negative "fix" that you find yourself playing it with other people in your life, continually taking one of the three roles—persecutor, rescuer, or victim—and then switching. Of course, we all play these games, and we're often totally unaware of it.

How Do You Find Your Playmates?

You can play these games anywhere. All you need is a playmate who wants to play in the same game—a sister, an employee, a friend. The fact that these games are particularly common in your intimate relationships may be an indication of how good of a match you have chosen in your partner. Basically, you've found someone who meets your needs—negative as well as positive. So, in the same way a well-organized person might be the ideal partner for someone who's prone to losing stuff and forgetting things, a partner who tends to believe that others are incompetent (a persecutor) will be the perfect playmate for someone who tends to believe they aren't deserving or good enough (a victim). Or a victim might hook up with someone who believes that other people always need help (a rescuer). In either partnership, the two playmates truly complement each other.

Once you've found someone who will take on the appropriate role, there are a variety of ways in which you can play out these little dramas. In the scene that opened this chapter—the person who'd had a bad day and the partner who was hoping to help—the game was "Why don't you . . . Yes, but . . ." ("Why don't you go to bed early?" "Yes, but that's a bad suggestion because I'll be up half the night sorting out this mess").

Sometimes you might not go as far as switching roles. You might just pass the time playing victim and rescuer with each other. This kind of routine could get tedious, but it's unlikely to be painful. In fact, you might call it "game lite." To get a true payoff you have to move to a new position. Every good story needs something to change if the conclusion is going to feel satisfying. In psychological games, it's that final switch of roles that brings the story to a painfully satisfying conclusion.

How to End or Avoid the Games

So, now that you know you're likely playing these wicked games with people, how do you stop the game play from messing up your relationships? First, realize that game playing isn't nice but it's absolutely normal—pretty much everyone plays games at one time or another. Recognizing that you're in a game at least gives you a way to understand what's going on. It may also reduce any resentment you feel toward the other person. After all, they're caught up in a game too.

It's great to understand that you're game playing, what roles you play, and that you're not evil because you play. Still, the goal is to stop the playing to avoid hurting someone, getting hurt, or building up a stockpile of resentment toward your playmates. Here are four steps that can help you "sit out" the next game:

Break the Gaming Habit

If your games are taking place at the unconscious level, you need to bring them into consciousness. Once you can identify the games, you can begin to take control of them and maybe even stop them before they begin. An easy way to remember this process is "Name it, claim it, and tame it." By observing what's going on, you reduce its impact. So, next time you find yourself asking, *How did I end up feeling so bad?* play the scene back and plot your roles on the drama triangle: persecutor, rescuer, or victim. Which role did you start in? Where did you end up? And what about your playmate? Can you think of other relationships in your life in which you play these roles?

Now share your knowledge. Talk to the other person about the game. Share your observations (e.g., "This is what I think is going on. Does that sound right to you?"). Between the two of you, identify when you tend to play this game and what triggers it. Then create a strategy to help you avoid it next time—maybe an alert that wakes you up to the fact that you're slipping into the game. You could agree on a word or a signal that indicates as much: "We're doing that thing again, aren't we? Let's stop, shall we?" Make sure to say "We're doing that thing," not *You're* doing that thing." Remember, it takes two to dance the toxic tango. Get skilled at alerting yourself in this way and you'll find it easier to sidestep the games. You'll also defuse the tension.

Stop the Game Before It Starts

Something lured you into the game—what was the hook? If you were the one who did the hooking, what bait did you use? If you can spot what got you into the game, you have a good chance of getting out of it. Although the game might feel irresistible, it's not. You may not be able to control what the other person does, but you do have control over your own behavior. Note that just because you've turned down the bait once, it doesn't mean it won't be offered again in another form. The other person wants to play, and the more you turn them down, the more determined they'll become. After all, you've had such fun together before: "Come on, you know you enjoy this game." It takes a lot of will, as well as skill, to avoid getting hooked. So, be prepared to hang on in there.

Listed here are some of the most popular hooks used in games, the typical responses from each of the three positions—persecutor (P), rescuer (R), and victim (V)—that ought to be avoided, and some suggestions for responses to help you stop a game from developing.

Persecutor

Hook	Typical Responses from Victims (V) and Rescuers (R)	What to Say to Stop the Game
"You dummy. Look what you've done again!"	"I'm sorry. I didn't mean to." (V) "I'll put it right straight away." (R)	"I have made a mistake." "I'm sorry. What can I do to fix it?" "I'll do (*a, b, c*) to resolve the problem."
"Why are you doing it that way?"	"I'm sorry. Am I doing it wrong?" (V) "I'm only trying to help you." (R)	"How do you think it should be done?"
"If it wasn't for you, I'd be free to . . ."	"I know I get in the way." (V) "Poor you. That must be awful." (R)	"What do you want to do?"

Rescuer

Hook	Typical Responses from Victims (V) and Persecutors (P)	What to Say to Stop the Game
"You look worried about something."	"You're so right." (V) "Mind your own business." (P)	"I'm dealing with a tricky problem and I'd like to ask your advice." "Thanks for your concern, but I'm okay."
"I think you'll find it easier if . . ."	"Yes, I thought I was doing it wrong." (V) "What makes you think you know better?" (P)	"Thanks. I'll come and ask you if I get stuck."
"Here, let me do that for you."	"Thanks. I'm terrible at doing these things." (V) "I doubt you'll do it better than me." (P)	"I'm doing okay right now, but thank you for the offer." "I'd like to do it myself but would like to hear your advice."

Victim

Hook	Typical Responses from Rescuers (R) and Persecutors (P)	What to Say to Stop the Game
"It's a disaster."	"How can I help?" (R) "Well, you should have seen it coming." (P)	"Oh boy, what are you going to do about it?" "Tell me what happened."
"What do I do now?"	"One idea would be . . ." (R) "Figure it out yourself!" (P)	"What are your options?" "What do you think would be the best approach?"
"I'm stuck."	"Let me do it for you." (R) "I'm not surprised. You'll never figure it out." (P)	"What can you do to get unstuck?" "What strategies have you not tried yet?" "What other ways can you approach this?"

Perhaps you've realized that you're the one doing the hooking. You know from experience that your bait leads to a game that ends with both of you feeling badly, and you'd like to stop playing.

Next time you feel yourself slipping into a role and reaching for the bait, ask yourself, *What do I really want right now?* If you're playing a game, you want attention, but is there a less toxic way of getting it? For example, perhaps you've noticed your tendency to act like a jerk toward another person when you feel tired after a long day. You know your partner always tries to help, but it never feels good enough, and you always end up feeling angry and unappreciated. Perhaps what you want is simply a hug. Or maybe you want five uninterrupted minutes with an audience so you can complain to your heart's content and then you can forget about it. Or being left alone in silence for fifteen minutes to unwind might do the trick. Identify what it is you really want and see if you can negotiate a positive way to get it from the other person. You'll save time, energy, and quite possibly your relationship.

Leave the Game Halfway Through

Switching to a new position is the final maneuver in these psychological games. Once you've made the switch, there's nothing much you can do; you're in a painful position and the game is over. Up until that point, though, you still have a chance to escape without harm. You can get out. It's hard, and the other person isn't going to like it, but it can be done.

If you feel you're in the middle of a game, press the pause button. Then tune in to yourself. Become aware of what you are about to say and realize that it is totally the wrong thing to say. It will only continue the game. Use skill and will to choose an alternative response that won't propel the game into further motion. The previous list of hooks and responses should give you some ideas. When you find a response option that works, remember it. You're going to need it again.

What If You Don't Get Out in Time?

You're probably feeling bruised, battered, and exhausted after last night's game. But don't give up. Tomorrow is another day and experience makes avoiding the games easier. In the meantime, reduce the pain by recognizing the past as just a losing streak. You've been hustled in your own game. Try laughing it off with the understanding that you'll be smarter the next time and won't get sucked into the game: *Okay, so I was caught again. I got hooked into the old "If it wasn't for you" routine. It's strangely funny and there's no point in feeling torn up about it now. I know what happened. And I can stop it next time.*

Games Over

The games we play in our relationships—at work and at home—are perhaps the hardest behavioral patterns to change. They often sit outside our conscious awareness, and we only become aware that we've just played a game after it's over and we are feeling upset. By spotting the games and making an effort to not get hooked into them, your relationships will feel more positive and more fulfilling.

GIVE YOUR MIND A WORKOUT

Beginner: Identify the Game

1. Identify a game you play in your life—it could be with a partner, a friend, a work colleague. Look for something you play regularly.

2. Identify the hook.

3. Identify the positions both you and your game-playing partner start in. Where do you end up?

Advanced: Stop the Game

1. Think about a relationship game you regularly find yourself in. Analyze the triggers that start the game. There will likely be a trigger in you, the environment, or the situation, and in the other person.

2. Analyze what it is about these triggers that hooks you. Ask yourself a series of "why" questions to get at the root of this trigger.

3. Visualize yourself reacting to the trigger like you typically do. Now change the visualization. Imagine yourself reacting differently, in a way that subverts the game. What does this look like? Repeat this visualization a few times, and then commit to yourself to put it into action the next time the trigger occurs.

4. Start a dialogue with the other person about the game dynamic and what you can both do to prevent it in the future. Be sure to first explain to them the concepts detailed in this chapter so your dialogue doesn't feel like an attack.

PART SIX

Let the Creative Juices Flow

IMAGINE YOUR alarm clock buzzing. Instead of getting out of bed, you wonder, *What else could an alarm clock do? What if it could answer my emails? What if it could alert me that I'll have a stressful day? What if it could wake me up by telling me how much money is in my bank account, what my blood pressure is, and how today's humidity will affect my hair? What if I could create something that eliminates bad hair days altogether?*

While this stream of ideas may seem appealing, you'd quickly get overwhelmed by the noise of it. So, to survive in this world, you have trained your brain to make practical shortcuts. And as you progress through life, you learn more mental shortcuts that help you do the regular things faster. Once you know how to make a cup of coffee, you don't rethink the whole process each time you fill the pot. You have better things to do.

Nevertheless, there are many situations in life in which the shortcuts you've created become harmful, in which the lack of creative thinking could be a detriment. Maybe you're tasked with a new project at work. Do you approach it the same way you have approached all your previous projects? What if you want to plan a special birthday party for your significant other? Do you want to plan it so it's just like last year's party?

As our world becomes more systematized, hyper fast, and process driven, the ability to think creatively becomes a premium skill—a valuable asset in the workplace and in your personal life—because for all the benefits of big data and the latest technology, the ability to engage in higher-order imagination is still unique to humans.

It pays to be creative when you want to

- solve a problem;

- spot (or discover) an opportunity;

- find a better, quicker, or easier way of doing something;

- be imaginative (write a story, decorate a cake, design your kitchen);

- add a little sparkle, humor, or romance; or

- make life more interesting.

This part of the book is for those of you who want to expand your creative potential. It will also help you improve your work, impress the world, and spice up your relationships and life.

In the following chapters, you'll discover ways to spot those mental shortcuts—or "filters"—that have become second nature, and remove them. You'll learn techniques to help you generate original ideas—techniques that actively encourage logical and free-thinking creativity. Plus, you'll learn how to tap into your unconscious mind so you can think the unthinkable.

Take your time with this section. Dive in. And let your creative juices flow.

CHAPTER 15

Overcome Creative Blocks

A man is driving a black car on a blackened road. There are no street-lights and no headlights on his car. A black cat crosses the road in front of his car and still he is able to apply the brakes to save the cat. How come? In this chapter, you'll discover the answer to this intriguing brainteaser and, more important, the way to solve it: how to think about things creatively.

There's an old saying that people looking at the past nostalgically are looking through rose-colored glasses. Similarly, the patterns in understanding future decisions and situations are often filtered by something we like to call a "filter bubble." Basically, your mind works much like an Internet search engine, only reporting back to you the information you expect to find based on the words you type into the search bar. Although you may not realize you are filtering, a "filter bubble" is a useful (but distorted) view of reality. The trick to thinking creatively is to remove all the filters and perceive the world with a fresh set of eyes and a fresh set of unexpected data.

Would you want to remove these filters permanently? Definitely not. Just like a pair of eyeglasses, these filters help you see the world in a way that is useful, recognizable, and clear. However, when you want to be creative, you want to remove your glasses and see all the fuzzy edges, the different shapes, the mass of interlocking colors that breaks down your assumptions and makes you think differently about the world around you and the challenges you face.

This chapter explores the different kinds of reality filters and how you can take them off to get more creative. Let's start by shedding some light on why that black cat wasn't run over.

Five Filters Through Which We See the World

Obviously we all see the world from different perspectives. Different life experiences create different filters that allow us to quickly relate situations to other situations. Maybe you've worked with a boss who was abusive. You leave the job, find a new one, and the moment your new boss says something that reminds you of your former employer, you assume you've once again entered a toxic environment. You use filters to get through life. They can allow you to quickly assess situations that may be dangerous or heighten your awareness to a situation that may be similar to one you've dealt with before. But they can also limit your ability to be creative.

Here are five filters through which we all see the world:

Filter One: I Know the Problem

A donkey is tied to a rope that is six feet long and there is a bale of hay eight feet away. How can the donkey get to the hay if he does not bite through or undo the rope?

Can you figure out the answer? It has nothing to do with using his hind legs or gusts of wind blowing the hay in his direction. If you can't figure out the answer, then try to work out what assumptions you have made about this situation. The brainteaser has been deliberately worded to encourage you to think in a certain way, but it is the wrong way to think if you want to solve the problem.

What are the assumptions you have made about the donkey? That a donkey has four legs, perhaps. And what about the rope? You know it is tied to the donkey, but what is it tied to at the other end? Aha! It doesn't say, and therein lies the answer to the question. The rope is not tied to anything, so the donkey has no problem getting to the bale of hay.

As frustrating as this brainteaser might be, it highlights a common filter that hinders creativity: knowing the problem. We often make assumptions about a problem before we try to solve it. Doing this automatically reduces the range of possible answers. If your assumptions are correct, they may help you get to an answer faster. But if they are wrong, they prevent you from ever getting an answer.

Sometimes there is a conscious effort to mislead. Let's go back to the black car and the black cat at the beginning of the chapter. Can you spot the assumption that most people make when defining this problem? Because the word "black" occurs so often and because there is a mention of streetlights and headlights, most of us assume that it is nighttime. However, it doesn't say the scene takes place at night. Once you realize that it could be daytime, you can solve the puzzle immediately.

Except in brainteasers, the narrow definition of a problem isn't usually deliberate. The narrowness occurs because you haven't challenged the way a problem has been expressed or what lies behind the expression.

The idea of introducing ATMs came out of some rather tired market research. Bank customers had said for years that they wished their branches were open longer and on weekends. But when the banks calculated the cost of extending business hours, they decided it wasn't worth it. It was only when someone spotted that the customers didn't necessarily want the branches to be open but wanted to be able to withdraw cash outside normal banking hours that the idea of the ATM took off.

Were you told at school to make sure that you read the question on the exam properly before answering? With our busy lives there is often a similar rush to answer, and we assume we know what the question is without checking. The consequence is the same: the wrong answer.

Filter Two: I Know the Solution

Look at the two following lines. Which do you think is longer, A or B?

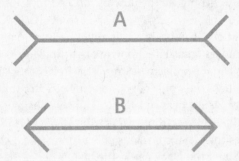

Now measure them. Go ahead. Use the edge of your mobile phone, a pen, the spine of another book, or any other straight edge, and find out for sure which line is longer.

Were you surprised? Most people think the lines are the same length because they have seen a puzzle that looks like this before where the lines were the same length. But this is not the same puzzle. And these lines are not the same length.

The *I know the solution* filter comes into play when you assume that either you know how to solve a problem or you already know what the solution is. While you might use this filter at the same time as the *I know the problem* filter, they are quite distinct.

Consider the story of Jake, a software engineer who was unhappy with his job because, even though he was earning good money and liked the company, he hated his boss. Eventually, Jake decided to consult with an executive recruiter, who assured him that he would have no problem finding a new job given the shortage of people with his skills and experience. That night, Jake reexamined the assumptions he was making about how to solve his problem. After thinking through his options carefully, he went back to the recruiter the next day, and while discussing potential job opportunities, he gave the recruiter his boss's name and praised him highly. A few days later, his boss was surprised when he was called about a new job opening, and he accepted a position with another company.

Jake was able to facilitate this happy solution for everyone con-cerned—he is now happy at his job and his boss is happy at a new company—because he thought differently about how to approach a familiar problem.

Filter Three: I Live in the Real World

When Einstein developed his theory of relativity, he did it in such a way that he left reality behind. He pictured himself chasing after a beam of light and imagined the journey he was going to take. Your thinking is often influenced by the "reality" you inhabit. Consider an exercise in which a group of people is asked to generate ideas for a new tourist attraction. First, they are asked to come up with alternative hours of operation. The group groans. What could be more boring than coming up with times that a tourist attraction might be open? With their real-ity filter firmly on, they list all the possible variations they can imagine. An abridged version of their brainstorm looks something like this:

- 9 A.M. to 5 P.M.   • Evenings

- 10 A.M. to 6 P.M.   • Mornings

- 8 A.M. to 6 P.M.   • Afternoons

- 5 P.M. to 9 A.M. (all night)   • Weekends

- 10 P.M. to 3 A.M.   • Lunchtime

- 24/7, every day   • Breakfast time

By the end of this exercise, the group feels they have been rather creative. Who would have thought of opening a tourist attraction only for the breakfast hours? There's nothing wrong with the group's list, but it doesn't exactly sparkle with originality. Why? Because all these ideas are based around typical hours of operation.

So, what would happen if they dismissed all their knowledge about what opening and closing times usually look like and thought about alternative times to operate the attraction? The next list looks very different. Here is an example of truly creative thinking:

- For the first fifteen minutes of every hour
- Only when there are twenty people ready to enter
- When half the group is under ten years old
- For groups of six
- When the moon is full
- During months with an *r* in them

Of course, some of these ideas wouldn't work. Nevertheless, the list sparkles with new ideas. Operating the attraction when the moon is full prompted an offer of a surfing competition held at night under the full moon. They could call it Night Surfari. And the idea of being open only for the first fifteen minutes of every hour might help with congestion, thereby allowing an effective flow of people through the attraction.

By letting go of the reality you're used to, the ideas you generate are likely to be more quirky, different, and engaging.

Filter Four: I Am an Expert

Sometimes your knowledge or expertise can get in the way of seeing different solutions or cause you to make assumptions about a particular problem.

A group of expert magicians was asked to watch one of their fellow illusionists perform a trick in which the ace card appears from the middle of a shuffled deck. A group of novices was also asked to observe the same trick. When asked what technique the magician had used to get the ace to appear, the experts gave long, convoluted explanations that involved complex and skillful sleight of hand. The novices simply said that the pack contained only aces. In this instance, the novices were right—the expertise of the magicians hindered their ability to think creatively.

Maybe you've heard the tale of older boys in a school teasing a younger boy by offering him a nickel and a dime and telling him he could have whichever coin he picked. The younger boy chose the nickel "because it's bigger." The older boys gave him the coin and laughed at him for being so stupid. The older boys played the game again and again, and each time the younger boy chose the nickel.

A kind teacher noticed the game the boys were playing and, feeling sorry for the younger boy, asked him, "Do you know that a dime is worth more than a nickel?"

"Of course," said the young boy.

"So, why do you keep picking the nickel?" asked the teacher.

"Because if I took the dime, they'd stop offering me the money."

The older boys and the teacher had their *I am an expert* filters on. They knew that a dime is worth more than a nickel. But the younger boy had removed his filter—he'd stopped thinking about whether the dime is worth more money than the nickel and instead considered the best possible way to get the boys to give him the largest amount of money. Picking the nickel proved to be the creative solution to the problem at hand.

The *I am an expert* filter dulls your creative ability when you assume you have special knowledge and can see something better than people who don't possess your knowledge.

Filter Five: What Is It?

Take a look at the following picture. What do you see?

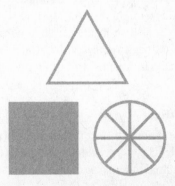

Some people say "a triangle, a shaded square, and a circle with lines in it" or "three geometric images." Others say "a tractor on a sunny morning," "a set of children's building blocks," or "a clown's face."

When it comes to thinking creatively, being too literal doesn't pay.

Don't worry if you still can't see a clown's face in the picture; that isn't really the point. Creativity is not about being right or wrong; it's about seeing things differently. Looking at a picture and imagining what it could be, as opposed to what it actually is, can release a fresh train of thought.

Children often exhibit this kind of "could be" creativity. They are uninhibited by assumptions about what is or a concern about getting things wrong (there is no "wrong"). A twig becomes an airplane, the water from a hose is a mountain stream, a hole in a wall is a dark and dangerous cave, and the petals from a flower are the hidden treasure.

You can gain creative insight by becoming uninhibited as well. Richard James was a naval engineer who was working on tension springs to support equipment on battleships. When one of the springs accidentally fell to the ground and kept on moving, Richard had a thought: *This tension spring could be a children's toy.* The result? The invention of the Slinky and one rich naval engineer.[1]

Pick up an object in front of you. What is it? What could it be?

Guidelines for Boosting Your Creativity

With your filters removed, creativity can flourish. Well, at least that's how it would seem. You might be wondering how, then, without filters (which act as constraints or guidelines to show us how *not* to think), do you generate creative ideas from a blank slate? Here are six guidelines that, when followed, will inspire you to create faster, fresher, more innovative ideas:[2]

Have an Objective

Aimless creativity is usually just that. A sense of purpose, or a problem to solve, greatly increases the odds of coming up with something that is not only original but also worthwhile.

Establish a Time Limit to Generate Ideas

Too much pressure makes people panic, but some pressure often helps you perform better (see chapter 18). Maybe tell yourself that you need to create a list of ninety ideas in fifteen minutes.

Go for Quantity

According to two-time Nobel Prize–winner Linus Pauling, the best way to have good ideas is "to have a lot of ideas and throw away the bad ones." When it comes to creativity, more is better, partly because you never know when you are going to discover something great and partly because, by going for volume, you force yourself to think without restrictions.

Don't Judge or Evaluate Your Ideas as You Brainstorm

This is the hardest rule to stick to. How often have you had a zany idea and instantly dismissed it as absurd? All ideas are good ideas because at the moment you have them you don't know where they might lead. If you catch yourself evaluating an idea, give yourself a penalty—like having to generate three more ideas in the next thirty seconds. After generating several ideas, set a period of time during which you don't allow yourself to assess them.

Write Down or Record Your Ideas

If you don't, you might end up spending all your time trying to remember them. Plus, an idea that won't work now may be the springboard for an amazing idea later.

Love Half Answers

Your moment of genius may come from letting an earlier thought that you liked (but weren't quite sure why) gestate. Ambiguity is great. Don't dismiss partial solutions, because they can often lead to the complete answer.

Prepare for Creative Takeoff: Removing the Spectacles

Once you know your filters and how they affect the way you think, it will become relatively easy to remove them. The challenge is noticing those rose-colored glasses in the first place.

Sometimes just noticing a filter is enough to remove it. Nevertheless, for the times when noticing isn't enough, here are four techniques to help you both spot the filter and turn it off.

Rephrase the Problem or Issue

Imagine, for example, explaining a problem out loud to someone who doesn't speak very good English. As you do so, look for the assumptions you are making that may not be true (not about their English but about the problem). By using simpler language to restate your problem, you may notice the filter that's stopping you from being creative. Or by restating the problem, you might spur an idea that removes the filter; your filter may have simply been the language you commonly use to explain the problem.

Look for Answers That Don't Work and Ask "Why Don't They Work?"

Once you can see why the ideas you are generating aren't solving your problem, you may start to see a new set of problems. Don't be discouraged by these new problems. They will typically expose your filter and give you a fresh path of thinking differently.

Keep Asking the Question "What Assumptions Am I Making?"

Making a list of your assumptions is a good place to start because it helps you search for assumptions ("A man is driving a black car on a blackened road" doesn't express that his headlights were on or that he could even see at all—he might be blind). Probe further, examining the definition of each word of a problem or any alternative meanings. This may help you spot your filters by forcing you to cull through your assumptions and remove those that are retraining your creative thinking.

Explore Other People's Perspectives

How would a doctor look at this challenge? What about a police officer? Or a third-grader? How would someone who has never seen anything like this before think about it? By using your imagination to shift perspectives, you adopt a different way of looking at the world. This, in turn, leads to fresh and different ideas.

The following two chapters are packed with more complex techniques that can help you think differently by removing or changing your filters.

GIVE YOUR MIND A WORKOUT

Beginner: Find the Filter

Can you spot the filters that the following brainteasers are encouraging you to put on? Can you take them off and solve these problems?

1. Which three numbers are next in the sequence 1 0 1 1 1 2 1 2 ?

2. There are three lightbulbs in a room and three separate light switches on the other side of a solid wooden door. You cannot see any of the lightbulbs from the light switches. You are on one side of the door and can go into the room only once and cannot come back. How will you find out which switch is for which lightbulb in one go?

3. A woman has five children and half of them are male. Is this possible? If so, how?

4. A woman with no driver's license goes the wrong way down a one-way street and turns left at a corner with a no-left-turn sign. A policeman sees her but does nothing. Why?

5. What's the next letter in this sequence: W, T, N, L, I, T?

6. There is a barrel with no lid and some wine in it. Without any measuring tools and without removing any wine from the barrel, how can you easily decide whether it is more or less than half full?

Find the answers on the next page.

Advanced: Open Your Mind

1. Divide a piece of paper into four rectangular boxes.

2. Draw a random squiggle or shape in each box without any thought for what you are drawing.

3. Then turn each squiggle or shape into a picture of something. Don't settle for a smiley face or a house; use your imagination and make something unique.

4. For an extra challenge, see if you can connect all four drawings into a scene. Don't worry if it's bizarre and doesn't make sense—that's the point.

Answers from Previous Page:

1. 3, 4, 5 (Imagine a clock counting from 10, 11, 12, 1, 2)

2. Turn on the first two switches and leave them on for five minutes. Then turn off the second switch and leave on the first switch. So, you have one switch turned on, one that was recently turned off, and one that was never turned on. Then go into the room and feel the two bulbs that are not turned on. The hot one is the one that was recently turned off, the one that is cool was never turned on, and the one that is bright is the switch that is still on.

3. All of them are male.

4. She is walking.

5. *S* ("what's the next letter in this *Sequence*")

6. Tilt it sideways. If the wine is aligned with the top inner edge of the barrel while not spilling out, it is exactly half full.

CHAPTER 16

Master the Tools of Creativity

Am I creative?" asked Marty. "No, I'm not creative at all. I'm a guy who likes facts and numbers."

"Am I logical?" asked Melanie. "No, I'm not very organized. I'm a free thinker. I like to be expressive and artistic."

When it comes to creativity, there are no rules. You don't have to be a certain type of person. You don't have to look a certain part. You don't have to like poetry or theatre. You can be a mathematical genius. You can love organization and structure. You don't have to wear outrageous clothing or have strange "Einstein" hair.

The good news about creative people is that they look and behave like anyone else. They can be both logical and free thinkers. They can be expressive, outrageous, and artistic, or reserved and refined. Creativity is achieved not by the way your brain operates or the way you present yourself to the world as much as by the tools and processes you use to overcome challenges.

This chapter explores creativity tools that, when used properly, will engage any person in the creative process. People who struggle with idea generation will discover new insights. People who are already creative will experience enhanced creativity.

Playing the Opposites

Opposites attract. Every action needs an equal and opposite reaction. Heroes have their villains. Yins have their yangs. Jon Stewart has Stephen Colbert. Whether you're talking physics, folklore, or cliché (there's two sides to every story), opposites exist, and they are a driving force of true creative potential, because they give you a starting point to bounce your ideas off of.

The opposites creativity tool considers the typical and traditional way of solving a problem and then bounces it off its opposite to create new and different solutions to that problem.[1] For example, deep-fried ice cream is a unique dessert because it is a combination of exact opposites: hot and cold. Pairing the heavy metal band Metallica with a symphony orchestra is an attention grabber because the two styles of music are so different.

The key to using this creativity tool is generating opposites. The opposite of black is white, the opposite of rich is poor, the opposite of tall is short, etc. At first glance, generating opposites seems simple enough; you are probably considering the most obvious answer. Try it yourself. What are the opposites of the following three words?

High _____   Early _____   Day _____

The challenge with this creativity tool is to come up with as many other opposites as possible. Don't stick to the literal opposite but find other alternatives. The literal opposite of black may be white, for example, but other colors would be considered opposites too. For example, in financial terms, you're either in the black or in the red. Or in culinary terms, the opposite of rich might be bland. Here are some other opposites of black, rich, and tall; can you think of more?

Black	White, red, green, orange, pink, light
Rich	Poor, well-off, comfortable, respected, shrewd, generous, understated, barren, plain, happy, light, sincere, bland
Tall	Short, long, strong, tiny, microscopic, giant, wide, narrow, true

High	
Early	
Day	

The power of playing the opposites is more evident when you have a problem to solve. Imagine you are planning a vacation and you want to do something different from last year's week at a lake cabin. You can use this creativity tool to look at opposites and think creatively of alternatives for your next vacation. For example:

Cabin	Hotel, resort, RV, tent, bed and breakfast, cruise
Lake	Ocean, mountain, desert, foreign country

The key to this tool is to remember that the goal is to come up with innovative ideas rather than a comprehensive list of accurate opposites. So, as you come up with opposites, don't stop to consider whether they are good or bad.

Here are four steps to get the most from this technique:

1. Ensure your objective is clear. If you are working in a group, make sure everyone understands what the objective is. For example, everyone needs to know that the goal is to plan your next vacation.

2. Brainstorm the ideas you would normally produce. Maybe you go to Las Vegas often, so your instinct is to not include it as an opposite of the cabin by the lake. But including it might spark some other ideas.

3. List the opposites. Remember, it's okay if something isn't an exact opposite. If your typical trip to California is to Santa Monica, then Venice Beach (right next door, but with a completely different vibe) would be considered an opposite.

4. Evaluate your opposites. Your instincts might tell you to cross things you don't like off the list as you are generating it. Resist the urge. For example, you or someone in your group might suggest that the

Bronx is the opposite of New York. Maybe you have absolutely no interest in visiting the Bronx. You can make that evaluation when you're finished.

Case Study: Opening a Restaurant

A group was asked to come up with ideas for opening a new restaurant. Their first assigned task was to use the opposites creativity tool to consider alternative types of food, operating hours, and prices for the various menu items.

You might think that the price of a dish isn't the most exciting place to begin, but it surprisingly generated the most interesting ideas. First, the group discussed whether to set prices for whole meals or individual dishes. Thinking a little more creatively, someone suggested that rather than set prices, why not have different prices for different days: cheaper meals on Mondays, for example, when the restaurant would be quiet. Starting to think outrageously, someone suggested that rather than having different prices on different days, why not have different prices on the same day? An idea that came out of this was a restaurant in a financial district where the prices are on an electronic board and go up and down based on how much each option is ordered. Each table would have an electronic box so customers could place orders when they want and get the price showing at the time. Should you order your dessert now or wait to see if it gets cheaper? This approach would also allow the restaurant to manage their inventory by lowering the prices of slow-selling dishes and raising prices when they have only one of that item left. How much would you pay for the last lobster tail? The restaurant would also save money on staff, since they wouldn't need waiters to take orders. There could also be a price based on loyalty. If customers came to the restaurant more than once a week, they would get cheaper meals, which would encourage them to eat there more often.

Sound far-fetched? It's not. Although the group wasn't aware of it, there used to be a bar in Paris called Le Footsie (as in "FTSE," the London exchange) that operated on a similar principle: the items on the bar's menu were modeled on stock shares, which rose and fell in price depending on how many people bought them. If such a great concept can come from thinking creatively about something as everyday as price, who knows what other innovative ideas might emerge when considering the restaurant's ambiance or menu items?

People often find they are very surprised at both the quantity of ideas they produce using this technique and the broad range of ideas they may not otherwise have considered. There are, however, some common problems people run into when using this tool.

Advantages and Disadvantages of the Opposites Tool

The main advantage of using the opposites creativity tool is that it is simple and easy to use and it generates a wide variety of ideas. The disadvantage is that the ideas produced tend to be based on an initial concept (e.g., opening a restaurant), meaning you may not always move far enough away from your traditional solution (e.g., why not operate a food truck instead?).

Here are some other common problems you may experience when using this tool and the solutions to overcome them:

Problem	I seemed to come up with the most obvious opposites but not more creative alternatives.
Solution	Don't take the word "opposite" too literally. Consider the broader category of the problem you are trying to solve. For example, if you are trying to come up with creative alternatives to your lake cabin vacation, consider all the possibilities within the category of lodgings and locations. The obvious opposite to "lake cabin" might be "no lake cabin," but a more creative opposite of "cabin" could include anything from a castle to a windmill to a hole in the ground. Now, these opposites are sure to spark more creative ideas for your next vacation.
Problem	All the ideas seem useless.
Solution	Unfortunately, that's creativity. If you come up with a fantastic idea every time you try, it's probably not that fantastic of an idea or not that different from a load of ideas you've had before. Persevere. Try coming back to it later, using a different tool, or thinking about your goal from a different perspective.

Problem	The ideas didn't seem very different from one another.
Solution	Think through your opposites again. Are you considering opposite ideas for every component of the original idea (not just "lake cabin" but "lake" and "cabin"). Have you articulated your objective clearly (e.g., we need ideas for a new topping that will be baked in the middle of a pizza)? If you are clear about your objectives, the ideas should get different quickly. The alternative is to try a different tool.
Problem	It was difficult coming up with the original ideas.
Solution	You're probably using the wrong tool. Try brainstorming without any filters from your own life experiences. Maybe you should choose to start not with opposites of your last vacation but of Kate Hudson's last vacation or Jimmy Kimmel's last vacation. Then pick out the more fitting ones to your life or wants and take them through the opposites process.
Problem	There were too many alternatives for each of the original ideas.
Solution	This is a great problem to have. Record your ideas in an orderly fashion (as much as possible). Then consider what criteria you should use to evaluate them. For example, one of your must haves for a vacation might be a high level of comfort. You could run through your list of ideas and remove many using that criteria (for example, the idea of a tent at the lake would get the ax right away).

The Morphological Matrix[2]

The morphological matrix is an ugly name for a very elegant creativity tool. It has been used by everyone from philosophers to car designers to scriptwriters. Its method is simple: break down a goal into its component parts, consider these parts separately, and then recombine them to find new solutions.

This tool helps you generate ideas super fast. On an idea-generated-per-second basis, no other technique can beat the morphological matrix.

The Key to the Matrix

Here is the simple key to the matrix: attributes. An attribute is a component part of a problem. So, if you're tasked with generating ideas for a surprise party, an attribute of the party might be the theme, the location, or the music. An attribute is different from an item, which is a possible answer to each attribute question. Therefore, for the attribute "location," two items that might fit are "boat" and "rooftop." Making the matrix work is all about understanding the difference between attributes and items, and not confusing the two.

Let's suppose, then, that your objective is to host that surprise party. Select three or four of the best attributes ("best" could mean anything from the most interesting to what makes the most sense given your objective). In this instance, you might choose dress, location, and music. Once the best attributes have been selected, come up with a list of items for each attribute.

Dress	Location	Music
Wild West	Boat	String quartet
1920s	Underground club	Jazz band
Celebrity	In the country	DJ
School	Rooftop terrace	Acoustic
Starts with the letter *p*	Warehouse	Pianist
Someone else	Posh hotel	Gospel choir
Disco	At home	ABBA tribute band
Medieval banquet	At the seaside	Blues guitarist
Toga	Favorite bar	Karaoke
Black tie	Shop window	Sounds of nature

Then take one item from each column to generate many more new ideas. For example:

- A Wild West party on a rooftop terrace with a blues guitarist in the corner

- A toga party in a shop window with a gospel choir singing in the background

• Everyone dressed as something beginning with the letter *p*, in a posh hotel with a pianist playing on a grand piano

There are ten items in each of these three attributes, so you have a thousand possible combinations or solutions to your objective. Add one more attribute and you have ten thousand possible ideas. And by using the morphological matrix tool in this way, you are sure to generate ideas that you would not normally have considered. Professional party planners can eat their party hats.

Free Association[3]

So far, we've dealt with creativity in a structured and rational way. But your mind has the ability to reach even further. To fully harness the power of creativity and come up with even more exciting and original ideas, you need to tap into your intuition as well.

Six Degrees of Kevin Bacon is a popular film trivia game. Building on the idea of six degrees of separation (the theory that anyone can contact anyone else in the world through six relationships or fewer), the game challenges players to link any film star to actor Kevin Bacon. So, for example, if the star in question is Tobey Maguire, then you could link him to Kevin Bacon as follows: Tobey Maguire was in *Spider-Man,* as was James Franco. James Franco was in *Rise of the Planet of the Apes,* as was John Lithgow. John Lithgow was in the original *Footloose,* as was Kevin Bacon.

In the same way the Six Degrees of Kevin Bacon game uses your film knowledge to link two seemingly unconnected actors, your mind pulls seemingly disparate objects together to create something new when using the morphological matrix. Pick three nouns randomly from a dictionary and see if you can find a way to connect them. For example, let's choose "electricity," "herring," and "one-armed bandit."

Can you link the three together? It's tricky, yes, but not impossible. One way of linking them could be that a particular one-armed bandit, which needs electricity to operate, has a fish theme and the jackpot is when you get three herrings in a row. Or maybe there was a bandit who liked nothing more than frying herrings on his electric cooker, because it only required the use of one arm. The words in question are so divergent, you could never have connected them using logic. By thinking more freely, you can.

Try it yourself with these sets of words:

• Wrench, dove, artichoke

• Monkey, door, world atlas

Mental freewheeling, or generating random "could be" connections and ideas, is similar to the mind-set jazz musicians use when they perform solos. Stand-up comedians also use this tool a lot, because it provides for hilarious scenarios. In fact, this is the foundation of improv comedy. To be effective, you need to let your mind go on an adventure where you have an objective and a starting point but the destination remains unknown.

What Is Free Association and How Can You Use It in Your Life?

Free association is a bit like connecting apparently unrelated words (or films), except you have only one word to start with and no final destination in mind. You start with that one word and use it to generate ideas related to whatever you want to think about creatively (your objective). Because there isn't a predetermined end point, you can let your mind explore in all sorts of different directions, and if you get stuck or bored, you can go back to the original word or stimulant and start over.

All this sounds great and creative, but how does it relate to your everyday life? Here is an example of using free association to help with a real challenge. A "spark" used in this instance is a random word.

One of your best friends runs a small local theatre. The plays are fantastic, but he's not getting enough business and the company is facing closure. In desperation, your friend asks if you would set some time aside and help him come up with some original ideas to promote the theatre. Being the good friend you are, you agree (in return for two free tickets and a backstage pass).

You would first likely come up with traditional ideas, such as your friend appearing on television and radio, getting press coverage and reviews, and telling all his friends about it. But you decide to look at things in a different way, by using something from one of the plays to

kick-start your thoughts. You pluck three numbers out of your head—
127, 16, and 6—which will represent a page number, a line number,
and a word number. You then turn to the script the cast is currently
rehearsing and discover the corresponding word is "out." That's kind
of a vague word, which might make this process seem difficult. But try
connecting the word "out" to your objective. What does "out" remind
you of, and how could that have anything to do with marketing the theatre? One thought is that "out" makes you think of exits, so you could
stand by the exits of stadiums or other theatres and distribute flyers.
What about "outside" or "out in the open"—why not have an open-air
performance in order to generate interest? This gets you thinking of
the U.S. Open golf tournament and maybe a competition at the end
of a performance of the play in which audience members could win
tickets to the event. Then, you might think of outpatients—maybe
your friend's theatre company could perform five-minute sketches in
a local hospital waiting room, where people are bored and want to be
entertained, and then hand out flyers afterward.

As you can see, you very quickly moved away from conventional to
truly innovative ideas by free-associating from your original word. You
also managed to remove your internal filters—any thoughts, concerns,
or preconceptions that may hinder your creative thinking. At no point
did you evaluate any of these thoughts or worry about whether they
would be effective. You can evaluate them later. For now, you let your
creative juices flow and came up with a fresh selection of new solutions.

Free Association Is More than Words: How to Get Really Creative

There are a number of different triggers besides words that you can use
to get your mind free-associating. Since we all associate with the world
in different ways, you will find some triggers more helpful than others.
The only way to discover which work best for you is to give them all a
try. Here are some of them:

Sound

Noises can be a great stimulus for new ideas. While considering
sound, however, it is best to avoid music, because you may already have
mental connections to certain songs, music types, or bands. Ideally

choose sounds that aren't immediately recognizable. For each sound, listen to it, spend a minute writing down every idea that comes to mind, and then think about how the sound relates to your objective.

For example, let's say your objective is to come up with a surprise present for your partner's birthday, and the sound trigger makes you think of a train speeding along the tracks. Putting aside obvious thoughts you might have, such as tickets for a train ride, let your mind wander further. One idea you might come up with is a choo-choo train, which then reminds you of chewing food, which then makes you recall the caramels your partner loved from that fancy food store.

Sight

Using visual images can also help you break down your traditional patterns of thinking. If the image you choose to trigger your free association is slightly abstract, your mind will wander in many more directions. This is because the less specific and more abstract the trigger, the more likely you are to think conceptually, as well as practically, and come up with something original. Again, look at the image and, for one minute, write down as many ideas as you can, then sift through them for the most appropriate idea. You might also try playing music while looking; combining stimuli has been shown to help creative problem solving. Say there's a crack in the sidewalk outside your home. It may not look like anything at first glance, but when you free-associate with the shape of the crack, ideas flood your mind. The shape almost resembles a triangle. The triangle reminds you of the album cover of Pink Floyd's *The Dark Side of the Moon*. The moon reminds you of cheese, and you recall driving past the new wine and cheese shop downtown. What a great birthday treat.

Scramble

This is a process of using letters to kick-start your ideas. Select a random handful of Scrabble tiles, or letters written on scraps of paper, and spread them out on a table in front of you. Then, rather than trying to form complete words, use the letters to make sounds or parts of words (for example, the letters might form the first or last portion of a word). Build on these to develop some ideas.

The letters *s, t,* and *a* could make you think of stamps, stamina, stacks, stands, stanza, and stampede. The letters *b, e,* and *e* could make you think of beer, beetles, beeping, and honey bees. The letters *g, n,* and *i* (reversed to *i, n, g*) could make you think of skiing, surfing, flirting, working, biking, drinking, and shopping.

Touch

Like sound and vision, objects can be used to help break patterns. They also have the advantage of adding a tactile (touch) dimension to creativity. Hold and feel the chosen object in your hands. Use simple things like rubber balls, paper clips, and sandwich bags.

Smell

Another sense you can draw on is your sense of smell. Choose a particular scent, be it eucalyptus, orange, or whatever, and think of not only ideas but also memories the scent evokes. This may lead you to a train of thought you hadn't previously considered. Try smelling simple things, like celery, and complicated things, like whiskey. Close your eyes and let the aroma lead your mind.

Keep the Creativity Flowing

If you get stuck or come to a standstill at any point during your free association, don't worry. Try the same problem using a different word. Alternatively, use sounds, objects, or pictures. If you do use sounds, slightly abstract ones work best, because different people respond to them in very different ways. Remember, patience is also a virtue in creativity. If you think you are going to generate award-winning ideas every time you think creatively, you are going to be disappointed. And if you're generating great ideas every time you think creatively, you're probably not thinking creatively often enough.

Logical Thinker or Free Thinker?

When it comes to thinking creatively, you can have your cake and eat it too if you use the three tools in this chapter. One type of thinking doesn't preclude the other; in fact, it can help it. One tool may give you very different results from another. Your best results will arrive when you combine everything into one massive creative exploration.

Beginner: Try Out the Morphological Matrix

1. Consider a goal or problem you are facing at the moment. Describe your objective as either a "how" question or a statement. For example, a question would be "How can we decorate our living room?" An objective would be "To generate ideas for decorating our living room." Objectives become unhelpful if either they are too specific or they can be answered with a yes or a no (for example, "Should we decorate the living room?").

2. What are the attributes of your objective? If you are considering what the attributes are for the objective of decorating the living room, "lawn chairs" would not be an attribute but an item within an attribute (furniture).

3. Select the best attributes—anything from the most interesting to what makes the most sense given your objective. (For your first try, probably start with three or four attributes.)

4. Brainstorm items within each attribute. Work through one attribute at a time, coming up with as many ideas as possible.

Objective:		
Attribute One:	Attribute Two:	Attribute Three:

Advanced: Free Associate

1. Choose another objective that you want to consider creatively. For example, "Ideas for throwing a great party" or "Easy ways to move

to a new house." Very complex, controversial, or overly simple objectives, such as "Finding ways to create world peace" or "How should
I eat this carrot?" should probably be left alone, at least for now.

2. Write down some of your traditional ideas. Writing down some of
   these first gets them out of the way (and there may be an excellent
   idea in there), but it also gives you something to compare with later.

3. Now look at the problem again using some random input. Try to
   generate ideas that link the word to your objective.

4. See what you can come up with using random words (such as
   "bird," "frying pan," or "bounce"), random sounds (such as thunder
   or a car alarm), a picture from a magazine, or a random smell (such
   as cinnamon).

CHAPTER 17

Tap Your Unconscious Mind

Daydreaming and watching the world pass by are not normally considered the best methods of getting ahead in life. Nevertheless, one person who was often found staring into space was Albert Einstein. Yes, this was when he got his best ideas.

Many other great thinkers are at their most creative when they aren't really "working" at all. Why is this? Because when you escape your conscious train of thought, you can tap into your unconscious mind. This chapter shows you how to do it. But be warned. Tapping into your subconscious isn't for everyone. It's risky. It may well feel uncomfortable. The outcome is uncertain, and for most of us, it's definitely very different from how we normally go about thinking creatively.

But it's also a fantastic way of generating new ideas and coming up with the sort of creative leaps you are unlikely to make if you stick with conscious thinking.

Three Ways in Which We Think

In his book *Hare Brain, Tortoise Mind,* cognitive psychologist Guy Claxton describes three different modes of thinking.[1]

The first mode is your wits—the almost instinctual part of your brain that is constantly aware, even when you're not paying attention. Have you ever noticed how you are able to navigate a busy shopping center or airport without having to think about it? You adjust your stride, pace, and direction according to the movements of hundreds of people around you without thinking. Of course, the moment you start thinking about what you're doing, you can't seem to stop bumping into people. Wits are also responsible for jamming on the brakes if someone pulls out in front of you in a car. There's no time to think and then react; you react first and then think afterward about what happened.

The second mode of thinking is your intelligent conscious. This is where you actively problem-solve. How can you get to work in the least amount of time? Where should you go on vacation? How do you organize the process of your current work project? The intelligent conscious is interested in solving the problem. It's literal and explicit thinking—in which explaining and coming up with solutions are more important than simply observing. The intelligent conscious is where you spend most of your thinking time; it is what you have been trained to use in school and at work. In Guy Claxton's book, he describes this type of thinking as the "hare-brain" mode. It's quick, decisive, and focused.

The third form of thinking is your intelligent unconscious. The intelligent unconscious is more interested in the problem than necessarily finding a solution. It tends to be imaginative and playful—meandering around a particular topic or issue to get to an answer. Intelligent unconscious is more useful when you're dealing with complicated or tough issues, in which attempting to solve the problem directly creates frustration and little else. This third mode of thinking Claxton calls the "tortoise mind." Basically, this means that rather than hurrying to try to solve an issue, you mull it over and ruminate on it.

It is here, in the third mode, according to Claxton, that your most creative ideas occur.

Your education and work have trained you to execute the intelligent conscious mode very well. But the unconscious methods of problem solving are typically ignored. In school, you learned how to solve problems logically, whether it was figuring out a math question or completing a comprehension test. Speed and showing how you worked out a problem were appreciated. However, a more playful and meandering approach (in particular, daydreaming) was discouraged.

Imagine you told your colleagues at work that you were going to spend the day sitting under a tree in the park thinking, and you were going to take the whole team with you to do the same. Then imagine, when you got back to the office, you freely admitted that you didn't come up with any useful ideas the whole day.

This would not be popular.

But if you came back with an earth-shatteringly brilliant and original idea, you would be heralded as a genius.

While the process of reaching into your unconscious mind may be uncomfortable for many people, and your boss or partner might not be too fond of your new sitting-under-a-tree habit, being able to use this very productive but underappreciated mode of thinking can be remarkably powerful—especially when your normal, quick, solution-oriented approach doesn't seem to be generating any answers.

Where do you start? Here are three tools to open up your unconscious mind:

Let the Idea Incubate

Einstein said that some of his best ideas occurred not just when he was staring into space but when he was taking a shower. Nobel Prize–winner Leó Szilárd revealed that the concept of a nuclear chain reaction came to him while he was waiting at a London traffic light. Mozart and Tchaikovsky both said that their most creative sequences emerged as spontaneous passages they could hear in their heads. You don't have to be one of the world's geniuses for ideas to arrive at unexpected moments. Watching TV in the middle of the night, walking the dog, or driving in rush-hour traffic might unleash your unconscious mind.

This first tool is based on a process called "incubation." Basically, incubation is allowing your mind to mull over a problem while you're doing something else. Scheduling incubation time for a problem-solving exercise can be a worthwhile investment. In fact, try to recall your best ideas. Most likely those ideas came to you outside of the office, when you were doing something mundane like buying groceries or taking a bike ride or riding the subway. When you frame a problem and then go about your daily business, other areas of your brain are activated and create connections that can help solve your problem.

In order to get the benefits of incubation, follow these principles:

1. Build in time to allow for incubation. Start thinking about the problem or challenge before you need an answer.

2. Don't allow yourself to get frustrated or feel under pressure to get an answer. If you do try to force an answer, it is likely to be the wrong one, or at least a weaker version of what you could come up with.

3. Have faith in your unconscious mind. Let it process undisturbed and unhurried.

The most important thing about allowing your intelligent unconscious to shine is getting yourself into the right frame of mind, which means giving your intelligent unconscious the chance to work.[2]

Think of it this way: You put dinner in the oven and expect it to be cooked in half an hour. Or you plant a tree and assume that if you keep watering it, it will grow on its own. In a similar way, you need to leave a thought in your mind and trust that a creative idea will emerge without trying to force it. You can't force your dinner to cook faster or a tree to grow more quickly.

Sure, you can go back to that thought every once in a while (like watering a plant), but if you constantly watch it, the growth will seemingly take an eternity.

Believe in the Daydream

Another way of dipping into your unconscious mind is sometimes called "reverie" or even "daydreaming." In this state of thinking, you can generate great creative leaps, in which you make sense of concepts, link different thoughts together, and produce truly original ideas.

"Whenever I get a challenge from a client, I visit churches," said the creative director from an ad agency. He found that wandering around these holy places was how his best ideas came to him. A CEO we spoke with from Arizona said that when he needs to daydream, he hikes up the side of a mountain. And Sarah, a boutique owner from California, told us that she swims laps in the pool at her gym. All of us will find different ways to stimulate the reverie state of mind. The question is, where will *you* find it?

Daydreaming is a state you surely recognize: that moment between wakefulness and slumber when you half dream, or when you peer out a window and your imagination takes you on a bizarre and quite unexpected journey. We are not talking about reminiscing about the past but about the kind of daydreaming in which you construct a new reality for yourself. You might imagine yourself as a pirate or an astronaut—you can distort or amend reality in such a way that a new situation occurs in your daydream, however freaky or strange that might be. Because you're imagining being someone other than yourself, all kinds of new situations might appear. Let them appear. This is your creative mind at work.

So, how do you get yourself into this state of daydreaming? The answer is in visualization, or "unconscious imagining," as it's sometimes called.

There are three elements that will help you get into the kind of daydreaming that is likely to generate ideas:

Relaxation

The first step in this creative visualization process is to quiet your mind (in other words, stop consciously thinking). One way of achieving this is by focusing on your breathing. When you concentrate on your breathing, you can begin to let all your other thoughts disappear. Sure, it sounds a bit simple. However, when you focus on something so basic, your mind can begin to wander.

A Special Location

A special location is a visualized setting where you can relax and think clearly while feeling safe and comfortable. Your location can be real or imagined, like a beach, park, stream, cave, forest, or a place you have read about in a book, seen in a film, or simply created yourself.

A Creative Guide

A creative guide is a visualized guide whom you trust, value, and respect. It is someone who is wise and original. Again, the guide can be based on a real or an imaginary person. They can be a person, a character, an animal, or another type of being.

DAYDREAMING: LEARN THE PROCESS AND EXPERIENCE THE WONDER

The process of creative daydreaming requires you to use all your senses as much as possible to bring ideas to life. By using sight, sound, touch, smell, and taste, you make the experience much richer and more engaging. Let's look at the process of daydreaming in step-by-step detail:

Step One   Breathe in deeply through your nose, filling both the top and bottom of your lungs. Breathe out easily through your mouth. Concentrate on the rhythm of your breaths; really focus on inhaling and exhaling, and nothing else.

Step Two   Let your thoughts drift away. If a thought comes into your mind, imagine it as a cloud that will be blown away with your next breath. Don't fight your thoughts; just let them drift in and then drift away again.

Step Three   Imagine arriving at your special location. Use all your senses to visualize this place with as much detail as possible so you feel like you are really there. You should imagine how it smells, what sounds you can hear, and how calm and relaxed you feel. Spend a few moments enjoying the tranquillity of your special location and drifting into a deeper state of relaxation.

Step Four   Now imagine you can see a figure moving toward you from the distance. As the figure gets closer, you see that it is your creative guide, who has come to help you with your objective. Imagine your guide arriving next to you, wherever you are, and you greeting them. You feel relaxed and inspired in the presence of your guide and are very happy to be in their company.

Step Five   Imagine you are explaining your objective to your guide. You may want to explain this verbally or write it down to inform your guide—whatever you prefer.

Step Six   Wait for a response, confident that your guide will help you come up with an original and innovative solution.

Your guide may talk to you, give you an object, or even show you a scene. The symbol, object, or scene may be abstract or cryptic, and you may need to spend a few minutes deciphering the various symbols. Having thought about what the symbol or gesture may represent, you can then relate it back to your objective and see what it may mean. You mustn't worry about your ideas being too strange or difficult to implement—part of the creative process is simply generating ideas.

People find that they come up with ideas they never would have reached using the more logical approaches to problem solving, or at least an initial thought that, with incubation, leads to a great idea. You might find it difficult to self-censor ideas when using this mode of thinking, which is a good thing. Censor-free, you'll surely generate interesting and quirky ideas.

This process doesn't work for everyone right away. It improves with practice; so if you enjoyed it, use it regularly. The more practiced you become at visualization, the more likely you are to generate useful, interesting, and creative ideas.

Stream-of-Consciousness Writing

In 1965, Bob Dylan found himself writing the words to a song and "a long piece of vomit twenty pages long" is how he later described his outpourings. To begin with, there was no structure, no rhyme, no direction—just "an ill-formed mass of words," in the opinion of one critic. But as Dylan went back to what he'd written, sifted through it, and started to edit and shape it, he knew he'd come up with something special. His "vomit" became the lyrics to "Like a Rolling Stone." What Dylan did was something called stream-of-consciousness writing.

Stream-of-consciousness writing is like recording a stream of your consciousness. When you capture all your thoughts as they occur, it is difficult to self-evaluate or self-correct. In fact, as you capture your thoughts in real time, you are more likely to drift into new and unexpected places in your unconscious mind.

To do this type of writing, find a space where you are comfortable, making sure you have a pen and some paper. Then get into a relaxed state of mind (the previous daydreaming exercise will help you accomplish this).

Start writing as quickly as you can and without thinking. If the flow of writing is broken, then stop, go to a new line, and start writing again. If you want to, use a trigger word to get your sentences going. Be prepared for your ideas to come from a deeper, more intuitive place, and don't be alarmed if they are odd—when you explore in this more extreme form of free association, you are more likely to produce ideas that are unusual and out of context; after all, that's the point.

A Few Tips

- Let go. No one is watching and no one will see what you've written. Let it rip.

- Write as fast as you can.

- Have a trigger word. If you dry up, don't worry, but use your trigger word to get you going again.

- There should be some grammatical sense (rather than just a string of words), but it doesn't need to be perfect or a work of literature.

- Use this writing as a starting point. It won't give you "the answer," but it may lead you to it.

- Review, amend, or adjust afterward, not as you're writing.

In the 2000 film *Finding Forrester,* Sean Connery plays the character of a successful author who is teaching a young man how to write. He explains, "You write your first draft with your heart. You rewrite with your head." Stream-of-consciousness writing is like writing with your heart.

More than Half a Brain

People often find that the unconscious mind is a great place to start the creative process. Still, your ideas then need to be significantly refined, improved, discarded, or amended before they can be used. In other words, once your tortoise mind has come up with the ideas, it is time to switch to hare-brain mode to analyze them. For the first time in a long while you will be turning your daydreams into reality.

GIVE YOUR MIND A WORKOUT

Beginner: Discover Your Stream

1. Commit to one week of doing stream-of-consciousness writing five minutes every day.

2. Set a recurring time, pick a random word or image, and just start to write. Do this early in the day, when your mind isn't bogged down, or right before you need to do something requiring a creative mindset. Notice how you become more comfortable with the technique as the week progresses.

Advanced: Open-Minded Analysis

This chapter, and this book, include many different techniques for coming up with creative ideas. Typically it's your tortoise mind that comes up with the ideas and your hare brain that analyzes them, but what would happen if you used your tortoise mind as a first stage of analysis? Using the skills you learned about incubation and daydreaming, take a recent solution to a thorny problem and practice a *what if* reflection.

A *what if* reflection involves imagining the outcome of a decision and seeing how you feel about it, how your body reacts.

1. First, find a quiet place free from distractions.

2. Take a moment in this place to consider the idea or solution you came up with, and think of other similar decisions you've had to make.

3. Then consider the solution or other choices that are available and play each out in your mind as if it is happening. Visualize the solution or outcome of the decision in detail.

4. As you mull over and visualize each potential outcome, notice how your body reacts. Your analytical mind is good at generating an idea of the future, but give your intuitive mind some time and space to provide a feeling about this outcome. Try different outcomes and see which one feels best.

5. Then ask yourself honest, probing questions about why certain outcomes don't feel right and why other ones do feel right.

This is a good technique to use whenever you want to encourage your intuitive mind to speak up or you're faced with a tricky situation and cannot decide which path to take.

PART SEVEN

Minimize Stress, Maximize Bliss

ORNING COFFEE, viral YouTube videos, and a seemingly endless string of updates on Facebook have become a daily ritual. But something not so pleasant has also become a morning ritual: stress. A survey by the American Psychological Association suggests that stress levels have actually declined—but it's not because Americans are feeling less stress. Instead, the survey suggests it's because we're getting used to it.[1]

Certainly there are plenty of things that can elevate your stress every day: your commute, the pile of emails waiting in your inbox, the lunchtime rush to get to the gym before everyone else does, and your horrible boss. Let's not overlook some of the biggest stressors in life: finances and relationships. Still, there's something intriguing about stress—many of us thrive on it. We want to be challenged. We want to feel the pressure. We want to improve. And, believe it or not, stress can be good for you.

Of course, there are times when stress can be bad for your health, but stress is also, in different forms, essential for your happiness, success, and fulfillment. If you eliminate all stress, you actually become less able to deal with it. And without it, you can't enjoy the thrills, pressures, and challenges that make life and work worthwhile and meaningful. No stress, in other words, can equal no joy.

The chapters in this part of the book explore both stress and relaxation. "Make Stress Work for You" describes how stress can be both positive and negative, and the chapter offers tools to help you work out which type you are feeling and how to make it work to your advantage. The more you know about your stress, the better equipped you are to deal with it.

"Combat Stress" focuses on getting down to business. Basically, you'll learn how to avoid letting stress get in the way of your productivity. The chapter includes surefire strategies to deal with the negative kinds of stress that paralyze you. This is the go-to chapter when you're experiencing bad stress and want practical advice about coping with it.

Finally, "Switch Your Mind Off" offers two very practical techniques for instant relief from negative stress that can be used anywhere, at any time. It may sound silly that you need to teach yourself to relax. However, after using the techniques in this chapter, you'll quickly understand how powerful true relaxation can be—and you'll wish you'd read this chapter years ago.

We feel it. You feel it. Everyone feels stress. The questions are: Do you understand the stress you feel and how to manage it? Do you understand how to leverage it to your advantage? Do you know how to truly relax?

Take a deep breath, because you're about to find out.

CHAPTER 18

Make Stress Work for You

Alice grew up in New York City. Now, at the age of twenty-eight, she is finally getting her driver's license—a requirement for her exciting new job as a family counselor in Atlanta. Today she's taking her final driving lesson before the test. She arrives early to chat with her instructor. After fifteen lessons, Alice is feeling pretty confident. She gets in the car and starts to drive. Two minutes later, while talking about what she was watching on TV last night, Alice fails to spot a van pulling out of a driveway and she has to jam on the brakes. Then she starts to concentrate. Without even thinking, she checks her rearview mirror, gently releases the brake, uses her blinker with plenty of warning, steers smoothly around a corner, and, altogether, drives like a professional.

Parking proves to be a little trickier. Even though she's done it perfectly on the last three occasions, she almost hits the curb. Nevertheless, she recovers. The rest of her final lesson is a little jerky, but she finishes without another incident. She thinks she's made it to the end. She feels okay. But when she pulls in to a final stop, she forgets to shift out of drive before she tries to take the key out of the ignition. Obviously she can't remove the key. Nervous now and not knowing what to do, she takes her foot off the brake. The car begins to roll forward. She screams in frustration, and her instructor has to calm her down and help.

If we wanted to plot Alice's driving lesson on a chart, it would look something like this:

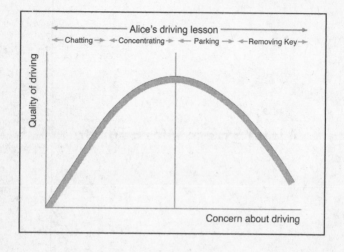

A hundred years ago two psychologists, Robert Yerkes and John Dodson, created a similar-looking graph to show how our level of "arousal"— our physiological and psychological level of alertness—affects what and how much we achieve.[1] In the same way that the quality of Alice's driving increased once she stopped chatting and started concentrating, Yerkes and Dodson suggested that as our arousal goes up, so does our performance. (Okay, chuckle at that last sentence. It's fair to assume that double entendres went unnoticed when Yerkes and Dodson were writing at the beginning of the twentieth century.) The effect arousal has on performance is clear in Alice's example: Her attitude changed from confident to concerned when she failed to spot the van, and then from concerned to stressed when she struggled to park the car. High levels of arousal (again, it's okay to chuckle) led to a decline in her performance. In fact, excessive arousal, such as Alice being unable to get the key out of the ignition, leads to no performance at all.

Yerkes and Dodson's model of how arousal impacts performance was developed further by psychologist Hans Selye. Selye correlated levels of arousal to distinctive stages of stress: The section of the chart where performance is improved by increased arousal are what he named the "calm" and "eustress" stages. Selye defined "eustress" as euphoric stress, or positive stress.[2] An example of the eustress stage would be the increased adrenaline rush you feel while playing basketball and sinking three-pointers like a pro. Selye called the section of the graph where arousal starts damaging your performance the "distress" and "extreme distress" stages (see the following figure). An example of the distress stage is when the time on the scoreboard is running down. Everyone is counting on you to make the final shot, the fans of the opposing team are booing you, and as a result, you find it hard to focus.

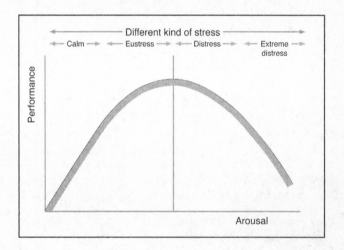

By identifying these four distinct stages of stress, Selye showed that stress can be both good and bad. There's an optimum point where the right amount of arousal results in increased performance. If you have much more arousal than that, it will have a negative effect on you. But if you stay below the optimum point in your arousal graph, gradually *increasing* your arousal levels until you've reached your optimum point will produce a positive result.

Somewhere along the way, however, Selye's impressive findings got lost. As the pace of all our working lives increased to frenetic, his subtle distinctions between the four stages of stress were left behind. In fact, the term "stress" has become a single catchall term to encompass both eustress and distress; "distress" now refers to what Selye called "extreme distress."[3]

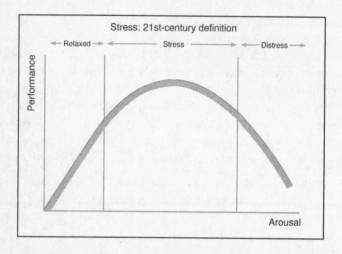

By losing this distinction, we've also lost the ability to distinguish between positive stress and negative stress; instead, we are left with the false assumption that all stress is bad. And if we can't diagnose the stress correctly, then we are highly likely to prescribe the wrong solution.

WHAT DO YOU DO UNDER PRESSURE?[4]

A study published in *Frontiers in Psychology* proved that pressure does increase performance.[5] Participants of the study were put under pressure to succeed at a physical task of throwing a ball at a target and meeting an accuracy goal. Randomly, some participants were told that their personality assessments indicated they were the type of person who would do well under pressure, and a control group was told unrelated/nonspecific personality assessment feedback. In the control group, only 27 percent of the participants met the accuracy goal, compared with nearly 90 percent of the participants in the group that was told they'd perform well under pressure.

What Happens When You Confuse Stress?

Sally is an actress auditioning for a role in a musical. If she gets the part, it would be her big break and she could finally quit her job as a waitress. Given that the stakes are high, she's been rehearsing hard and is bouncing off the walls with adrenaline. At this point, her arousal level is high—and so is her performance:

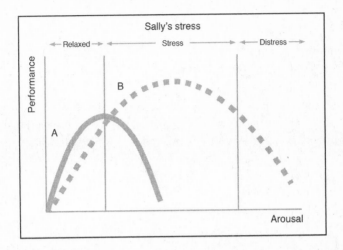

This is where our modern one-size-fits-all definition of stress comes into play. If you asked Sally if she was stressed, she'd probably reply "Yes." She assumes, like most of us do, that stress is a bad thing. Her response to any stress is to relax, in hopes that by reducing stress she'll improve her performance. So, she decides to go shopping to calm her nerves.

Sally's mistaken analysis of the situation (that she is stressed) leads her to pursue the wrong action (relaxing), which creates the opposite effect to what she intends (decreasing her stress and lowering her arousal, curve A), marginalizing her performance instead of honing and perfecting it. In fact, Sally was coping well with the adrenaline of rehearsing, and by continuing to focus she could have greatly improved her performance. In other words, by *adding* stress Sally could have improved her performance (curve B).

Although Sally assumes that all stress is bad, she is still considered "laid-back" compared to many other people who don't handle stress well. In a similar situation to Sally's, these people might avoid any and all stress until their resilience to stress is negligible—they can no longer deal with any. At that point, waiting tables during the quiet periods could be too stressful.

There are, however, two pieces of good news. First, if you can identify where you are on the stress curve, you can take the right steps to improve your performance. Second, just as you can mentally redraw your stress curve downward (that is, relax), you can also redraw it upward and become more resilient.

Welcome to Club Stress

As we mentioned earlier, the key to coping with stress is to identify where you are on the stress curve. In order to do so, it is useful to consider the curve as having four distinct zones. Think of these four zones as four different rooms in a club, and each has its own ambience and atmosphere (see the following figure). By looking at each zone in detail, you can make a decision as to where you are and where you want to be at any particular moment.

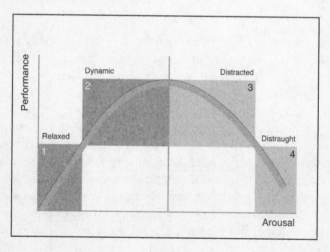

Relaxed: The Chill Zone

There's no doubt about it: the Chill Zone is a great place to be. The music is smooth and gentle. The lighting is soft. Everyone's talking quietly rather than shouting to be heard. There are cozy sofas and soft chairs to sit on. The hustle of the rest of the world seems a million miles away. Everyone is happy, unwinding, laid-back, and relaxed.

The people hanging out in the Chill Zone are pretty much at their lowest level of arousal. If they are thinking at all, their thoughts might resemble these:

• It's not that important. It's not my problem.

• Life is good.

• Yeah, whatever. I'm not bothered.

• Isn't the world a beautiful place?

• No need to worry. It'll all work out in the end.

• I'm bored, bored, bored.

Some people spend most of their lives in the relaxed zone. James, a participant at a Mind Gym event, told us that he never really experienced stress. The only thing he felt even remotely stressed about was the fact that his peers had all progressed further than him at work. This made perfect sense to us. In order not to experience stress of any kind, James must spend most of his time in the relaxed zone. As a result, his performance rarely reaches that of his peers, who, willing to experience stress, had improved their performance and had been promoted as a result.

Most popular advice on managing stress suggests that the relaxed zone is your ideal default position. This isn't quite true. People who spend most of their lives in this zone, like James, are in danger of letting the world pass them by. The relaxed zone is a good place to be every now and then, when you're on vacation, for example, or at the end of a tough day. Everyone needs time and space to unwind. But to do so, there needs to be something to unwind from.

Dynamic: The Thrill Zone

If the Chill Zone is cool, then the Thrill Zone is hot. The music is upbeat, the lights are sharp, and everybody's dancing.

Remember Hans Selye, the psychologist we introduced earlier in the chapter who came up with the idea of eustress? This is his room. It's the place to be when the adrenaline's pumping and you're in top form. This is the zone where "go-getters" reside—people who are fulfilling their potential at work and are pushing for promotion. People here feel these sorts of things:

- I'm excited, exhilarated, and enjoying myself.
- I'm nervous.
- I'm under pressure / being tested / being pushed to succeed.
- I'm determined.
- Every moment counts.
- Time is distorted; long periods of time feel like a few seconds.

This is Mindy's room. She's a doctor friend of ours who told us, "I'm bored of people telling me they're tired. In my opinion, if you're not tired, you're not living." She's right: don't be put off with all the advice from the stress scaremongers; the dynamic zone can be a great and rewarding place to be. If you want to achieve challenging goals and aren't satisfied with just "getting by," you need to spend considerable time in this zone.

Distracted: The Spill Zone

At first glance, this zone doesn't look too different from the previous one. But while the Thrill Zone was hot, at the Spill Zone, things are just starting to boil over. It's a little bit competitive at the bar. People keep bumping into you and spilling your drink. There is still a lot of talent on the dance floor, but you're trying to impress too many people at the same time. Whereas the Thrill Zone felt fun, here you're starting to feel hassled.

If you spend a lot of time in the dynamic zone, you will, almost inevitably, slip into the distracted zone every once in a while. It's not a fantastic place to be. When you are in this zone, you tend to spend a lot of time worrying. You focus on the impossibility of your situation rather than what you can do to get out of it. These are the types of things people in the distracted zone might be thinking:

- I don't know where to start.
- No one appreciates the pressure I'm under.
- This is going to be a disaster. I'm not sure that I can see a way out.
- I have so much to do. How on earth am I going to do it all?

Quite simply, *Argghhhh!*

The trick is to make your visits to the distracted zone occasional and short (that's what the following chapters are all about).

Distraught: The Kill Zone

Now things are going from bad to worse. In the Kill Zone, it's too hot, the lights are too bright, the music is too noisy, and the dance floor is too crowded. You've been waiting half an hour at the bar, but no one will serve you. Your head is starting to thump and the taxi you booked is still two hours away.

One of the big differences between the distracted zone and the distraught zone is that when you are in the distracted zone, you recognize that you are worrying or stressing about a specific, temporary situation. When you are in the distraught zone, however, it seems like the stress and worrying will go on forever. Everything is on top of you and you can't see a way out. The situation is so grave that it stretches into your foreseeable future—there is no escape.

Here are the sorts of things people might be thinking in this zone:

- My life is a mess/disaster.

- There's no way out.

- The world is out to get me.

- I am useless.

- I just can't cope anymore.

- Everything I touch goes wrong.

- I can't concentrate on anything.

- Even simple tasks take ages.

Many of us have been in the distraught zone briefly, but usually we see some hope or relief and get out quickly. Staying in the distraught zone for extended periods of time is dangerous. It can be like quicksand, dragging you into a sense of hopelessness from which, after a while, it is not easy to pull back.

WHERE IS HAPPINESS?

Mihaly Csikszentmihalyi isn't just a potentially award-winning Scrabble word. He's also the former chairman of the Department of Psychology at the University of Chicago. Csikszentmihalyi has spent thirty years conducting research with thousands of people across the world to find out what happens at their moments of greatest enjoyment. What he discovered was that one, two, or up to eight of the factors in the following list are involved:[6]

1. We have a chance of completing the tasks we are confronting.

2. We can concentrate on what we are doing.

3. We have clear goals.

4. We receive immediate feedback.

5. We feel a deep and effortless involvement that is all-embracing.

6. We have a sense of control over our actions.

7. We don't think about ourselves during the activity but think better of ourselves after we have completed it.

8. Our sense of the duration of time is altered.

With each of the factors listed, the people involved in the study experienced significant amounts of eustress; they were firmly in the dynamic zone. However, Csikszentmihalyi also believes that if you are satisfied with passive pleasure—enjoying an experience without having to actively engage with it, like lying on a beach—which he rates as a much weaker contributor to happiness, you are likely to find pleasure when you are relaxed.

So, where is happiness? Somewhere below the point at which your performance drops off, depending on what kind of person you are.

Your Zone

Different people have different propensities toward particular zones. Take a look at the following questions and statements and decide which responses best describe your thoughts in each situation. You'll discover which zone you're likely to spend most of your time in, and that will give you a good idea of how to better manage your stress. Circle your most likely response to the situation provided.

1. You are stuck in traffic and will arrive late to your appointment. What do you think?

   a. What are a few minutes? There's not much I can do about it anyway.

   b. Let me see if there's another route. I'll call to warn them.

   c. This is so unlucky. If only I'd left earlier.

   d. I can't believe it. I'm going to be really late. This is a disaster.

2. You have an important deadline that is fast approaching and no idea how you are going to deliver good-quality results on time.

   a. I'm sure it will all work out somehow or other.

   b. This is an exciting challenge. Let's get going.

   c. I don't know where to begin.

   d. This is impossible. It's going to be a catastrophe.

3. Someone asks you to do something urgent, which means that you will need to change your plans significantly.

   a. Yeah, sure.

   b. I'll rise to the challenge and make it work.

   c. I can't believe you're doing this to me. I have my own things to do too.

   d. This is the final straw. I can't possibly do it as well.

4. Your flight was delayed, the villa is nothing like the picture in the brochure, and it's raining.

   a. We're on vacation. It doesn't really matter. Let's just enjoy ourselves.

   b. This is no good. I'll get the tour operator to sort this out.

   c. The airline is incompetent and the travel agency is crooked. I am furious.

   d. This is the worst vacation of my life. I wish I'd stayed at home.

5. You check your bank balance and it's looking much worse than you thought.

   a. Who cares about money? At least I have my health.

   b. I'll sort this out. Not quite sure how yet, but I'll get on this right away.

   c. And that's before I pay the bills at the end of the month. What am I going to do?

   d. Everything in my life is going wrong. I'm a walking disaster zone.

6. Which of the following best describes your view on life?

   a. Life's a breeze (though it can be a bit boring sometimes).

   b. My life is a constant stream of exciting, fresh challenges.

   c. I have too much going on at the moment and I don't know how I'll cope.

   d. My life is a mess.

Check Your Zone

Mostly a's: Relaxed

For people who spend most of their time in the relaxed zone, the question is whether or not you are happy. If you are, then great, though you might wonder if you are fulfilling your potential. If you would like to spend more time in the dynamic zone, you may want to set yourself some challenges that really stretch you.

Mostly b's: Dynamic

People here are definitely experiencing stress, but they have nothing to worry about and potentially lots to celebrate. This is a great place to be, provided there is an occasional dip into the relaxed zone to recharge. High performers who spend a lot of time in this zone may well slip into the distracted zone now and again. As long as this is spotted and acted on, there is no reason for concern.

Mostly c's: Distracted

People here feel stressed quite a lot, and it isn't the good stress. Anyone who spends a lot of time here may want to rethink how their life is structured. The tips and techniques in the following chapters will be a great help in reducing negative stress and moving back to the dynamic zone.

Mostly d's: Distraught

People here are likely to be suffering from stress. They should stop and remember when life was more enjoyable. It may not be easy, but there are definitely ways to make life good again, or better. It might be wise to talk things through with someone—family, friends, or a professional.

Sort Out Your Stress

The good news is that the person who can do the most to affect your stress zones, and leverage the good stress while managing the bad, is you. And if you can combine that knowledge with the tactics and techniques in the next few chapters, you can learn to not only understand and manage stress (both good and bad) but also leverage it to your advantage.

GIVE YOUR MIND A WORKOUT

Beginner: Remembering Your Dynamic Zone

1. Think back to a time you were experiencing eustress. Close your eyes and imagine it; replay it in your head.

2. Now answer the following questions: What were you doing? How did you feel? How did the eustress you felt in one area of your life positively influence other areas of your life?

3. Assess what you can start doing now to bring some eustress into your life (i.e., is there a new challenge you could take on, or can you look at a stressor in a different light so it becomes a source of eustress instead of distress?)

4. Do it.

Advanced: Where Are You on the Curve?

Go through your average day and write which zone you think you are in *every thirty minutes*. Set an alarm, perhaps in your phone, to remind you when to document which zone you are in, what you're doing, and what you're thinking and feeling at the time. At the end of day, look at your graph and answer the following questions:

- Are you spending most of the day in the relaxed or dynamic zones?

- At what times do you move into the distracted or distraught zones?

- What is going on in your mind and body at those moments?

The next chapter will show you what you can do to move closer to the dynamic zone, but for now, this exercise will help you become more aware of exactly when you transition through zones and why you transition.

CHAPTER 19

Combat Stress

Fred is sitting in solid traffic on his way to his brother's wedding. If it doesn't clear soon, he will miss the start of the ceremony. It's a very small gathering at their local church. If he doesn't make it, he's going to be in a world of trouble. Why didn't he take the train or leave half an hour earlier? He feels completely helpless. The more he realizes that there is nothing he can do, the angrier he gets. He imagines his father's reaction. He imagines his mother's disappointment. Soon, Fred's frustration turns to dread, and his dread turns to panic.

Fred's other brother, Chris, is in a car about fifteen miles behind Fred. He's stuck in the same traffic jam. Like Fred, he is going to the wedding and he's expected to read in the ceremony. Chris decides, however, that since there is nothing he can do about the traffic, there is no point in worrying. He is better off doing something useful. He sits back and starts to practice his speech.

Chris and Fred's half sister, Anne, is twelve cars ahead of Fred. Yep, she's stuck too. Anne has spent the last ten minutes on the phone to a traffic hotline to try to find out how long she'll be stuck. She's left a message for her mother to tell her the situation and to see if the ceremony can be pushed back. Then it occurs to her that Fred might also be stuck in traffic, so she picks up her phone again and dials.

Fred, Chris, and Anne are all stranded in the same situation. Yet they each have very different approaches to dealing with it. In the previous chapter we discussed how to differentiate between positive stress (which boosts your performance) and negative stress (which inhibits your performance). Anne is a good example of someone who is experiencing positive stress. She is alert and focused on productive activity; she has figured out what she can do given the circumstances and has started to implement her plan. Fred, on the other hand, is working himself into a frenzy that will only end up making things worse. Fred's way of dealing with this stressful situation is not really dealing with it at all. Finally, Chris's reaction is to relax rather than stress about the situation.

We have all, at different times, experienced each of these reactions. At one stage or another, we have freaked like Fred, chilled like Chris, and reacted effectively to a situation like Anne. However, we probably didn't think about whether our reaction was the best approach for that specific situation. Instead, we jumped into doing whatever felt right at the time. The purpose of this chapter is to give you more choices for how to respond when you are about to become, or already are, negatively stressed.

HOW DO YOU SEE STRESSFUL SITUATIONS?

Most of us would find skydiving fairly stressful. However, if a skydiving instructor was about to make her 300th jump, the chances are she would barely be stressed at all.

Psychologists Richard Lazarus and Susan Folkman suggest that the way in which you view a situation makes just as much difference to your level of stress as the situation itself. They call this concept "cognitive appraisal."[1]

Among the most influential factors in determining how stressed you feel are your personal beliefs (e.g., jumping out of planes is dangerous) and situational factors—how familiar or predictable the event is (e.g., the first jump versus the 300th).

This difference in perception is one of the main reasons why, in identical situations, some people remain totally calm while others become highly distressed. The beautiful thing about this theory is that you can alter your level of stress simply by choosing to think about the situation differently.[2]

In the pages that follow, we present nine tactics of tackling stress—we call them stressbusters. Each has its own strengths. Of course, one stressbuster will be more useful than another in different situations. Or you may need a combination of stressbusters to help you out of a proverbial jam. The nine stressbusters are ordered, roughly, from those that require thinking about a situation differently, like Chris in the example earlier, to those that focus on taking action, like Anne. If you master these stressbusters and discover how to combine them to create the best effect, you'll discover a new level of control in your life.

Stressbuster One: Minimize the Situation

Distress occurs when we believe not only that we aren't capable of dealing with a situation but also that the situation itself is important. One simple way of reducing your level of stress is by changing your assessment of the *situation* (which has the bonus effect of making the outcome seem less crucial).

Quite often, of course, the opposite is the case. The more you think about the thing you're stressed about, the more important it feels. Fred is anxious about missing his brother's wedding because, of course, a wedding is an important family milestone. While he is stuck in traffic, his mind might be telling him, *Well, don't worry about being late for the next family gathering. You won't be invited. Your father's will? Forget about it. He'll probably just leave you his watch to remind you what an idiot you've been.* This type of runaway thinking is known as a "catastrophic fantasy." We all create catastrophic fantasies in our heads when faced with certain stressful situations. Consider your thoughts the last time you were late for a meeting. Consider the nights you laid in bed awake worrying how you might lose your job because of some minor miscommunication.

If you are in a stressful situation and working out a catastrophic fantasy in your mind, the first step is to remind yourself that the scenario you're imagining may sound catastrophic but it is also just a fantasy. So, dismiss it. If you can pause and listen to yourself, you will probably realize that it is a highly unlikely scenario.

The second step is to reverse the fantasy: Rather than paint the most negative version of the situation, go the other way and give the situation the most positive twist possible. As an example, Fred could change his thinking to this: *I'm going to be late for the wedding, but I'm not the first person to be late for a wedding and I won't be the last. They can either delay things until I get there or they can proceed without me. My brother will be annoyed, but at the end of the day, he is my brother, and he knows I want to be there. He'll forgive me. Or if he does hold a grudge because I'm a few minutes late, well, that's his problem not mine. I know I've done my best. If being late for my brother's wedding is the worst thing I've ever done to him, then I guess it shows what a good relationship we have.*

By playing the situation down, reducing the importance and impact of being a few minutes late, Fred could avoid becoming so distraught.

Stressbuster Two: Minimize the Outcome

Much like exaggerating the importance of an event, you might also tend to exaggerate the probability of a negative outcome.

Marie, a participant in a Mind Gym event, recounted a horror story about sending out a company e-newsletter. After sending the e-newsletter to the company's employees, Marie realized that she'd made a major mistake. The graphs on the lead story were wrong: rather than illustrating one business's success, the graph suggested a massive failure. In a state of panic, Marie offered to send a personal email to that business, explaining her mistake. But rather than take her up on her offer, her boss told her not to worry. "To be quite honest," he continued, "I'm not sure how many people will notice." He was right: out of the twenty thousand people who received the e-newsletter, not one mentioned it.

Marie was correct in her perception that it would be extremely bad news if everyone had thought that the business was a failure. But she was also wrong to assume that everyone, or indeed anyone, would notice her error. Playing down the probability of a bad outcome is a very powerful way to counteract distress.

Stressbuster Three: Reframe the Situation

Imagine someone is trying to rent out their house but is having problems attracting interest because of the small size of the bedrooms. By repainting the walls in a lighter color and removing some of the furniture and clutter, the owner can make the rooms feel bigger and more attractive. In a similar way, a stressful situation can appear much less daunting if you think about it, or "reframe" it, in a different way.

For example, you are trying to organize a vacation but everything is going wrong. The cheap tickets you spotted online are now twice the price. The hotel your friend recommended as "the only place worth staying at" is fully booked. A close friend has announced that he is having his birthday party in the middle of your proposed vacation dates. And just when you thought nothing else could go wrong, you discover that your passport is due to expire in three weeks.

Your initial reaction to all this may be to give up—everything's getting too stressful and conspiring against you. But by reframing the situation, things could look far more positive and, therefore, far less stressful. The cheap airline tickets are gone: flying first class rather than coach might be more expensive but at least you'll really enjoy the eight-hour flight. The hotel is fully booked: you can probably find a hidden gem that won't be so touristy. Your close friend is having a birthday party: you can celebrate separately, without having to deal with or listen to his crazy sister. Your passport is expiring: It's about time! You can finally get rid of that terrible picture.

Reframing is not creating Pollyanna optimism, in which everything is roses and there's no other way to see the world; instead, it's thinking differently about the external facts and focusing on what is good about them rather than what is not.

Stressbuster Four: Celebrate the Positive

Feeling stressed leaves us feeling depressed. One way of tackling this feeling of depression is to think of all the good things that are going on in your life at the moment. For example, the offer you made on a house fell through and it seems that finding a decent place to live is impossible. But what are the good things in life at the moment? Get a piece of paper and write them all down. Do you have close friends? An interesting job? Are you in love? Hey, you still have enough money to buy a new house. All the waiting and planning you did before you made the offer has put you in a great financial position.

Chances are that your list will be longer than you expect. Thinking about the positive things in your life will take the attention away from the negative stress, which in turn makes you feel better. When things are going right, don't be afraid to celebrate. Rather than worry about the next thing you need to tackle, pat yourself on the back. It will help boost your energy level for the next challenge.

At the end of a busy day set aside a couple of minutes to think through what you have achieved rather than what you have to do tomorrow. This will reduce your level of anxiety and help you sleep better too.

Stressbuster Five: Use Your Mental Energy Wisely

If the first four stressbusters don't seem to be enough, try asking the following question: *Is worrying about the situation helping me? Is there something better I could be doing with all this mental energy?* You have only so much mental energy to go around. If you're using it all worrying, then you won't have the energy to address the issues that are causing all the grief in the first place. If you save your energy for something more worthwhile, you're more likely to get the situation fixed, and you'll feel better about yourself in the process.

Stressbuster Six: Take a Break

Sometimes the best way of dealing with excessive stress is to escape from it. Sure, you could literally try to walk away from it—a change of scenery and getting some oxygen into your brain might just help you see things differently. But you can also choose a mental escape, resolving not to think about the situation for a while. Or a break may involve taking time out (an evening off or a night out on the town), so that when you return to the situation, you have a fresh perspective. Of course, escaping for too long can be dangerous. The causes of distress may have increased while you were away, making your level of distress even greater. But a short break can also help to put things into perspective and bring long-term benefits.

Stressbuster Seven: Seek Support from Friends[3]

Sometimes the best way of dealing with a stressful situation is to share your thoughts with someone else rather than carry the burden alone.[4] It sounds too simple to work, but talking through a situation will actually help you feel better.[5] Most of us have played a support role for our friends, colleagues, and family. There is no reason why they wouldn't be delighted to do the same for you. But remember, your friends (okay, at least *our* friends) aren't clairvoyant. You will need to ask them for support if you are going to benefit from their help. Here are some ways a friend or colleague can offer support:

- Listen and empathize: "He really called you that? No wonder you feel terrible. They don't know how lucky they are to have you there."

- Challenge your assumptions about what is happening: "Are you sure that is what he meant? Things written in emails can sound far more aggressive than they actually are."

- Facilitate a solution to the situation: "Why don't I ask him if he wants to join us for coffee or a drink after work to clear the air?"

- Help come up with solutions: "Let's get together and see if we can think up some more creative alternatives."

- Actually do things on your behalf: "I'll make some posters and put them on trees around the area. Does he answer to another name besides Rover?"

- Lend or give you the physical or financial support that would alleviate the cause of your distress: "I've just done my expenses, so I'm fine for money at the moment. I'll pay to have the red wine stain removed and you can pay me back when you want. He'll never know it happened."

This is what friends are for (well, one of the reasons), so don't be afraid to ask for help.

Stressbuster Eight: Ask the Right Questions (and Act on the Answers)

When we get distressed, we often ask ourselves the wrong questions, if we ask any questions at all. By asking the right questions, you can get to the heart of why you are distressed. And once you know this, you can take the appropriate action to reduce the distress.

So, what are the right questions? Well, they're not the ones in which you start beating yourself up about the situation (e.g., *How could I have been so stupid? What made me think I could cope with this?*) Instead, the questions to ask are straightforward and involve doing something practical. Questions (and answers) like these:

- What is the real cause of my stress? (I might miss the wedding, as opposed to being a few minutes late.)

- What could I do to reduce the demands of the situation? (Maybe I should call ahead and try to get the wedding moved back an hour.)

- What alternative ways are there to address the cause of my stress? (I should look at a map and see if I can turn off at the next exit and find another route.)

- What can I do to increase my resources? (I could call a traffic hotline to find out what is causing the delay and how long I might be waiting here.)

- What can others do to help? (While I am listening to the traffic hotline, someone at the wedding can alert the minister that people are going to be late.)

- What should I do and in what sequence? (I should call my father first and explain the situation to see if there is any way the start of the wedding can be delayed. Next, I'll call the traffic hotline to see how long the delay is likely to be. Finally, I'll call Fred and Chris to see if they are in the same situation.)

In our original wedding example, Anne discovers one of those perfect circles in order to cope with stress. By getting things done, she is able to keep calm. And by keeping calm, she is able to get things done. But however smart Anne is in coping with the situation, she could still be smarter by asking herself two more questions, once the wedding is over:

- Is this cause of stress, or something similar, likely to happen again?

- If so, what can I do to prepare for it?

By learning from your experiences, you can start to build up your stress immune system, which means that you are less likely to experience distress in the future, or at least you'll be better equipped to deal with it when you do.

Stressbuster Nine: Confront the Situation

You can either accept the demands and pressures that people put on you or you can challenge them. Sometimes confronting the issue head-on is the best way of reducing the distress you feel. For example, you might tell a coworker, "I know I said we'd meet this afternoon, but I'm afraid I can't any longer." By confronting the issue head-on, quite often you'll discover the situation is not as bad as you first thought.

A common situation this tactic helps with is in your relationship with your boss. You desire not to look weak in front of him or her, and you try to carry on as if nothing is wrong. The truth is, it's far better to let your boss know how you feel. Nine times out of ten they will respect you more for being honest.

Create a Stressbusting Strategy

Reading this section might raise your awareness of aspects of your life that you need to deal with. Maybe you feel with some aspects it's already too late. Or maybe a situation has just arisen. Either way, it's good to create a game plan—a strategy of stressbusters.

Imagine the following situation:

For a week I put off opening the letter from the bank. I finally decide to look inside and see how bad the situation is. Oh my goodness, they must have made a mistake! I know I've been spending a lot on my credit card, but this is crazy. It can't be right, can it? What am I going to do?

They'll stop my card. I won't be able to keep up with my mortgage payments. They'll repossess the house and I'll go bankrupt. It'll be virtually impossible to borrow ever again.

I should have opened the bank letter when it arrived. By not responding quickly, I've made the situation even worse. And now I'm late for my class at the gym. Not that I'm going to be able to concentrate properly, not while I'm worrying about this . . .

It's a tough and potentially scary situation. The question is, What is the best way to deal with it? Before reading on, it might be worth skimming back through the nine stressbusters and deciding which you think would be most useful in this case. There is no "right" answer, but here are some suggestions:

Minimize the Outcome

Let's be realistic. I'm a long way off having my house repossessed. The worst scenario in the short term is that I can't withdraw cash or write checks for a week or two. Well, I never write checks anyway, and I'll just use one of my other credit cards if things get tight.

Celebrate the Positive

It's not all bad. I have a good job that is relatively secure. I'm healthy and fit. The sun is shining, and I've just come back from a fantastic vacation.

Reframe the Situation

It's not like I haven't been in this situation before. I was deeply in debt when I left college and I managed to pay that off eventually. If I can do it once, I'm sure I can do it again.

Seek Support from Friends

I'll call Jim. His wife works in a bank and he may be able to find out how these things work.

Ask the Right Questions (and Act on the Answers)

What is the real cause of my stress? In the short term, I might not be able to cover a round of beers at the bar. In the medium term, I might not be able to pay my mortgage and my house might be repossessed. What if the bank has made a mistake? I should check the letter thoroughly and call them if I have any questions.

What can I do to cut my costs? I won't eat out for the next few weeks. I will cancel my cable TV subscription. What can I do to increase my income? I can rent out the spare room if the mortgage becomes a problem. I also have some stocks—I could cash some of those in. What can I do to keep the bank off my back? I could write to them and let them know what I am doing to address the situation.

Take a Break

Once I've done all this, I'll go to the gym—maybe tomorrow—and lose myself totally in a class and not think about my debts again until afterward.

This combination of stressbusters is just one suggested strategy for approaching this situation. Of course, there are others that would be equally useful. And what they should show is this: each of the nine stressbusters is great by itself, but they are most effective when combined to deal with the stress of a situation.

Trip Wires and Alarm Calls

This chapter is filled with stressbusters to cope with a situation once your stress levels are already up. But there is another way to look at dealing with stress: Attack it before it actually occurs. If you can teach yourself what the telltale signs are of getting stressed, you can take preemptive action and stop the stress before it ever starts. There are two kinds of early warning systems for distress: trip wires and alarm calls.

Trip Wires

Your shoulders get tense. You can't sit down for more than a minute before you are up again, and you pace back and forth. You chew the end of the pen until it, like you, is a gnarly mess.

Whatever mannerisms or habits surface when you are stressed, it's your job to spot them. And when you see them arising, pause, think about your situation, and take the necessary steps before the distress occurs.

Alarm Calls

We all recognize signs that our partner, colleague, or child is about to have an emotional reaction. If you can recognize signs in them, they can do the same for you. Alarm calls are like trip wires except instead of recognizing your own stress habits, other people point them out for you. The people who know you best can warn you when you're about to get into a dangerous or distressed state. Yes, you may have to ask nicely to get them to tell you, but it's invaluable to have someone on the lookout.

After all, tapping someone on the arm and saying "Be careful, now; I think you are about to lose it" may be exactly what tips someone over the edge. To make the best use of your alarm calls, don't just ask friends, colleagues, or family members to warn you when they think you are heading into emotionally troubled waters but also suggest how they can tell you. Maybe they could open a bottle of expensive wine or give you a neck massage. The point is to agree on a simple way of warning you without prompting an overreaction, and everyone will benefit.

Stress comes in all shapes and sizes. It affects each of us differently. And each of us will prefer to combat stress in different ways. The good news is that you don't have to let it overrun your life. Call on the nine stressbusters. The more you practice them, the better you'll become at regaining control and giving yourself some relief.

GIVE YOUR MIND A WORKOUT

Beginner: Rethink the Past

1. Think about a recent event in your live that really stressed you out.

2. Use the strategies in this chapter to come up with better ways you could have handled the situation.

How could you have thought about it differently?_____

How could you have reacted differently?_____

What would have been the impact?_____

Advanced: Know Your Trip Wires and Alarm Calls

1. Think about a *recurring* stress in your life, and analyze the trip wires and alarm calls that are also recurring.

   Trip wires: _____

   Alarm calls: _____

2. Now think about what occurs before, during, and after this recurring stressor. What stressbusters can you put in place to manage your reaction?

   Before the stressor:_____

   During the stressor:_____

   After the stressor:_____

CHAPTER 20

Switch Your Mind Off

By this point in the book, you've learned a lot of new ways to exercise your mind. Now it's time to learn how to relax. Yes, it sounds simple. But due to our high-speed culture, constant connection to technology, and stressful lifestyles, you might be surprised by how many people struggle to relax. And if you think you're not a person who struggles, you might also be surprised to find out that by reading this chapter, you could experience a deeper level of relaxation. The human mind and body are equipped with some powerful tools: breathing and visualization. Use them correctly and you can send yourself on a vacation from stress any time you choose.

Breathing: It's Not Just Something That Happens

Breathing is less fattening than eating a tub of ice cream. It won't give you a hangover like a bottle of wine. It is less exhausting than an hour on the treadmill at the gym. And it's less expensive than an afternoon of shopping. Breathing is free, simple, and, if used properly, can instantly calm you down when life gets to be too much.

Consider the saying "Take a deep breath and count to ten." Most of us understand that statement to mean we should pause before we do something that we might later regret. What is often forgotten is the "deep breath" part of the sentence, yet it is of equal, if not greater, benefit.

Breathing 101: Learn the Basics

When you feel distressed, you breathe in a manner called "chest" breathing. The focus, as the name implies, is around your chest: Your breathing becomes shallow, irregular, and rapid. Less air is able to reach your lungs, and this in turn leads to an increased heart rate and greater muscle tension. However, it's not just distressing situations that create this physical situation. Chest breathing is also common when you are inactive. Take for instance many peoples' lives—and posture—at the office. Sitting at a desk and working at a computer encourages a breathing style that actually increases stress rather than helps you to unwind.

The alternative to chest breathing is a form of breathing known as "diaphragmatic" breathing. Rather than the emphasis being on your chest, you breathe with your diaphragm—a membrane that separates your lungs from your digestive system. The diaphragm is naturally taut and expands when you breathe in, then gently moves back into place when you breathe out.

While chest breathing is shallow, irregular, and rapid, diaphragmatic breathing is deep, even, and loose. It allows the respiratory system to work as effectively as possible. (It does this by using the full amount of oxygen to oxygenate the bloodstream, which helps waste products like carbon dioxide be removed.) Chest breathing leads to increased heart rate and muscle tension; diaphragmatic breathing lowers your heart rate and normalizes your blood pressure.

Learn How to Breath

The goal is to learn (and remember) to breathe using your diaphragm. If you do, you can gain control, choosing to position your body in a state closer to relaxation rather than to stress.

The first step is to become aware of the way you breathe. To do this, lie on the floor or sit in a relaxed posture in a chair, legs uncrossed. Place your right hand on your abdomen or stomach, just above your waistline, and your left hand on your chest. Close your eyes and notice how you are breathing. Which hand is rising and falling as you inhale and exhale?

Most of the time, adults breathe with their chests (so your left hand will move more than your right hand). Now try pushing out your stomach as you breathe so that you feel your right hand moving instead of your left. Can you feel the difference between the two types of breathing? At first it might seem strange to be pushing out your stomach to breathe, but after a while it will become more natural and less forced. Try not to make the breathing jerky or use your stomach muscles too much. Instead, allow your diaphragm to take over. Find a gentle rhythm and continue to do this for a couple of minutes. Soon the rhythm will feel comfortable—almost like you're not trying.

To understand the effect distress has on your breathing, try to think of something stressful, like being stuck in a traffic jam when you are late for a date. Most people who practice these exercises will find that their diaphragmatic breathing automatically reverts to chest breathing—in other words, their left hand starts to move more.

Over the next couple of days, pay attention to your breathing at different times and in different situations. Are you breathing from your chest more than your diaphragm?

Once you know how you are breathing, you can focus on how to make it better. What follows are two ways of doing so, thus helping you to relax.

Suggestive Breathing: Getting Your Brain Involved

The key to better breathing is to focus on your diaphragm rather than your chest. But you can make it even better by adding a mental process to the physical process.

During your diaphragmatic breathing, try saying or thinking the words "Breathe out tension." Bizarre as it may seem, it will help you relax. Basically, if you imagine an event, your brain reacts in much the same way as if the event is actually happening. By imagining yourself breathing out tension, you can make your brain respond as if you really were breathing out tension. After all, it doesn't matter whether the situation is real or imaginary; the important thing is that it helps you relax.

In the suggestive breathing exercise, as you inhale, become aware of tension in your body and say to yourself, "Breathe in for relaxation." Pause with the breath held inside you, and then exhale, letting go of any tension, saying to yourself, "Breathe out tension." Be prepared for funny looks if you say this out loud in a public place.

Some people go to the next stage when practicing this exercise, adding visualization to their breathing. As they exhale, they imagine their stress and tension being released from them, often as red mist. This red tension mist then slowly wafts away and eventually disappears from view.

Better Breathing Breath-less

"It was a nightmare," said Emma about her presentation. "I had fully prepared for weeks and thought I was ready to make an impact. But then, right before it was my turn to speak, I felt a tightening in my chest. It was very difficult to breathe, and I wondered whether I could stand in front of the group. I tried breathing in deeply, but I still didn't feel like I could get enough air. I continued taking deep breaths, again and again. When it was my turn to present, I sounded really breathy and nervous."

Emma is describing a common situation. When people feel panic or are put under stress, they have a tendency to gasp—take in a breath and hold on to it. The resulting sensation of fullness and inability to get enough air produces quick, shallow breathing. This can trigger a stress response that makes the situation even worse. Once again, diaphragmatic breathing is the solution. But this time rather than using a suggestion, such as "Breathe out tension," try what is known as the "ten-second cycle." First, inhale through your nose counting *one . . . two . . . three*. Pause for four, and exhale through your mouth, counting *five . . . six . . . seven . . . eight*. Pause for nine and ten, and then inhale again.

What you are trying to do is exhale for longer than you inhale. By taking deeper breaths than you need to, you are attempting to reduce the number of breaths you need to take. People tend to breathe more than they need to. Most of us, on average, take a breath every six to eight seconds, but in a recent survey, doctors found that the optimal breathing rate was significantly slower. In the study—published in *The Lancet,* one of the medical community's highly respected journals—researchers working with patients with heart disease discovered that patients using breathing techniques were able to increase their blood oxygen and perform better on exercise tests.[1] The researchers found that a breathing rate of about six breaths per minute, or one every ten seconds, was around the optimum frequency. The closer you can get to this optimum number of breaths per minute, and the longer the pauses between your breaths, the more relaxed you will feel.

Every Breath You Take

The real payoff of better breathing comes when you don't use it just as a last resort for dealing with stress but regularly, to position your body close to a state of relaxation most of the time.

How can you create reminders for yourself to regulate your breathing? Tim, a friend of ours, uses Post-it notes stuck on his computer to remind him about diaphragmatic breathing and posture. Think about where and when such reminders might be useful, and give them a try. And remember this: if you can improve your breathing, the most basic of human functions, you will be infinitely better equipped to deal with stress, whenever it occurs.

Visualization: The Mental Cure for Stress

If breathing is the physical tool to reduce stress, then visualization is the mental tool. Consider this scenario:

It's Friday night after work. You're on your way to meet a friend for a weekend trip to Las Vegas. Well, it's a good thing Las Vegas never sleeps, because your plane hasn't left the tarmac. The pilot apologizes for the delay, and it's no big deal at first. Time and time again the pilot apologizes. Ten minutes have now turned into ninety minutes. You check your watch, notice the amount of time that has slipped away, and realize that your first night of partying is being held hostage by an overcrowded runway. In such a moment, your stress is instant, and you want instant relief.

Visualization, like better breathing, acts as a sort of psychological medicine. Wherever you are, whatever the situation, it offers immediate relief and a rapid reduction of your stress level. Scientifically proven, the visualization technique may take a little time to master, but it's well worth it—because when you learn how to do it, it has great power.[2]

Visualization 101: How to Create Your Perfect Daydream

It may be a summer's day in the park. It may be a deep and luxurious bath. It may be sunbathing on a Caribbean beach. When you have a hectic and stressful day, you have an image in your head about where you'd rather be. This is visualization—in essence, it's creating your most pleasant daydream.

Here's how it works. Every time you see an image, your mind gives it a meaning (in terms of what it means to you), and this meaning triggers an emotional or physical response. Look at the two following images, for example. What responses do they conjure up in you? Hunger? Nausea? Yum? Ugh?

Imagined images can trigger exactly the same reactions as real ones. In the same way that the image of a rotten apple can trigger disgust, the right type of visualization can trigger a state of relaxation. All you need to do is create images that you associate with calm and tranquillity. And unlike the real world, where a quick trip to the soothing shores of the Caribbean is out of your reach, visualization can take you wherever you want to go, immediately.

Emile Coué, a French pharmacist, came up with the idea of visualization, along with a whole host of positive thinking techniques.[3] Coué knew that the imagination is one of the strongest mental "tools" at your disposal. His stroke of genius was realizing that your imagination is more powerful than your will. Basically, this means that you can't will your way into a relaxed state of mind, but given practice, you can imagine your way into one.

Eyes Wide Shut: Yes, You Can See Whatever You Choose

Some people think they can't visualize. This is, of course, nonsense. They think visualization is more complicated than it actually is. At its simplest, visualization is imagining something that isn't actually there in front of you. It does require some effort—more than, say, watching a film, which is an almost entirely passive experience—but it is not difficult.

Here is a very simple example of visualization: Close your eyes. Imagine you are standing in front of the door to your home. What color is the door? Where is the keyhole? Is there a handle or doorknob? If so, what does it look like?

Well done. You have just visualized. Sure, it was a simple visualization, but you did it.

Now make your visualization more sophisticated. For instance, add in movement and start "visualizing" with your other senses (so far the focus has been entirely on sight). Read the following points, and then close your eyes again.

- You take your key out and hold it in your hand. What temperature is it against your skin? How heavy? What do the edges feel like?

- You put the key into the lock. What does this feel like? Does it slide in gently or is there some resistance?

- You turn the key. What do you hear?

- You push the door open. How does this feel? Where is the pressure? In your arms or elsewhere? The door opens; you step in. What is the smell?

You probably were able to clearly visualize at least one of these points—without ever leaving the comfort of your own mind. Maybe your strongest experience came from visualizing the feel of the key in your hand. Maybe your strongest was visualizing the smell of chocolate chip cookies in the oven as you pushed open the door. With practice, all the outcomes to the questions in each point will be crystal clear.

Here are some general tips that will help you visualize all these points and beyond:

Avoid Distractions

You will visualize better if you are not distracted by what you are actually looking at or hearing in real life. Find a quiet place to close your eyes.

Use Better Breathing

Earlier in this chapter we showed you how to breathe properly. Breathing prepares you to move into a state of relaxation, in which you are more likely to visualize effectively.

Involve All the Senses

Although the technique is called visualization, include also sound, touch, taste, and smell. When thinking of an apple, for example, what is the sound when you bite into it? Is its texture smooth? Does it taste fresh? Is there a soft, sweet smell?

Add Details, Movement, Depth, and Contrast

Vividness comes from adding details, and your eyes are attracted to movement (how things operate or how far away they are). By adding depth, contrast, and movement, your visualization becomes much fuller and three-dimensional. Imagine again taking a bite out of an apple. What do the teeth marks look like after you've taken that bite? How deep are they? What is the contrast between the outside and the inside of the apple? If you put the apple down, does it roll gently across the table before stopping?

Include Positive Emotions

Don't just see an apple, for example, but think how you might feel when you bite into it: satisfied, happy, content? Negative emotions in a visualization can add stress, so keep your mind searching for the good stuff.

Use Metaphors and Different Styles

Your visualization doesn't always have to be real. Anger could be a dark cloud rolling away into the distance and disappearing. Or, if it relaxes you, why not visualize in a specific style—like an impressionist artist painted your visualization or it's a movie shot to represent a specific genre.

Be Positive

In order to get the most from visualization, approach everything that occurs from a positive perspective. Rather than the sea being "rough," make the sea "strong." Music isn't "loud"; it's "empowering."

Suspend Judgment

Visualizations are not the time to critique, analyze, scrutinize, or evaluate. If you judge your visualization, you are more likely to restrict your imagination rather than unleash it.

Practice

As with most things, your ability to visualize will get better with time and effort.

Be Patient

You can't force visualization to happen; it takes time, and at first it may feel a little awkward and clumsy. Persevere. There will come a day when it will be a powerfully positive tool in your life.

Doing It: You Understand Visualizing, but Can You Do It?

Of course, it is impossible to read the guidelines for these visualizations and keep your eyes closed at the same time. Here is another, more in-depth visualization that you can use as practice. It focuses on a situation that we are all too familiar with. If you really want to experience it, use an audio recording device to record the steps and play them back when you're ready. (You could even speak it into a video on your smartphone; your eyes will be closed when you listen to it, so you won't be watching it anyway.) This example makes more use of all your senses and might take some practice to get right. But by learning to focus on the small details, you're going a long way toward improving your visualization.

Step One: Close your eyes and imagine a familiar bathroom sink in front of you.

Step Two: Imagine the water taps and some soap. Note the contours of the sink and how the color of the porcelain changes shades at different points. Look at the taps: the design, the reflection they may give, and the shadows they make. What color is the soap? What shape? Does it look like it is stuck to the sink, or is it loose?

Step Three: Now reach over and pull the drain lever to plug the sink. Then turn on the taps. Hear the splash of the water falling into the sink. How does the sound change as the sink starts to fill? Look at where the edge of the water touches the side of the sink. Is it a straight line or a wave? How quickly is the water level rising? Notice how the light flickers on the water's surface. When the sink is fairly full, turn off the taps.

Step Four: Put your hand into the water and check the temperature. If it is too hot or too cold, turn on the taps again until the water reaches the right temperature. Put both hands into the basin so the water laps against your wrists. How does this feel?

Step Five: Now take your hands out of the basin and pick up the soap. Notice its color, its shape, and its texture. Bring the bar up to your nose. What does it smell like?

Step Six: Roll the soap over in your hands and notice how it lathers and how your hands glide over each other. Put the soap down and notice the sound it makes as it is set on the sink. Continue washing your hands.

Step Seven: Put your hands back into the water. Hear the noise as they break the surface of the water. Note how it feels as you leave them in the water and how your hands change as you start to rub them together to remove the remaining lather from the soap. Notice how the water changes color and bubbles appear on the surface. What else can you see as you look into the sink?

Step Eight: Take your hands out of the water. Pick up a towel, noting its color and texture. Use it to dry your hands. Note how this feels and the patterns the towel makes as you use it.

Step Nine: Release the drain plug. Watch the water disappear. What do you hear? What does the sink look like now? How is it different from when you started, when it was empty a few moments ago?

Step Ten: Open your eyes and come out of the visualization.

This visualization went into far more detail than the previous one about opening the front door. Once you get used to the process, it becomes easier to delve deeper into visualizations and create specific sensations.

You can also purposefully alter the circumstances of your visualization, which leads to a whole new string of experiences within your visualization (for example, the soap bar could slide out of your hand and fall onto the floor). If you aren't yet comfortable with visualizing, keep practicing with these two scenarios or try something else to visualize, like peeling an orange or making a pot of fresh coffee. Sometimes the simplest things can create powerful visualizations.

Find a Peaceful Place to Go

Some people find the visualization about washing their hands in itself a relaxing experience. This is partly because it takes their mind off things that worry them and partly because they find the experience (putting their hands in warm water) and the pace (fairly slow and reflective) calming.

Using visualization to help you relax is the process of creating a place (real, imaginary, or a bit of both) where you feel completely at ease. This place is unique to you. And although you create it through a fairly detailed visualization, once you have imagined it fully, you can return whenever you want to feel calmer.

The visualization exercise that follows is a bit longer and more detailed. However, it will help you create your place of peace, so we highly recommend practicing it over and over. Ready to go?

Step One: Visualize yourself walking down a path. What do you see? What do you smell? What is the weather like? What's the temperature? What is the path made of? What are you wearing on your feet, or are you barefoot? What sound do you make as you walk? What else can you hear? What else are you wearing? Is your mouth dry? Can you taste anything?

Step Two: You come to a bend in the path. Maybe you speed up, because you're eager to find out what is around the corner. You see a building. It is a building where you instantly know you will be relaxed, happy, and calm. What kind of building is it? What does it look like? What are the walls made of? Are there windows and doors? What do they look like? What is the roof made of, if it has one? Is smoke coming out of the chimney or a flag blowing in the breeze or anything else moving?

Step Three: You walk up to the door and push it open, knowing it will be safe inside. What is the door made of? Is it heavy, or does it swing open easily? Is there a squeak, another sound, or is it silent? You step over the threshold and into the building and close the door behind you.

Step Four: Look around the place and take in the doors, walls, and windows. What do you see? What is on the walls, if anything? What kind of flooring? What is the ceiling like? If things are unclear, experiment with what is on the walls. Feel free to change what you see. If you don't like something, just remove it and put something else in its place.

Step Five: Add some furniture and other decorations. Turn around and look up and down so you have a good idea of the entire interior of the building. If you want to, walk around and look in some other rooms. Once you are familiar with the inside of the building, go to each window and look outside. What do you see? If you want, each window can have a very different view. Are the windows open? If so, what can you see or feel or smell of the outside?

Step Six: Now add some sound: Have something that creates noise, whether it be wind chimes, farm animals, a high-tech sound system, or even a live band. Play some music in your mind. It could be jazz, pop, opera, or the latest country music hit.

Step Seven: Tell yourself that when you're in this place you can do anything you want and no one will care. Here you can be relaxed, content, and creative. Sit or lie down somewhere where you are completely comfortable. If you are hungry or thirsty, help yourself to a delicious meal or snack or drink.

Step Eight: It is now time to create a symbol for stress. The blinds or curtains or shutters close and block the view through the windows. Now imagine, for example, a pile of metal knives, forks, and spoons on a table, each with a life of its own, wrapping themselves around each other, stretching and twisting, with the prongs of a fork trying to trap a spoon, or a knife trying to cut off one of the prongs of a fork. You can hear the screeching sound of metal scraping against metal and perhaps even the cries of anguish and determination as they do battle. They are tying themselves up in ever-increasing knots, sliding in and out of one another faster and faster, like snakes, forming more and more distorted shapes, each trying to get the better of another.

Step Nine: There is then a release of tension—relate the image to how you feel. Imagine, for example, that the knives, forks, and spoons are uncoiling from one another, sighing with relief, gently flopping away from one another and resuming their original shapes. Perhaps they all lie down together, the spoons neatly fitting against the spoons and the forks against the forks. Or maybe they form a neat table setting—a knife, a fork, and a spoon resting happily together or rolled up in a comfortable, thick napkin. Focus on the knives, forks, and spoons finding their comfortable place and, as they do so, the blinds or curtains or shutters open to let in warm sunshine. And you feel totally calm, peaceful, and at ease.

Step Ten: Look around you again. Stand up and wander around your room, make improvements and changes wherever you like, and perhaps look out a window at the view. Notice what you see. Enjoy the feeling of calm control.

Step Eleven: When you are ready, open your eyes. This visualization should create a sense of calm. If it didn't work for you, then it's worth another try. Perhaps the real you needs to be in a place where you are less likely to be distracted, or you need more time to indulge your senses.

Some people find that trying to come up with an imaginary place is too demanding. If you feel like this, then envision a place you know. Maybe you want to visualize sitting in the backyard or being at your grandparents' house or walking in a nearby park with the smell of recently cut grass or lying in bed on Sunday morning with the aroma of toast and freshly ground coffee. As long as it is somewhere you associate with being relaxed, it should work.

Breathing and Visualization: A Recap

Visualization has many uses. Athletes, for example, often visualize the race they are about to run or the game they are about to play. They do it because it works. Scientific research proves that effective visualization increases your chances of achieving your goals in all walks of life (poor visualization, however, can decrease them, so beware). And possibly the most important aspect of visualization is its power to help people experience relaxation. This, combined with proper breathing, will allow you to experience a whole new level of calm and a whole new level of control over stress—wherever you are and whenever you want.

GIVE YOUR MIND A WORKOUT

Beginner: Breathe

1. Schedule a daily five-minute deep-breathing break at a time when you are normally tired or stressed. Put a reminder somewhere where you'll see it and turn off all distractions (or at least as many as you can).

2. Practice breathing to a count of ten using this cadence: Breathe in and say in your mind *one,* breathe out and say *two,* in on *three,* and so on, until you get to ten, then start over. Try to focus only on your breath and the number. Notice how good it feels to breathe slowly and deeply—and also notice how quickly your mind wanders. You might find yourself wandering and counting out *thirteen* in your head; if this happens, just start again at one and keep trying.

3. Once you can reliably count to ten without your mind wandering while doing this exercise, increase your time to ten minutes—or do multiple five-minute sessions throughout the day.

Advanced: Get Peaceful

Create your perfect mental peace place by answering the following questions. Once you've created it, take it for a test-drive and watch your stress disappear.

1. As you walk toward your place, what does it look like?

2. How do you enter your place?

3. What can you see as you walk in and look around?

4. What are the details of, for example, the pictures, the furniture, the floor?

5. Does your place have a particular smell?

6. What can you hear?

7. What can you see out of the windows?

8. What time of day is it?

9. What is the weather like outside?

10. How do you feel as you walk around or sit down in this place?

And remember, you can always change any details you don't like. Try painting the walls a different color and see how this changes your mood. Some people also find it useful to write down what their place is like, to help jog their memory for the next time.

Back to the Beginning

Imagine you are at your high school reunion. It might be ten or twenty or even thirty years since you've seen many of your class-mates. You bump into Kevin, the wimpy guy everyone picked on. You stumble into Donny, the guitar player who had rock-star hair. You briefly say hello to Ryan, the valedictorian and Eagle Scout. You might carefully approach Kate, who was ultrashy and didn't have many friends. Oh, and then you notice Jody, the party animal. Maybe you wind your way through the event, talking to all your classmates. And each time you bump into someone from your past, you realize something profound: They aren't the more mature versions of your adolescent perceptions. In fact, Kevin is now over six feet tall with a commanding presence. Donny the rock star is now a financial analyst at a major brokerage firm. Ryan currently travels with a rock band as their sound manager. Kate, the shiest person in your class, is actually running for political office in her state. And Jody is an attorney at a large law firm in Los Angeles.

The changes in your perceptions, however profound they may be, still can't compete with your perceptions from the past. You still view them as the people they were in high school. And they view *you* as the person you were in high school. For some, these reunions are grand experiences, where they are able to revisit a triumphant youth. For others, reunions are painful reminders. And here lies the point.

Your mind is consistently being introduced to and challenged by new situations, new relationships, and new stimuli. Your life follows a path, and along that path, your experiences change and shape the way you think.

If you read this book once, your mind will expand. But it will only expand in ways that relate to your current situations and relationships. Read it again in six months, a year, or five years, and your understanding of the insights, tools, and exercises will be completely different.

Quite simply, if you met your classmates today, your perceptions of them would be quite different from what they were in the past. And if you met yourself two, three, or ten years from now, the same would be true.

Use this book now. Use this book then. Use it when you need it. Use it when you simply feel that change is necessary or confusion is high or frustration is present.

Working out (both physically and mentally) is not a one-time endeavor. It's a lifestyle. And when you feel you're getting a little flabby, head to the gym. Go back to the beginning. It's time to get in shape.

Acknowledgments

Mind Gym would never have happened without the insight, support, and energy of many others:

The academic board, including

Professor Guy Claxton, Professor Michael West, and Professor Janet Reibstein.

The Mind Gym core team, including

David Atkinson, Paula McLoughlin, Cathy Walton, Cile Johnson, Rich Hodgson, Pui-Wai Yuen, Hannah-Leigh Bovington, Davina Whitten-Eisenacher, Jennifer Cheung, Sinead Keenan, Geethika Jayatilaka, Daniel Leatherdale, Oliver Fisk, Dawn Haynes, Sarah Donovan, Deborah Buchanan, Emma Burgess, Jayne Callum, Shahveer Ratnagar, Ryan Boughan, Hywel Berry, Dominic Harris, Preet Satiarthi, Ellen Wilsker, Robert Windeyer, Phil Banks, Alex Franklin, Nikolai Koval, Kate Williams, Jacqueline Arnott, Kieran Roche, Kate Lafferty, Hannah Roderick, Diti Sangoi, Arron Dowdall, Louise Parry, Emily Mora, Laura Barone, Alexandra Evans, Cordelia Hutchinson, Ian Friday, Kate Marples, Beth Maguire, Polly Clarke, Louisa Spiteri, Brittany Sandstrom, Rachel Loughrey, Steven Craig, Nicola Sutherland, Melissa Goddard, Deepak

Lall, Catherine Hible, Becky Starr, Georgina Law, Alicia Holloway, Danielle Raye, Lauren Frieslander, Rachel de Minckwitz, Eleanor Daniel, Naomi Guckenheim, Kelci Davidson, Rosie Santos, Tessa Roberts, Rachel Morris, Bex Field, Annamaria Mattera, Ceri Williams, Lindsay White, Martha Wright, Cara Struthers, Tom Waghorn, Kirsty Hannah, Mimi Schilz, Camille Malet, Francesca Bliss, Eileen Tan, Isabel English, George Clarkson, Marek Rembiasz, Anastasia Tielman, Shuyun Kong, Lamia Khaled, Lucinda Barrett-Cheney, Natasha Idnani, Colleen Cagney, Iain Smith, Ekaterina Solomeina, Robert Irven, Paige Rinke, Karine Haberland, Oliver Brincat, Charlotte Sandbach, Alexandra Loy, Alice Kingsnorth, Anthony Suppiah, April Robinson, Cara Beeton, Caroline Amer, Emlyn Middleton, Marius Bett, Maryam Yaqub, Natasha Elvin, Roper Peckham-Cooper, Ann Strackhouse, Belinda Chiu, Brian Alvela, Greta Raaen, Ryan Ross, Leslie Schaffer, Belinda Chiu, Erin Wickham, Michael Kofsky, Rory Sisco, and Erica Zalma.

Our clients, who have supported and advocated Mind Gym since our launch in North America:

Michael Molinaro (New York Life); Kate Minnikin, Michele Isaacs, Patsy Doerr, and Vera Vitels (Thomson Reuters); Rachel Lee, Jane Clements, Arnold Dhanesar, Elizabeth Nieto, and David Henderson (MetLife); Pete Heller, Kyran O'Neill, Zaakera Stratman, and Stacey Gardner (Microsoft); Rachel Levy, Joe Garbus, and Philippe van Holle (Celgene); Susan Connor (Hanover Insurance Group); Regina Brab, Rebecca Campbell, and John Hoguet (SunGard Data Systems); Kathy Oates, Jaison Williams, Sarah Leonard, and Tim Haynes (GSK); Allison Bebo and Evan Izquierdo (ANN Inc.); EJ Henry, Chris Leady, and Elizabeth Walker (Campbell Soup Company); Meredith Lubitz (News Corporation); Mary Slaughter and Michele Resnick (SunTrust Banks); Melissa Janis (McGraw-Hill Education); Juliana Melo and Chris Wortmann (Diageo); Melissa Frescholtz and Susan Amori (AOL); Steve Uren (Schlumberger); Lisa Ciampolillo (Hasbro); Mark Sullivan (Sunovion Pharmaceuticals); Eric Tolman and Jennifer Duncan (Arthur J. Gallagher & Co.); Steve Dealph (The Walt Disney Company); Michael Futterman (Allianz Global Investors of America); Don Carter (MasterCard); Moira McFarlin (Lincoln National); Lori Bradley and Jennifer Underwood (PVH); Monika Czarkowski (Northern Trust); Yvan Mau and Jennifer Blakey (Irvine); Juan Barajas (Cisco); Per Wingerup (CBS); Rohit Singh

(Massachusetts Mutual Life); Michael Byars (Children's National Medical Center); Kara Schillaci (PepsiCo); Carol Ryan Ertz and Karen Bradbury (Unum Group); Tara Stevens (Interpublic Group of Companies); Clyde Haynes (RetailMeNot); Kevin Hitchmough and Vicky Lodor-Martinecz (L'Oréal USA); Beth Messich, Heather Robsahm, and Chrissie Leibman (The Gap); Erin Deemer (Biogen Idec); Rolf Huelsenbec and Christine Locher (BCG); Princess Cullum (Cancer Treatment Centers of America); Daniel Gandarilla (Texas Health Resources); Leslie Solomon (Palomar Health); Carol Wells (Genentech); Anita Flagg (Fidelity Investments); Lindsay Flannery and Lisa Edler (Avery Dennison); Lori Bober and Laurie Jerome (Experian); Regis Courtemanche (BuzzFeed); Holly Rush and Bernadette Phillips (Luxottica); Connie Chartrand (Morgan Stanley); Stacy Critzer (Avalere Health); Kimo Kippen and Winnie Larsen (Hilton Worldwide); Lorna Hagen (OnDeck Capital); Ken Fendick (Bank of America); Nick Pope (Unilever); and Mike Foley, Kathleen Savio, and Tracy Lampert (Zurich).

Mind Gym coaches in the Americas, who have delivered the workouts in 20 different countries in 270 organizations. In particular,

Anil Saxena, Becca Niederkrom, Becky Heino, Bennett McClellan, Beth Adler, Bob Wiesner, Cara Barrineau, Carolyn Laughlin, Cathy Marshall, Edwardyne Cowan, Elaine Arons, Ellen Lee, Erin Gelzer, Fernando Caramazana, Frank Leitzman, Gene Moncrief, George Rossi, Gigi Gilliard, Gina Caceci, Hywel Berry, Ingrid Wiese, Jack Flanagan, Janet Oldenbroek, Jeanne Jones, Joe Bill, John Ford, Jolene Shouman, Kate Duffy, Katelyn Donald, Kim McConnell, Kim Perkins, Kristina Katayama, Laura A. Davis, Laura Lewis-Barr, Laurie Carrick, Leif Everest, Lisa Mickey, Lou Orzech, Louise Litt, Lucy Counter, Margaret Cooke, Martha Mendoza, Matt Horan, Michelle Benning, Olivia Lockwood, Paige Chen, Pamela Miller, Pat Travis, Peter Margaritis, Renee Torchia, Robin Knudsen, Russ Johnson, Tal Hershko, Theresa Picone, Wayne Meledandri, Windy Warner, Beatriz Terinelli, Eng-An Chou, Jorge Gibbons, Marina Hoyos, Alfredo Lago, Juliana Taioli, Liz Bittar, Barbara Henders, Chris Irwin, Dayna Patterson, Jill Hooper, Carlos Garcia, Tara Donato, Sharon Weber, Christina Olex, Joan Findley, Denis Olaizola, Hope Miller, Julia Douglas, Sandra Birckhead, Gabriela Pagot, Susan Boras, and Rebecca Wirtel.

Joanne: a sage Non-Exec Director for Mind Gym, a deeply supportive wife, and a remarkable mother to the mind gym of my non-working life, our deliciously curious daughter, Brontë.

Juliet, Genevieve, and Miranda, who bring laughter, joy, and meaning to my every day.

The indefatigable Lacy Lynch of Dupree Miller, who is an agent to wish for, particularly with her rare combination of wise counsel and commercial savvy. Much of the writing was aided by Todd Nordstrom, who got our British jokes and idioms and translated them for an American ear, along with Katelyn Thomas, who sought out obscure original references and examined the rigor of more recent theories.

The team at HarperOne, who instantly saw the potential and believed in the concept from the outset, with particular thanks to our magnificent editor, Genoveva Llosa, who had a significant hand in shaping the structure and tone of the book.

The greatest thanks of all are due to the hundreds of thousands of people who take part in Mind Gym experiences and share, every day, what they do and don't like. These honest (sometimes very honest) views are the basis on which Mind Gym is constantly revised, refreshed, and renewed. We hope that, as a reader of this book, you too will share your opinions and so make sure that Mind Gym constantly improves and consistently gives you what you want. Well, as near as.

Notes

The ideas contained in this book use thousands of psychological articles as an evidence base or for inspiration. A constraint of space means that only a few can be included here, so below is a selection we believe will interest readers with an appetite for more detail.

Chapter 1: Flip the Switch on Automatic Thinking

1. John M. Darley and C. Daniel Batson, "From Jerusalem to Jericho: A Study of Situational and Dispositional Variables in Helping Behavior," *Journal of Personality and Social Psychology* 27, no. 1 (1973): 100–108.
2. This is the original paper where the term "impostor syndrome" was coined. At the time, the researchers thought the syndrome was unique to high-achieving women. Since 1978, the syndrome has been studied extensively and found to affect men as well, of all ages, in nearly any situation in which someone is challenged to a high degree. Pauline R. Clance and Suzanne A. Imes, "The Imposter Phenomenon in High Achieving Women: Dynamics and Therapeutic Intervention," *Psychotherapy Theory, Research, and Practice* 15, no. 3 (1978): 241–47.
3. Pauline Clance, *The Impostor Phenomenon: Overcoming the Fear That Haunts Your Success* (Atlanta: Peachtree Publishers, 1985).
4. John Gravois, "You're Not Fooling Anyone," *Chronicle of Higher Education* 54, no. 11 (2007): A1.
5. Mihaly Csikszentmihalyi, *Flow: The Classic Work on How to Achieve Happiness* (London: Rider, 2002).

Chapter 2: Think like an Attentive Optimist

1. Richard Wiseman, *The Luck Factor* (London: Arrow Books, 2004).
2. Optimistic athletes show greater performance after negative feedback, which may relate to the way negative information is processed as something specific and non-pervasive, as well as the way optimists approach goals. Optimists, it turns out, have greater goal commitment and perseverance in the face of challenges. Basically, optimists get things done and achieve what they set their minds to. So, it's less about

having a Pollyanna personality and more about getting what you want out of life. Ying Zhang, Ayelet Fishbach, and Ravi Dhar, "When Thinking Beats Doing: The Role of Optimistic Expectations in Goal-Based Choice," *Journal of Consumer Research* 34, no. 4 (2007): 567–78.

3. Optimism is correlated with high levels of well-being, better coping with adversity, better physical health, more educational achievements, higher salary, and better relationships. Charles S. Carver, Michael F. Scheier, and Suzanne Segerstrom, "Optimism," *Clinical Psychology Review* 30, no. 7 (2010): 879–89.

4. T. Maruta, R. Colligan, M. Malinchoc, and K. Offord, "Optimists vs. Pessimists: Survival Rate Among Medical Patients over a Thirty-Year Period," *Mayo Clinic Proceedings* 75, no. 2 (2000): 140–43.

5. D. Danner, D. Snowdon, and W. Friesen, "Positive Emotions in Early Life and Longevity: Findings from the Nun Study," *Journal of Personality and Social Psychology* 80, no. 5 (2001): 804–13.

6. S. G. Jowsey et al., "Seligman's Theory of Attributional Style: Optimism, Pessimism, and Quality of Life After Heart Transplant," *Progress in Transplantation* 22, no. 1 (2012): 49–55.

7. Martin E. P. Seligman and Peter Schulman, "Explanatory Style as a Predictor of Productivity and Quitting Among Life Insurance Sales Agents," *Journal of Personality and Social Psychology* 50, no. 4 (1986): 832–38.

8. Randall A. Gordon, "Attributional Style and Athletic Performance: Strategic Optimism and Defensive Pessimism," *Psychology of Sport and Exercise* 9, no. 3 (2008): 336–50.

9. There's a dark side when you study optimists in certain circumstances. Some research indicates that in rapidly changing business environments the pessimists actually fare better, because optimists focus too much on previous experience and a positive belief in the future instead of on detail and negative information that may present itself. Keith M. Hmieleski, "A Contextual Study of Entrepreneur Dispositional Optimism: Implications for New Venture Performance," *Academy of Management Annual Meeting Proceedings* 8, no. 1 (2007): 1–6. Even with personal finances, pessimists outperform optimists by playing it safe. Optimists are more likely to run up a credit card tab, spend now, and avoid saving enough for the future. David T. Robinson and Manju Puri, "Optimism and Economic Choice," *Journal of Financial Economics* 86, no. 1 (2007): 71–99.

10. Martin E. P. Seligman, Tracy A. Steen, Nansook Park, and Christopher Peterson, "Positive Psychology Progress: Empirical Validation of Interventions," *American Psychologist* 60, no. 5 (2005): 410–21.

Chapter 3: Take Charge

1. Julian B. Rotter, *Social Learning and Clinical Psychology* (Englewood Cliffs, NJ: Prentice-Hall, 1954).

2. This meta-analysis did not just look at locus of control but also found that self-esteem, generalized self-efficacy, and emotional stability are predictors of job performance and job satisfaction. These four traits are highly correlated and are sometimes used together as a single construct known as "core self-evaluation." T. A. Judge and J. E. Bono, "Relationship of Core Self-Evaluations Traits—Self-Esteem, Generalized Self-Efficacy, Locus of Control, and Emotional Stability—with Job Satisfaction and Job Performance: A Meta-Analysis," *Journal of Applied Psychology* 86, no. 1 (2001): 80–92.

3. Combining forty years of locus of control research with more than thirty thousand people across eighteen cultural regions, this meta-analysis looked at the influence of culture on locus of control. In particular, the researchers were interested in the difference between individualistic cultures and cultures with a more collective orientation. Results showed that, across cultures, an external locus of control is correlated with depression and anxiety, though anxiety varied more with cultural orientation, with more individualistic societies (such as the United States) having a higher correlation of anxiety and external locus of control. Cecilia Cheng, Shu-Fai Cheung, Jasmine Hin-Man Chio, and Man-Pui Sally Chan, "Cultural Meaning of Perceived Control: A Meta-Analysis of Locus of Control and Psychological Symptoms Across Eighteen Cultural Regions," *Psychological Bulletin* 139, no. 1 (2013): 152–88, http://dx.doi.org/10.1037/a0028596.

4. Qiang Wang, Nathan A. Bowling, and Kevin J. Eschleman, "A Meta-Analytic Examination of Work and General Locus of Control," *Journal of Applied Psychology* 95, no. 4 (2010): 761–68.

5. Though many studies show that stress and illness are strongly related, this study looked at the role of one's locus of control and level of self-efficacy when it comes to stress and illness. Results showed that participants with high levels of stress reported higher levels of illness and were more likely to have an external locus of control and low levels of self-efficacy. Locus of control was found to be a partial mediator between stress and illness, meaning those who were highly stressed but had an *internal* locus of control reported less illness compared with those who had an *external* locus of control. Angela Roddenberry and Kimberly Renk, "Locus of Control and Self-Efficacy: Potential Mediators of Stress, Illness, and Utilization of Health Services in College Students," *Child Psychiatry and Human Development* 41, no. 4 (2010): 353–70.

Chapter 4: Start a New Chapter

1. Studies show that our upbringing leaves many of us fearful of letting others down, and we spend a lot of time attempting to avoid the stigma of failure. S. S. Sagar and J. Stoeber, "Perfectionism, Fear of Failure, and Affective Responses to Success and Failure: The Central Role of Fear of Experiencing Shame and Embarrassment," *Journal of Sport and Exercise Psychology* 31, no. 5 (2009): 602–27.

2. Beverley Stone, *Confronting Company Politics* (London: Palgrave Macmillan, 1997). The existential cycle is built on work in the learning sciences, including research by David Kolb. Kolb used studies from across five decades to look at how we learn from Experience. D. A. Kolb, *Experimental Learning: Experiences as the Source of Learning and Development,* (Englewood Cliffs, NJ: Prentice Hall, 1984).

3. Suetonius, "The Crossing of the Rubicon," in *Readings in Ancient History: Rome and the West,* ed. William Stearns Davis (Hawaii: University Press of the Pacific, 2004; New York: Allyn and Bacon, 1913).

Chapter 5: End Procrastination Now

1. Timothy A. Pychyl, Jonathan M. Lee, Rachelle Thibodeau, and Allan Blunt, "Five Days of Emotion: An Experience Sampling Study of Undergraduate Student Procrastination," *Journal of Social Behavior and Personality* 15, no. 5 (2000): 239–54.

2. Gregory Schraw, Theresa Wadkins, and Lori Olafson, "Doing the Things We Do: A Grounded Theory of Academic Procrastination," *Journal of Educational Psychology* 99, no. 1 (2007): 12–25.

3. This study asked participants to complete a math test and gave them a fifteen-minute head start with which to practice, play a video game, or work on a puzzle. Interestingly, when the math test was described as an important measurement of their mathematical and cognitive skills, the chronic procrastinators spent more time on the video game or the puzzle than the non-procrastinators. But when the math test was described as a fun game, there was no difference in the amount of time spent on the video game or puzzle by both chronic procrastinators and non-procrastinators. Joseph R. Ferrari and Dianne M. Tice, "Procrastination as a Self-Handicap for Men and Women: A Task-Avoidance Strategy in a Laboratory Setting," *Journal of Research in Personality* 34, no. 1 (2000): 73–83.
4. William J. Knaus, *End Procrastination Now! Get It Done with a Proven Psychological Approach* (New York: McGraw-Hill, 2010).
5. Piers Steel, "The Nature of Procrastination: A Meta-Analytic and Theoretical Review of Quintessential Self-Regulatory Failure," *Psychological Bulletin* 133, no. 1 (2007): 65–94.

Chapter 6: Get in the Right Relationship Mind-Set

1. John Bowlby, *Attachment* (London: Hogarth Press, 1982).
2. L. J. Berlin, J. Cassidy, and K. Appleyard, "The Influence of Early Attachments on Other Relationships," in *Handbook of Attachment: Theory, Research, and Clinical Applications,* eds. J. Cassidy and P. R. Shaver (New York: Guilford Press, 2008).
3. Bowlby believed that a child's attachment style would persist throughout his or her life and across all relationships. While this is mostly true, in some cases children have different attachment styles with different caregivers, so they might have experienced a secure attachment with one and an anxious attachment with another, for example. Also, attachment styles are fairly persistent across one's life but can change, becoming more or less secure with further relationships. H. Rudolph Schaffer, *Introducing Child Psychology* (Oxford: Blackwell, 2007).
4. The *I'm okay, you're okay* concepts were first introduced by the psychiatrist Thomas Harris. See T. A. Harris, *I'm OK—You're OK* (New York: Harper and Row, 1967).
5. Christopher Peterson and Martin E. P. Seligman, *Character Strengths and Virtues: A Handbook and Classification* (Washington, D.C.: American Psychological Association and Oxford University Press, 2004).

Chapter 7: Bid for Attention

1. John M. Gottman and Clifford I. Notarius, "Decade Review: Observing Marital Interaction," *Journal of Marriage and the Family* 62, no. 4 (2000): 927–47.
2. John M. Gottman and L. J. Krokoff, "Marital Interaction and Satisfaction: A Longitudinal View," *Journal of Consulting and Clinical Psychology* 57, no. 1 (1989): 47–52.
3. Joann Wu Shortt and John M. Gottman, "Closeness in Young Adult Sibling Relationships: Affective and Physiological Processes," *Social Development* 6, no. 2 (1997): 142–64.
4. Lynn F. Katz and John M. Gottman, "Patterns of Marital Conflict Predict Children's Internalizing and Externalizing Behaviors," *Developmental Psychology* 29, no. 6 (1993): 940–50.
5. John M. Gottman and Janice L. Driver, "Dysfunctional Marital Conflict and Everyday Marital Interaction," *Journal of Divorce and Remarriage* 43, nos. 3–4 (2005): 63–77.
6. John M. Gottman, "The Roles of Conflict Engagement, Escalation, and Avoidance in Marital Interaction: A Longitudinal View of Five Types of Couples," *Journal of Consulting and Clinical Psychology* 61, no. 1 (1993): 6–15.

7. John M. Gottman and R. W. Levenson, "Marital Processes Predictive of Later Dissolution: Behavior, Physiology, and Health," *Journal of Personality and Social Psychology* 63, no. 2 (1992): 221–33.

8. In 1998, John Gottman repeated the 1992 research and predicted divorce with an 83 percent success rate. John M. Gottman, James Coan, Sybil Carrere, and Catherine Swanson, "Predicting Marital Happiness and Stability from Newlywed Interactions," *Journal of Marriage and the Family* 60, no. 1 (1998): 5–22.

Chapter 9: Win Hearts and Minds

1. This paper replicated previous research in validating the influence tactics, especially as it concerns direction of who you're trying to influence: upward, downward, or laterally. Interestingly, it found that the two most used tactics regardless of direction of influence are rational persuasion and consultation, the latter having a focus on collaborative decision making or involving others to bring them around to your point of view. Gary Yukl and Cecilia M. Falbe, "Influence Tactics and Objectives in Upward, Downward, and Lateral Influence Attempts," *Journal of Applied Psychology* 75, no. 2 (1990): 132–40.

2. Except for simple requests, this approach can work wonders. In a study where a plain-clothes researcher wanted to skip to the front of a long line to use a copy machine, the researcher simply asked to skip to the front of the line, but the technique didn't work too well. Yet when the researcher said he wanted to skip to the front "because I need to make some copies," people frequently said yes. This example of weak reasoning shows the power of the word "because" with simple requests. Ellen J. Langer, Arthur Blank, and Benzion Chanowitz, "The Mindlessness of Ostensibly Thoughtful Action: The Role of 'Placebic' Information in Interpersonal Interaction," *Journal of Personality and Social Psychology* 36, no. 6 (1978): 635–42.

3. In this study, participants in a research lab were unknowingly influenced by a confederate they thought was another research participant. This confederate unexpectedly gave them a soft drink and then later asked them to buy raffle tickets. Participants were more likely to buy raffle tickets if they'd be given a soft drink. It's believed that social norms are at work here and participants buy raffle tickets to return the favor. Dennis T. Regan, "Effects of a Favor and Liking on Compliance," *Journal of Experimental Social Psychology* 7, no. 6 (1971): 627–39.

4. This groundbreaking study showed that by virtue of asking for a favor you can influence someone to like you more, even if you don't return the favor. Research participants won some money in a fake contest. Half were approached by the researcher afterward and asked to return the money because, he said, it had come out of his own pocket and he needed it for more studies. The other half got to keep the money. In both cases, participants were asked at the end to rate how much they liked the researcher, and those who were asked to give the money back liked the researcher substantially *more* than those who had been allowed to keep the money. Psychologists argue this works because people are driven to adjust their attitudes in accordance with their behaviors. So, the participants who gave the money back might have done so out of social pressure, but they then subconsciously readjusted their attitudes so it felt more like they did the researcher a favor because they liked him. Jon Jecker and David Landy, "Liking a Person as a Function of Doing Him a Favour," *Human Relations* 22, no. 4 (1969): 371–78.

Chapter 10: Impress Everyone

1. It used to be thought that charisma was innate; you either had it or you didn't. But psychologists and management experts have since changed their minds, arguing instead that charisma is based on certain key behaviors that can be learned. John Antonakis, Marika Fenley, and Sue Liechti, "Learning Charisma," *Harvard Business Review* 90, no. 6 (2012): 127–30.

2. The empirical studies explained in this paper show that the positive emotional expressions inherent to charisma influence others to feel more positive. As a result, people are more likely to look favorably on the person who exhibited charisma in the first place. Joyce E. Bono and Remus Ilies, "Charisma, Positive Emotions, and Mood Contagion," *The Leadership Quarterly* 17, no. 4 (2006): 317–34.

3. Deborah G. Ancona and Chee L. Chong, "Entrainment: Cycles and Synergy in Organizational Behavior," working papers 3443-92, Alfred P. Sloan School of Management, Massachusetts Institute of Technology, 1992, http://hdl.handle.net/1721.1/2421.

4. This interesting study showed that when college students delivered a fake campaign speech as a "charismatic leader" character—smiling broadly and intensely, making more eye contact than usual, etc.—those observing the speech also demonstrated the same charismatic behaviors. Paul D. Cherulnik, Kristina A. Donley, Tay Sha R. Wiewel, and Susan R. Miller, "Charisma Is Contagious: The Effect of Leaders' Charisma on Observers' Affect," *Journal of Applied Social Psychology* 31, no. 10 (2001): 2149–59.

5. Cynthia G. Emrich, Holly H. Brower, Jack M. Feldman, and Howard Garland, "Images in Words: Presidential Rhetoric, Charisma, and Greatness," *Administrative Science Quarterly* 46, no. 3 (2001): 527–57.

6. E. M. Forster, *Aspects of the Novel* (London: Edward Arnold, 1927).

Chapter 11: Give Great Feedback

1. This review article looks at years of feedback research and the evidence for its effectiveness as a performance enhancer and motivator. The review is very helpful, but what is most interesting is the feedback model the paper proposes, based on reaching recipients at four levels: task, process, self-regulation, and self. The paper argues that feedback aimed at the self-regulation level is the most effective type because it encourages a recipient's self-assessment. Recipients who are capable of honest self-assessment have the meta-cognitive skills to measure their own performance as they go and can eventually develop their own internal feedback systems as well as self-correcting behaviors. Feedback givers can use this self-regulation feedback to encourage these self-management behaviors in the recipient. John Hattie and Helen Timperley, "The Power of Feedback," *Review of Educational Research* 77, no. 1 (2007): 81–112.

2. Though there is some controversy over the power of immediate versus delayed feedback, in most cases immediate feedback is preferable. Delayed feedback might work better with high-achieving, highly capable recipients, particularly those grappling with complex issues that require new concept formation and new thinking, which proceeds a bit slower than procedural or behavioral changes. But when in doubt, go with immediate feedback. Valerie J. Shute, "Focus on Formative Feedback," *Review of Educational Research* 78, no. 1 (2008): 153–89.

3. This study showed the power of verbal praise as a feedback technique and found that graduate students given verbal praise performed better on examinations, spent more time on homework, and were more motivated in the classroom. Dawson R. Hancock,

"Influencing Graduate Students' Classroom Achievement, Homework Habits, and Motivation to Learn with Verbal Praise," *Educational Research* 44, no. 1 (2002): 83–95.

4. Valerie J. Shute, "Focus on Formative Feedback."

5. Results of this study showed that negative feedback from 360-degree reviews was perceived by the recipient as less accurate and less useful. These results question the efficacy of 360-degree feedback as a whole and the assumption that negative feedback leads to growth. J. F. Brett and L. E. Atwater, "360-Degree Feedback: Accuracy, Reactions, and Perceptions of Usefulness," *Journal of Applied Psychology* 86, no. 5 (2001): 930–42.

6. This empirical study showed that medical students given the feedback sandwich believed it was an effective and useful approach that would improve their future performance. But the feedback sandwich did not positively impact their future performance and was the least effective feedback method overall. Jay Parkes, Sara Abercrombie, and Teresita McCarty, "Feedback Sandwiches Affect Perceptions but Not Performance," *Advances in Health Sciences Education* 18, no. 3 (2013): 397–407.

Chapter 12: Detox Your Relationships

1. A. Ostell and S. Oakland, "Absolutist Thinking and Health," *British Journal of Medical Psychology* 72 (1999): 239–250.

2. Roy F. Baumeister, Karen Dale, and Kristin L. Sommer, "Freudian Defense Mechanisms and Empirical Findings in Modern Social Psychology: Reaction Formation, Projection, Displacement, Undoing, Isolation, Sublimation, and Denial," *Journal of Personality* 66, no. 6 (1998): 1081–124. Self-defense research, originally taken from Freud, is now applied to understanding stereotyping and prejudice, since it is thought that both spring from a defense mechanism whereby one suppresses and then projects one's unpleasant thoughts and feelings onto an alternative group or person. Interestingly, those that excelled at suppressing negative thoughts about themselves or their group were the most likely to project this negativity onto another group. Leonard S. Newman, Tracy L. Caldwall, Brian Chamberlin, and Thomas Griffin, "Thought Suppression, Projection, and the Development of Stereotypes," *Basic and Applied Social Psychology* 27, no. 3 (2010): 259–66.

Chapter 13: Navigate Difficult Conversations

1. "John Gottman on Couples Therapy," interview by Randall C. Wyatt, 2001, http://www.psycho therapy.net/interview/john-gottman.

2. This study looked at fifty-six newlywed couples over four years and found that aggression and communication had different roles to play in their marriages. Aggression levels mediated those couples that stayed together and those that headed for divorce. Communication was not correlated with this variable but, instead, mediated whether or not the couples were satisfied. Those with strong communication skills were more satisfied than those with poor communication. R. D. Rogge and T. N. Bradbury, "Till Violence Does Us Part: The Differing Roles of Communication and Aggression in Predicting Adverse Marital Outcomes," *Journal of Consulting and Clinical Psychology* 67, no. 3 (1999): 340–51.

Chapter 14: Take the Drama Out of Relationships

1. Eric Berne, *Games People Play: The Psychology of Human Relationships* (London: Quality Book Club, 1966).

2. Stephen B. Karpman, "Fairy Tales and Script Drama Analysis," *Transactional Analysis Bulletin* 7, no. 26 (1968): 39–43.

Chapter 15: Overcome Creative Blocks

1. "Inventor of the Week: The Slinky," Lemelson-MIT Program, Massachusetts Institute of Technology. Retrieved May 2, 2014 from http://web.mit.edu/invent/iow/slinky.html.
2. Eugene Sadler-Smith, *The Intuitive Mind* (West Sussex, UK: Wiley and Sons, 2010); Michael A. West, *Developing Creativity in Organisations* (Leicester: British Psychological Society, 1997); and Howard Gardner, *Creating Minds* (New York: Basic Books, 1993).

Chapter 16: Master the Tools of Creativity

1. Mark A. Runco, ed., *Divergent Thinking and Creative Potential* (New York: Hampton Press, 2012).
2. Fritz Zwicky, *Discovery, Invention, Research—Through the Morphological Approach* (Toronto: The Macmillan Company, 1969).
3. James C. Kaufman and Robert J. Sternberg, eds., *The Cambridge Handbook of Creativity* (New York: Cambridge University Press, 2010).

Chapter 17: Tap Your Unconscious Mind

1. Guy Claxton, *Hare Brain, Tortoise Mind* (London: Fourth Estate, 1998). The idea of separate mental systems is known as the "dual processor theory," first put forth by the father of American psychology, William James, and then coined by Jonathan Evans. For more on this theory of mind, see Jonathan St. B. T. Evans, "Heuristic and Analytic Processes in Reasoning," *British Journal of Psychology* 75, no. 4 (1984): 451–68; Keith E. Stanovich and Richard F. West, "Individual Differences in Reasoning: Implications for the Rationality Debate?" *Behavioral and Brain Sciences* 23, no. 5 (2000): 645–726; and Daniel Kahneman, *Thinking Fast and Slow* (New York: Farrar, Straus, and Giroux, 2011).
2. In this empirical study, participants were asked to generate a list of place names starting with the letter A. There were three groups of participants: (1) those who generated the names right away, (2) those who were given a few minutes to prepare, and (3) those who were distracted with something else. It was the latter—the group distracted for a few minutes—who came up with the best ideas (as decided by someone who was blind to what group they were in). The theory is that the distracted group is the only group that had time for their unconscious to mull over the task. Ap Dijksterhuis and Teun Meurs, "Where Creativity Resides: The Generative Power of Unconscious Thought," *Consciousness and Cognition* 15, no. 1 (2006): 135–46.

Part Seven: Minimize Stress, Maximize Bliss

1. Sharon Jayson, "Americans Are Stressed, but We're Getting Used to It," *USA Today*, January 11, 2012, http://usatoday30.usatoday.com/news/health/medical/health/medical/mentalhealth/story/2012-01-11/Americans-are-stressed-but-were-getting-used-to-it/52485486/1.

Chapter 18: Make Stress Work for You

1. Robert M. Yerkes and John D. Dodson, "The Relation of Strength of Stimulus to Rapidity of Habit Formation," *Journal of Comparative Neurology and Psychology* 18, no. 5 (1908): 459–82.
2. Hans Selye, *The Stress of Life* (New York: McGraw-Hill, 1978).

3. Mark Le Fevre, Jonathan Matheny, and Gregory S. Kolt, "Eustress, Distress, and Inter-pretation in Occupational Stress," *Journal of Managerial Psychology* 18, no. 7 (2003): 726–44.

4. The *Frontiers in Psychology* research study is just one of many studies that show stress can improve performance. For example, in the study cited in this note, participants were subjected to physical stress (inserting their dominant hand into ice water for sixty seconds) before being asked to complete a difficult virtual maze. The stressed group—compared to the control group, who did not undergo the freezing hand part—performed significantly better and faster on the maze. Some argue this is due to evo-lution and the adaptive advantage quick learning under stress could confer. Roman Duncko, Brian Cornwell, Lihong Cui, Kathleen R. Merikangas, and Christian Grillon, "Acute Exposure to Stress Improves Performance in Trace Eyeblink Conditioning and Spatial Learning Tasks in Healthy Men," *Learning and Memory* 14, no. 5 (2007): 329–35.

5. Brad McKay, Rebecca Lewthwaite, and Gabriele Wulf, "Enhanced Expectancies Improve Performance Under Pressure," *Frontiers in Psychology* 3, no. 8 (2012), doi: 10.3389/fpsyg.2012.00008.

6. Mihaly Csikszentmihalyi, *Flow: The Classic Work on How to Achieve Happiness* (London: Rider, 2002).

Chapter 19: Combat Stress

1. Richard Lazarus and Susan Folkman, *Stress, Appraisal, and Coping* (New York: Springer Publishing, 1984).

2. This study showed that the difference between distress and eustress is in the appraisal as well as the coping strategies invoked. When an event was perceived as distressing, the person saw it as a threat and used emotion-focused coping strategies to handle the distress. On the other hand, when an event was perceived as eustress, the person saw it as a challenge and invoked task-focused coping strategies (e.g., *I'll practice more in this area*). Jennifer McGowan, Dianne Gardner, and Richard Fletcher, "Positive and Negative Affective Outcomes of Occupational Stress," *New Zealand Journal of Psychol-ogy* 35, no. 2 (2006): 92–98.

3. Gallup research from 2010 to 2012 in the United States found that hav-ing a best friend at work leads to higher engagement, and higher engage-ment can help people cope with high stress levels. "State of the American Workplace: Employee Engagement Insights for U.S. Business Leaders," www.gal-lup.com/strategicconsulting/163007/state-american-workplace.aspx. Retrieved: May 2, 2014.

4. Friends aren't just good for lowering your stress level; they might even prolong your life. In a study of patients with coronary artery disease, social isolation resulted in a higher mortality rate. Even when experimentally controlling for things like smoking, poverty, obesity, etc., patients with a social circle of three or fewer people were at an elevated risk. Beverly H. Brummett et al., "Characteristics of Socially Isolated Patients with Coronary Artery Disease Who Are at Elevated Risk for Mortality," *Psychosomatic Medicine* 63, no. 2 (2001): 267–72.

5. In this study, participants had to complete a public speaking task, before which the experimental group interacted with a friend and the control group interacted with a stranger. Results showed that those who had interacted with a friend reported feeling less stress and fear of their upcoming speech compared to those who interacted with a stranger. Barbara A. Winstead, Valerian J. Derlega, Robin J. Lewis, Janis Sanchez-

Hucles, and Eva Clarke, "Friendship, Social Interaction, and Coping with Stress," *Communication Research* 19, no. 2 (1992): 193–211.

Chapter 20: Switch Your Mind Off

1. L. Bernardi, G. Spadacini, J. Bellwon, R. Hajric, H. Roskamm, and A. Frey, "Effect of Breathing Rate on Oxygen Saturation and Exercise Performance in Chronic Heart Failure," *The Lancet* 351 (1998): 1308–11.

2. João Luís Alves Apóstolo and Katharine Kolcaba, "The Effects of Guided Imagery on Comfort, Depression, Anxiety, and Stress of Psychiatric Inpatients with Depressive Disorders," *Archives of Psychiatric Nursing* 23, no. 6 (2009): 403–11.

3. Emile Coué, *Self-Mastery Through Conscious Autosuggestion* (Stilwell, Kansas: Digireads, 2006; New York: Malkan Publishing, 1922).

About the Authors

Sebastian Bailey, Ph.D., is cofounder of Mind Gym and President of Mind Gym, Inc. He is a featured contributor for Forbes.com, *Chief Learning Officer, Talent Management, Business Insider, Training Magazine,* and *HR Magazine.* He lives in New York with his wife and two daughters. Sebastian can be found on Twitter @DrSebBailey and you can email him at sebastian@themindgym.com.

Octavius Black is cofounder and CEO of Mind Gym. He has contributed to and been featured in *The Times,* the *Sunday Telegraph,* the *Daily Telegraph,* and the *Financial Times.* He lives in London, England, with his wife and daughter. Octavius can be found on Twitter @octaviusblack and you can email him at octavius@themindgym.com.

About Mind Gym

Mind Gym believes that people matter most in organizations. When you help individuals flourish, the companies they work for flourish, too.

Using groundbreaking psychology, Mind Gym's tools and solutions equip people to achieve more by thinking, feeling, and behaving differently. By configuring its uniquely developed bite-size products, Mind Gym has helped millions of individuals in hundreds of the world's most progressive organizations. Mind Gym operates globally with over four hundred certified associates and offices in New York, London, Dubai, and Singapore.

Mind Gym contributes 1% of all its income to their philanthropic program Parent Gym, a parenting program that changes lives in the most deprived parts of our society forever.

To find out more, visit www.themindgym.com.

Index

Page numbers in *italics* refer to illustrations.